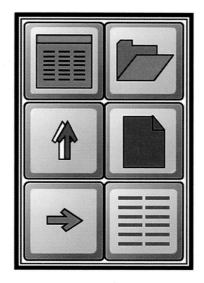

Introductory
# WordPerfect® 6.0
# for Windows™

S. Scott Zimmerman
Beverly B. Zimmerman
Brigham Young University

A
Susan
Solomon
Book

**Course Technology, Inc.** One Main Street, Cambridge, MA 02142

Course
TECHNOLOGY

*Introductory WordPerfect 6.0 for Windows* is published by Course Technology, Inc.

| | |
|---|---|
| *Vice President, Publisher* | Joseph B. Dougherty |
| *Series Consulting Editor* | Susan Solomon Communications |
| *Managing Editor* | Marjorie Schlaikjer |
| *Product Manager* | Katherine T. Pinard |
| *Editorial Assistant* | Ann Marie Buconjic |
| *Director of Production* | Myrna D'Addario |
| *Production Editor* | Pale Moon Productions |
| *Desktop Publishing Supervisor* | Debbie Masi |
| *Desktop Publishers* | Andrea Star Greitzer |
| | Susannah Lean |
| *Production Assistant* | Christine Spillett |
| *Copyeditor* | Karen L. Palmer |
| *Proofreader* | Andrea Goldman |
| *Indexer* | Alexandra Nickerson |
| *Product Testing and Support Supervisor* | Jeff Goding |
| *Technical Reviewers* | Godfrey Degamo |
| | James Valente |
| *Manufacturing Manager* | Elizabeth Martinez |
| *Text Designer* | Sally Steele |
| *Illustrations* | illustrious, inc. |
| *Cover Designer* | John Gamache |

*Introductory WordPerfect 6.0 for Windows* © 1994 Course Technology, Inc.

## Trademarks

## Disclaimer

ISBN 1-56527-082-7 (text)

Printed in the United States of America

10 9 8 7 6 5 4

# From the Publisher

At Course Technology, Inc., we believe that technology will transform the way that people teach and learn. We are very excited about bringing you, college professors and students, the most practical and affordable technology-related products available.

## The Course Technology Development Process

Our development process is unparalleled in the higher education publishing industry. Every product we create goes through an exacting process of design, development, review, and testing.

Reviewers give us direction and insight that shape our manuscripts and bring them up to the latest standards. Every manuscript is quality tested. Students whose backgrounds match the intended audience work through every keystroke, carefully checking for clarity and pointing out errors in logic and sequence. Together with our own technical reviewers, these testers help us ensure that everything that carries our name is error-free and easy to use.

## Course Technology Products

We show both *how* and *why* technology is critical to solving problems in college and in whatever field you choose to teach or pursue. Our time-tested, step-by-step instructions provide unparalleled clarity. Examples and applications are chosen and crafted to motivate students.

## The Course Technology Team

This book will suit your needs because it was delivered quickly, efficiently, and affordably. In every aspect of our business, we rely on a commitment to quality and the use of technology. Every employee contributes to this process. The names of all of our employees are listed below:

Tim Ashe, David Backer, Stephen M. Bayle, Josh Bernoff, Erin Bridgeford, Ann Marie Buconjic, Jody Buttafoco, Kerry Cannell, Jim Chrysikos, Susan Collins, John M. Connolly, David Crocco, Myrna D'Addario, Lisa D'Alessandro, Howard S. Diamond, Kathryn Dinovo, Katie Donovan, Joseph B. Dougherty, MaryJane Dwyer, Chris Elkhill, Don Fabricant, Kate Gallagher, Laura Ganson, Jeff Goding, Laurie Gomes, Eileen Gorham, Andrea Greitzer, Cathie Griffin, Tim Hale, Roslyn Hooley, Nicole Jones, Matt Kenslea, Susannah Lean, Suzanne Licht, Kim Mai, Elizabeth Martinez, Debbie Masi, Dan Mayo, Kathleen McCann, Jay McNamara, Mac Mendelsohn, Laurie Michelangelo, Kim Munsell, Amy Oliver, Kristine Otto, Debbie Parlee, Kristin Patrick, Charlie Patsios, Jodi Paulus, Darren Perl, Kevin Phaneuf, George J. Pilla, Cathy Prindle, Nancy Ray, Marjorie Schlaikjer, Christine Spillett, Susan Stroud, Michelle Tucker, David Upton, Mark Valentine, Renee Walkup, Lisa Yameen.

# Preface

Course Technology, Inc. is proud to present this new book in its Windows Series. *Introductory WordPerfect 6.0 for Windows* is designed for a first course on WordPerfect. This book capitalizes on the energy and enthusiasm students have for Windows-based applications and clearly teaches students how to take full advantage of WordPerfect's power. It assumes students have learned basic Windows skills and file management from *An Introduction to Microsoft Windows 3.1* or *A Guide to Microsoft Windows 3.1* by June Jamrich Parsons or from an *equivalent* book.

## Organization and Coverage

*Introductory WordPerfect 6.0 for Windows* contains six tutorials that present hands-on instruction. In these tutorials students learn how to plan, create, edit, format, preview, and print WordPerfect documents. Using this book, students will be able to do more advanced tasks sooner than they would using other introductory texts; a perusal of the table of contents affirms this. By the end of the book, students will have learned such formerly "advanced" tasks as defining and using styles, recording and playing macros, creating and merging data and form files, inserting graphic images, creating tables, and desktop publishing.

## Approach

*Introductory WordPerfect 6.0 for Windows* distinguishes itself from other Windows textbooks because of its unique two-pronged approach. First, it motivates students by demonstrating *why* they need to learn the concepts and skills. This book teaches word processing using a task-driven, rather than feature-driven, approach. By working through the tutorials—each motivated by a realistic case—students learn how to use WordPerfect in situations they are likely to encounter in the workplace, rather than learn a laundry list of features one-by-one, out of context. Second, the content, organization, and pedagogy of this book make full use of the Windows environment. What content is presented, when it's presented, and how it's presented capitalize on WordPerfect's power to perform complex editing and formatting tasks earlier and more easily than was possible under DOS.

## Features

*Introductory WordPerfect 6.0 for Windows* is an exceptional textbook also because it contains the following features:

■ **"Read This Before You Begin" Page** This page is consistent with Course Technology's unequaled commitment to helping instructors introduce technology into the classroom. Technical considerations and assumptions about hardware, software, and default settings are listed in one place to help instructors save time and eliminate unnecessary aggravation.

- **Tutorial Case** Each tutorial begins with a word-processing problem that students could reasonably encounter in business. Thus, the process of solving the problem will be meaningful to students. These cases touch on multicultural, international, and ethical issues—so important in today's business curriculum.

- **Step-by-Step Methodology** The unique Course Technology, Inc. methodology keeps students on track. They click or press keys always within the context of solving the problem posed in the Tutorial Case. The text constantly guides students, letting them know where they are in the process of solving the problem. The numerous screen shots include labels that direct students' attention to what they should look at on the screen.

- **Page Design** Each *full-color* page is designed to help students easily differentiate between what they are to *do* and what they are to *read*. The steps are clearly identified by their color background and numbered bullets. Windows' default colors are used in the screen shots so instructors can more easily assure that students' screens look like those in the book.

- **TROUBLE?** TROUBLE? paragraphs anticipate the mistakes that students are likely to make and help them recover from these mistakes. This feature facilitates independent learning and frees the instructor to focus on substantive conceptual issues rather than common procedural errors.

- **Reference Windows and Task Reference** Reference Windows appear throughout the book and provide short, generic summaries of frequently used procedures. The Task Reference appears at the end of the book and summarizes how to accomplish tasks using the Power and Button Bars, the pull-down menus, and the CUA and DOS keyboard templates. Both of these features are specially designed and written so students can use the book as a reference manual after completing the course.

- **Questions, Tutorial Assignments, and Case Problems** Each tutorial concludes with meaningful, conceptual Questions that test students' understanding of what they learned in the tutorial. The Questions are followed by Tutorial Assignments, which provide students with additional hands-on practice of the skills they learned in the tutorial. The Tutorial Assignments are followed by three or more complete Case Problems that have approximately the same scope as the Tutorial Case.

- **Exploration Exercises** Unlike DOS, the Windows environment allows students to learn by exploring and discovering what they can do. The Exploration Exercises are Questions, Tutorial Assignments, or Case Problems designated by an **E** that encourage students to explore the capabilities of the computing environment they are using and to extend their knowledge using the Windows on-line Help facility and other reference materials.

## The CTI WinApps Setup Disk

The CTI WinApps Setup Disk, bundled with the instructor's copy of this book, contains an innovative Student Disk generating program designed to save instructors time. Once this software is installed on a network or standalone workstation, students can double-click the "Make WordPerfect 6.0 Student Disk" icon in the CTI WinApps group window. Double-clicking this icon transfers all the data files students need to complete the tutorials, Tutorial Assignments, and Case Problems to a high-density disk in drive A or B. These files free students from tedious keystroking and allow them to concentrate on mastering the concept or task at hand. Tutorial 1 provides complete step-by-step instructions for making the Student Disk.

Adopters of this text are granted the right to install the CTI WinApps icon group on any standalone computer or network used by students who have purchased this text.

For more information on the CTI WinApps Setup Disk, see the section in this book called, "Read This Before You Begin."

## The Supplements

- **Instructor's Manual**  The Instructor's Manual is written by the authors and is quality assurance tested. It includes:
  - Answers and solutions to all the Questions, Tutorial Assignments, and Case Problems. Suggested solutions are also included for the Exploration Exercises.
  - A disk (3.5-inch or 5.25-inch) containing solutions to all the Questions, Tutorial Assignments, and Case Problems.
  - Tutorial Notes, which contain background information from the author about the Tutorial Case and the instructional progression of the tutorial.
  - Technical Notes, which include troubleshooting tips as well as information on how to customize the students' screens to closely emulate the screen shots in the book.
  - Transparency Masters of key concepts.
- **Test Bank**  The Test Bank contains 50 questions per tutorial in true/false, multiple choice, and fill-in-the-blank formats, plus two essay questions. Each question has been quality assurance tested by students to achieve clarity and accuracy.
- **Electronic Test Bank**  The Electronic Test Bank allows instructors to edit individual test questions, select questions individually or at random, and print out scrambled versions of the same test to any supported printer.

## Acknowledgments

Creating this book was a team effort. Many people deserve a hearty thanks for shepherding the text through its many stages of production.

The authors first want to thank the reviewers: Pam Lautsch-Bowman of Pennsylvania State University, Jackie Crowe of Spokane Community College, and Dave Cooper of New River Community College. Thank you for your helpful suggestions.

We would also like to thank Robin Geller for her superb production skills and the technical review team of Jeff Goding, Godfrey Degamo, and James Valente for keystroking all the tutorials and assignments. A special thanks also goes to Ann Marie Buconjic, Editorial Assistant, for ensuring that the numerous manuscripts and disk files flowed in and out of the Course Technology office with efficiency and effectiveness.

We would like to express appreciation to Joseph B. Dougherty, Editorial Director at Course Technology. His strong leadership has made this and many other projects possible. We also cherish our long association and friendship with the founders of Course Technology, Inc., John Connolly and Stephen Bayle, whose vision, knowledge, and determination have made possible the publication of premier textbooks on computer applications.

We owe a debt of gratitude to Susan Solomon for developing the basic model and design on which this text is based. Her dynamic leadership in guiding the Windows Series has been invaluable. We also wish to thank Marjorie Schlaikjer, the Windows Series Managing Editor, for her skillful work.

Finally, we wish to express our deepest appreciation to Katherine T. Pinard, the Product Manager for this text, for her faith and encouragement, her skillful and tactful guidance, and her numerous perceptive suggestions. The quality of this book owes much to her efforts. Thank you, Kitty. You're the greatest.

To all of you, and to many others too numerous to mention, we give our heartfelt thanks.

S. Scott Zimmerman and Beverly B. Zimmerman

# Brief Contents

# Contents

## TUTORIAL 2    Formatting and Editing a Document

**TUTORIAL 3**    **Using Additional Editing Features**

**TUTORIAL 4**          **Formatting Multiple-Page Documents**

## TUTORIAL 5 Using Special Word-Processing Features

# Index                                     WP 273

# Task Reference                            WP 281

# Reference Windows

# Introductory
# WordPerfect 6.0
# for Windows Tutorials

# Read This Before You Begin

## To the Student

To use this book, you must have a Student Disk. Your instructor will either provide you with one or ask you to make your own by following the instructions in the section "Your Student Disk" in the Tutorial 1. See your instructor or technical support person for further information. If you are going to work through this book using your own computer, you need a computer system running Microsoft Windows 3.1, WordPerfect 6.0 for Windows, and a Student Disk. *You will not be able to complete the tutorials and exercises in this book using your own computer until you have a Student Disk.*

## To the Instructor

***Making the Student Disk*** To complete the tutorials in this book, your students must have a copy of WordPerfect 6.0 for Windows and the Student Disk. To relieve you of having to make multiple Student Disks from a single master copy, we provide you with the CTI WinApps Setup Disk, which contains an automatic Student Disk generating program. Once you install the Setup Disk on a network or standalone workstation, students can easily make their own Student Disks by double-clicking the "Make WordPerfect 6.0 Student Disk" icon in the CTI WinApps icon group. Double-clicking this icon transfers all the data files students need to complete the tutorials, Tutorial Assignments, and Case Problems to a high-density disk in drive A or B. If some of your students will use their own computers to complete the tutorials and exercises in this book, they must first get the Student Disk. The section called "Your Student Disk" in Tutorial 1 provides complete instructions on how to make the Student Disk.

***Installing the CTI WinApps Setup Disk*** To install the CTI WinApps icon group from the Setup Disk, follow the instructions inside the disk envelope that was bundled with your book. By adopting this book, you are granted a license to install this software on any computer or network used by you or your students.

***README File*** A README.TXT file located on the Setup Disk provides additional technical notes, troubleshooting advice, and tips for using the CTI WinApps software in your school's computer lab. You can view the README.TXT file using any word processor you choose, and a printout of the README.TXT file is included with the Instructor's Manual.

## System Requirements

The minimum software and hardware requirements your computer system needs to install the CTI WinApps icon group are as follows:

- Microsoft Windows version 3.1 or later on a local hard drive or a network drive and DOS version 3.30 or later.
- A 286 (or higher) processor with a minimum of 2 MB RAM. (4 MB RAM or more is strongly recommended.)
- A mouse and printer supported by Windows 3.1.
- A VGA 640 × 480 16-color display is recommended; an 800 × 600 or 1024 × 768 SVGA, VGA monochrome, or EGA display is also acceptable.
- 1.5 MB of free hard disk space.
- Student workstations with at least one high-density 3.5-inch disk drive. If you need a 5.25-inch CTI WinApps Setup Disk, contact your CTI sales rep or call customer service at 1-800-648-7450. In Canada call Times Mirror Professional Publishing/Irwin Dorsey at 1-800-268-4178.
- To install the CTI WinApps Setup Disk on a network drive, your network must support Windows.

### OBJECTIVES

In this tutorial you will:
- Plan a document
- Launch WordPerfect
- Use the Button Bar, the Power Bar, function keys, and pull-down menus to execute WordPerfect commands
- Use word wrap
- Open, edit, and save a document
- Preview and print a document
- Exit WordPerfect
- Get help on WordPerfect features

# Creating a Document

## Writing a Business Letter

**Clearwater Valve Company** Steve Morgan recently received a degree in business management with a specialty in operations and production. He has been hired as the executive assistant to Andrea Simone, the operations manager for Clearwater Valve Company. Clearwater designs and manufactures specialty valves for industrial sprinkler, cooling, and plumbing systems.

One of Andrea's responsibilities is to train Clearwater's production plant employees on safety procedures. She decides to purchase training videos so she can conduct safety training easily and inexpensively. After looking through several catalogs, Andrea determines that Learning Videos, Inc. publishes a video that seems appropriate. Andrea asks Steve to write a letter requesting further information. She gives him a handwritten note with her questions.

In this tutorial you'll complete Steve's letter. You'll learn how to plan a letter and then how to use WordPerfect to write it.

# Using the Tutorials Effectively

These tutorials will help you learn about WordPerfect for Windows. They are designed to be used at your computer. Begin by reading the text that explains the concept. Then when you come to the numbered steps, follow the steps using your computer. Read each step carefully and completely before you try it.

In these step-by-step instructions:

- WordPerfect commands to be executed using pull-down menus often appear as a series of menu or dialog-box items. For example, if you see the instruction "Click **File**, then click **Open**," you would use the mouse pointer to point to the File menu item, press the left mouse button to "pull down" the File menu, and then click the item Open.

- Boldface text indicates keys that you press, options that you select, or words that you type. For example, you might see the instruction "Type **Clearwater Valve Company**." The words in boldface clearly indicate what you should type.

- Buttons from the WordPerfect toolbars appear as icons in the text. (Icons are small pictures or symbols that represent a command or feature.) For example, "Click ▦" means that you should move the mouse pointer to the designated icon on the Power Bar and click the left mouse button. You'll learn more about the Button Bar and Power Bar later in this tutorial.

- Special keyboard keys appear in brackets. For example, [Enter] indicates the Enter key, [F3] indicates the function key labeled F3, and [→] indicates the Right Arrow key. In the step-by-step instructions, these special keyboard keys appear in bold-face, indicating that you should press the key. For example, if you see the instruction, "Press **[Enter]**," you would press the Enter key.

- A key combination, such as **[Ctrl][F4]**, means that you press and hold down the first key, and then while still holding the first key, you press the second key. You then release both keys.

- A key or key combination used to execute a WordPerfect command is followed in parentheses by the name of the command. For example, **[Ctrl][F4]** (Close) means that you would press the key combination [Ctrl] and [F4] to execute the Close command, which closes a document window. (This procedure is explained later in the tutorial.)

As you work, compare your screen with the figures in the tutorial. Don't worry if your screen display differs slightly from the figures. The important parts of the display are labeled in each figure. Just be sure you have these parts on your screen.

Don't worry about making mistakes; that's part of the learning process. **TROUBLE?** paragraphs identify common problems and explain how to get back on track. Complete the steps in the **TROUBLE?** paragraph only if you're having the problem described. If you encounter other difficulties, try your best to figure out what is wrong and take corrective action. If that doesn't work, consult your instructor or technical support person.

After you read the conceptual information and complete the steps, you can do the exercises found at the end of each tutorial in the sections entitled "Questions," "Tutorial Assignments," and "Case Problems." The exercises are carefully structured to help you review what you learned in the tutorials and apply your knowledge to new situations.

When you are doing the exercises, refer to the Reference Window boxes. These boxes, which are found throughout the tutorials, summarize frequently used procedures. You can also use the Task Reference at the end of the tutorials; it tells you how to accomplish tasks using the mouse, the menus, and the keyboard.

Before you begin the tutorials, you should know how to use the menus, dialog boxes, Help facility, Program Manager, and File Manager in Microsoft Windows. Course Technology, Inc. publishes two excellent texts for learning Windows: *A Guide to Microsoft Windows 3.1* and *An Introduction to Microsoft Windows 3.1.*

## Your Student Disk

To complete the tutorials and exercises in this book, you must have a Student Disk. The Student Disk contains all the practice files you need for the tutorials, the Tutorial Assignments, and the Case Problems. If your instructor or technical support person provides you with your Student Disk, you can skip this section and go to the section entitled "Documents and Document Windows." If your instructor asks you to make your own Student Disk, you need to follow the steps in this section.

To make your Student Disk you need:
- A blank, formatted, high-density 3.5-inch or 5.25-inch disk
- A computer with Microsoft Windows 3.1, WordPerfect 6.0 for Windows, and the CTI WinApps icon group installed on it.

  ***If you are using your own computer,*** the CTI WinApps icon group will not be installed on it. Before you proceed, you must go to your school's computer lab and find a computer with the CTI WinApps icon group installed on it. Once you have made your own Student Disk, you can use it to complete all the tutorials and exercises in this book on any computer you choose.

To make your WordPerfect Student Disk:

❶ Launch Windows and make sure the Program Manager window is open.

  TROUBLE?  The exact steps you follow to launch Microsoft Windows 3.1 might vary depending on how your computer is set up. On many computer systems, you must get to the DOS prompt (for example, "C:\>") and type WIN, then press [Enter] to launch Windows. If you don't know how to launch Windows, ask your instructor or technical support person.

❷ Label your formatted disk "WordPerfect for Windows Student Disk" and write your name on it. Then place the disk in drive A.

  TROUBLE?  If your computer has more than one disk drive, drive A is usually on top. If your Student Disk doesn't fit into drive A, then place it in drive B and substitute "drive B" anywhere you see "drive A" in the tutorial steps.

❸ Look for an icon labeled "CTI WinApps," like the one in Figure 1-1, or a window labeled "CTI WinApps," like the one in Figure 1-2.

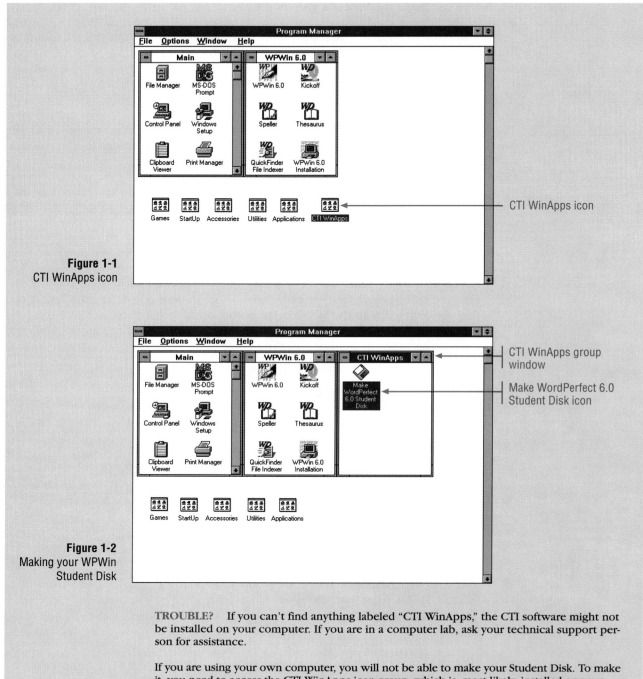

**Figure 1-1**
CTI WinApps icon

**Figure 1-2**
Making your WPWin
Student Disk

**TROUBLE?**    If you can't find anything labeled "CTI WinApps," the CTI software might not be installed on your computer. If you are in a computer lab, ask your technical support person for assistance.

If you are using your own computer, you will not be able to make your Student Disk. To make it, you need to access the CTI WinApps icon group, which is, most likely, installed on your school's lab computers. Ask your instructor or technical support person for further information on where to locate the CTI WinApps icon group. Once you create your Student Disk, you can use it to complete all the tutorials and exercises in this book on any computer you choose.

❹    If you see an icon labeled "CTI WinApps," double-click it to open the CTI WinApps group window. If the CTI WinApps window is already open, go to Step 5.

❺ Double-click the icon labeled "Make WordPerfect 6.0 Student Disk." The Make WordPerfect 6.0 Student Disk window opens. See Figure 1-3.

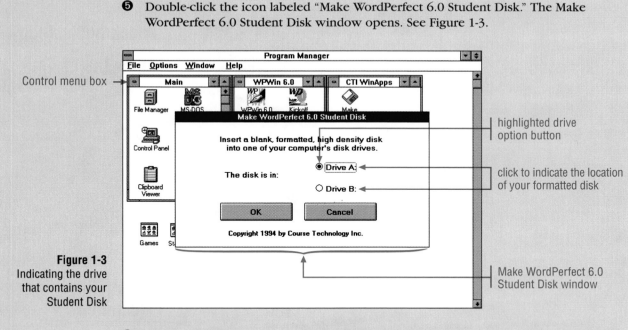

Control menu box →

highlighted drive option button

click to indicate the location of your formatted disk

Make WordPerfect 6.0 Student Disk window

**Figure 1-3**
Indicating the drive that contains your Student Disk

❻ Make sure the drive that contains your formatted disk corresponds to the drive option button that is highlighted in the dialog box on your screen.

❼ Click the **OK button** to copy the practice files to your formatted disk.

❽ When the copying is complete, a message indicates the number of files copied to your disk. Click the **OK button**.

❾ To close the CTI WinApps window, double-click the **Control menu box** on the CTI WinApps window.

## Documents and Document Windows

Before you begin this tutorial, you need to learn three key terms: document, document window, and document file. In WordPerfect terminology, the letter that you'll write is called a document. A **document** is any written item, such as a memo, letter, or report. You use the document window to create and edit documents. The **document window** is the visual display on the computer monitor where you see the text you type and the changes you make to your document. You save your WordPerfect documents in a **document file,** which is stored on the computer's hard disk or on a 3.5- or 5.25-inch disk. The document file contains the text itself, as well as formatting information about your document (Figure 1-4).

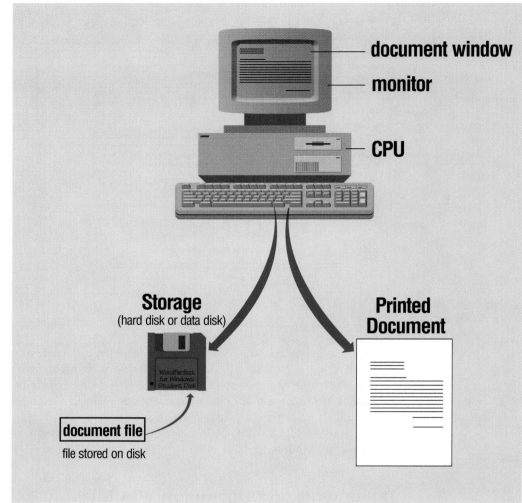

**Figure 1-4**
Document window on
the monitor, document
file on the disk, and
printed document

Let's begin with the first step in writing with WordPerfect—planning a document.

## Planning a Document

Planning a document before you write it improves the quality of your writing, makes your document more attractive and readable, and, in the long run, saves you time and effort. You can divide your planning into four parts: content, organization, style, and format.

### Content

Begin your planning by determining what you want to say in the document, that is, the content. The content should clearly convey your purpose in writing and be appropriate to your reader. Include enough information to achieve your objective, but not so much that your reader becomes overwhelmed or bored.

As Steve considers his purpose and his reader, he focuses on the handwritten note from Andrea (Figure 1-5). The note lists Andrea's questions and contains the catalog information about the training video. Steve decides that the questions will be the primary content of his letter and that the catalog information will help his reader identify the correct video. He knows that he should limit the letter to a few short paragraphs.

**Figure 1-5**
Handwritten note
from Andrea Simone
to Steve Morgan

> Steve, please write and find out the following:
>
> Does the video cover the most recent OSHA, HAZCOM, and EPA regulations on chemical safety?
>
> What instructor materials are available?
>
> The video is catalog number LV18427, "Safety in the Work Place." Our customer service rep is Peter Argyle. His address is Learning Videos, Inc., 862 Pinewood Road, Suite #210, Pecos, TX 79772

## Organization

After you have determined the content of your document, you should organize the information so that your ideas appear in a logical and coherent sequence. For a short letter or memo, you can organize the information in your head or make a few notes on paper or on the computer. For a longer document, you should create a complete outline (using WordPerfect) before you begin writing.

Steve decides to use the standard organization for a business letter, which begins with the date, the inside address, and the salutation, then presents the body or text of the letter, and concludes with a complimentary closing and the writer's name and title.

## Style

After you have settled on the content and the organization of your document, you should begin writing, using a style that satisfies your purpose and meets the needs of your audience. In business documents the style should be simple and direct. You can achieve this style by using simple words, clear sentences, and short paragraphs so your reader can easily grasp the meaning of the text while reading at a brisk, natural pace.

In addition to being direct, Steve will make the tone of his letter positive and pleasant, to encourage a quick response from Learning Videos, Inc.

## Format

Finally, you should make your document visually appealing. An attractive document is a readable document. Formatting features, such as ample white space, sufficient line spacing, and appropriate headings make your document readable and your message clear. Your reader will spend less time trying to understand your message and more time acting on it. Usually the longer and more complex a document is, the more attention you'll need to pay to its format. Making format adjustments is easy using WordPerfect. In these tutorials, you'll learn how to control the appearance of your documents.

Because Steve's letter to Learning Videos is short and simple, he decides to use the standard business letter format provided by WordPerfect. This format includes single-spaced lines and one-inch margins around all four edges of the page.

Having planned what he's going to write, Steve is ready to use WordPerfect to write the letter to Learning Videos. In this tutorial, you'll create Steve's letter, as shown in Figure 1-6.

CLEARWATER VALVE
1555 North Technology Ave., Nutley, NJ 07110
Phone (201) 347-1628   FAX (201)374-8261

September 2, 1994

Mr. Peter Argyle
Learning Videos, Inc.
862 Pinewood Road, Suite #210
Pecos, TX 79772

Dear Mr. Argyle:

I have read the catalog description of your training video number LV18427, entitled "Safety in the Work Place."  The video seems appropriate for our training needs at Clearwater Valve Company, but I would like additional information.

Specifically, please answer these questions:

1.  Does the video cover the most recent OSHA, HAZCOM, and EPA regulations on handling hazardous chemicals?

2.  What instructor materials are available for testing and documenting student performance?

3.  Do you provide a discount for volume purchases?  If so, what is the pricing structure for the discount?

Your attention to this matter is appreciated.  I hope to hear from you soon.

Sincerely yours,

Steve Morgan
Executive Assistant, Operations

**Figure 1-6**
Letter from
Steve Morgan to
Learning Videos, Inc.

Before you start this tutorial, make sure WordPerfect is installed on your computer system. If you're using a computer in a lab, check with your instructor or technical support person. If you're using your own computer, install WordPerfect by following the installation instructions that came with your copy of the software.

# Launching WordPerfect for Windows

To use WordPerfect to create documents, you have to start (launch) the WordPerfect software. Let's do that now.

To launch WordPerfect:

❶ Make sure you have the WordPerfect Student Disk ready.

   TROUBLE?   If you don't have a Student Disk, you need to get one. Your instructor will either give you one or ask you to make your own by following the steps earlier in this tutorial in the section called "Your Student Disk." See your instructor or technical support person for information.

❷ If necessary, turn on your computer and start Windows.

   The Windows Program Manager should appear on the screen. If it doesn't, consult your instructor or technical support person. Program group windows and group icons appear within the Program Manager window as shown in Figure 1-7.

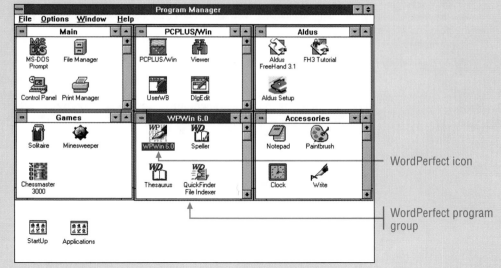

**Figure 1-7**
Windows Program Manager with the program group containing WordPerfect for Windows

The WordPerfect icons appear in the WordPerfect group window, as shown in Figure 1-7. The arrangement of windows and icons might be different than the one shown here.

   TROUBLE?   If the WordPerfect group window does not appear, open it by double-clicking the WordPerfect group icon. If you can't locate the WordPerfect program group or if the WordPerfect icon doesn't appear in the window, consult your instructor or technical support person.

❸ Double-click the **WordPerfect 6.0 for Windows (WPWin 6.0)** icon.

   This launches WordPerfect. After a moment or two, the WordPerfect window appears on the screen.

❹   If WordPerfect doesn't fill the entire monitor display, click the **maximize button** in the upper-right corner of the WordPerfect window. See Figure 1-8.

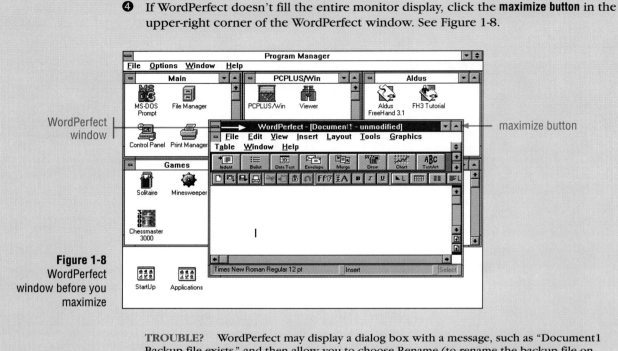

**Figure 1-8**
WordPerfect window before you maximize

**TROUBLE?**   WordPerfect may display a dialog box with a message, such as "Document1 Backup file exists," and then allow you to choose Rename (to rename the backup file on disk), Open (to open the document into a document window), or Delete (to erase the backup file from the disk). You should usually choose Open to inspect the backup document and decide if you want to save it to a disk or discard it.

WordPerfect is now running and ready to use. Let's look at the various parts of the WordPerfect window.

## The WordPerfect Window

Figure 1-9 shows the blank WordPerfect document window in which you create and edit WordPerfect documents. As you type words and characters, they become part of the document in the document window. The document window contains WordPerfect features, as well as features common to all Windows applications.

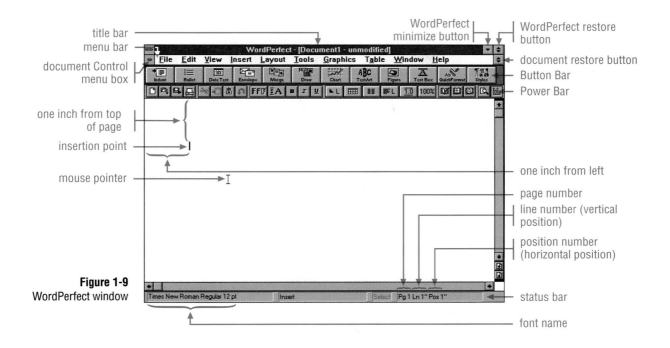

**Figure 1-9**
WordPerfect window

## Common Windows Features

Several features of the WordPerfect window are common to all Windows applications. For example, the WordPerfect Control menu box allows you to minimize, maximize, and restore the WordPerfect window, to close the WordPerfect window, or to switch to another application running under Windows. In addition, the minimize, maximize, and restore buttons, the document Control menu box, and the scroll bars function in WordPerfect the same way they do in other Windows applications.

Within the WordPerfect window, you can have up to nine document windows. You can use the document Control menu box to control and select the active document window within WordPerfect.

The title bar gives the name of the application, in this case "WordPerfect," and the name of the current document. If the document has never been saved to the disk and you're using only one document window, the document name is listed as "[Document1 - unmodified]."

## The Insertion Point

Notice the blinking vertical bar near the upper-left corner of the document window. This is called the **insertion point.** It marks the location in the document where the next character you type will appear.

## The Mouse Pointer

The mouse pointer changes shape in different regions of the screen. In some regions it appears as ↖. In the text region of the document window it appears as I. You'll see other shapes as you work through the tutorial.

## The Button Bar and Power Bar

The **Button Bar** and **Power Bar** are toolbars that appear just below the menu bar. WordPerfect provides twelve Button Bars, each containing a different set of commonly executed WordPerfect commands. Only one Button Bar appears on the screen at a time. Don't worry if your Button Bar doesn't appear along the top of the document window. You'll learn how to position it there later.

WordPerfect provides only one Power Bar. It contains the most important and most commonly executed commands in WordPerfect. The buttons on the Power Bar allow you to create a new document window, open an existing document from a disk, save the current document file to a disk, print the current document, change the line spacing, and so forth.

## The Status Bar

The bottom line of the screen is called the **status bar.** It tells you the current font, the page number, the line number, the position number where the insertion point is located, and other information to help you understand the status of your current WordPerfect document.

A **font** is a set of characters (letters, digits, and other characters such as !, @, and *) that have a certain design, size, and appearance. Each font has a name, such as Courier, Times Roman, or Helvetica (Figure 1-10). The font size is usually measured in **points,** where one point equals 1/72 of an inch in height. The font appearance refers to variations within a certain font design. For example, a font may have any one of the following appearances: normal, bold, italic, underline, double underline, or small caps. In Figure 1-9, the left side of the status bar lists the font as "Times New Roman Regular 12 pt." Your status bar might indicate a different font, depending on your printer and on how your copy of WordPerfect was installed. If the name of the font appears normal rather than, for example, bold, underlined, or italicized, the next character you type at the insertion point will have a normal appearance.

**Figure 1-10**
Three sample fonts

This is Courier
This is Times Roman
This is Helvetica

*Pg 1* in the status bar in Figure 1-9 means that the insertion point is currently on page 1—the first printed page—of your document. If your document has more than one page, this message will change as you move the insertion point to other pages of the document.

The line number is the distance in inches (accurate to within 0.01 inch) from the top of the page to the current location of the insertion point. *Ln 1″* means that the text you type will be one inch from the top of the page when you print the document. As you add lines of text to the document, the insertion point moves farther down the screen and the line number increases. Unless you specify otherwise, your document will automatically have a one-inch margin at the top and bottom of each page.

The position number is the distance from the left edge of the page to the current location of the insertion point. *Pos 1″* means that the next character you type will be one inch from the left edge of the printed page when you print the document. As you type each character in a line of text, the insertion point moves to the right, and the position number increases. Unless you specify otherwise, your document will automatically have a one-inch margin along the left and right edges of the page.

## The Default Settings

Part of planning a document is deciding its format, including the width of the margins, the line spacing, and the justification (how the text is aligned along the left and right margins). WordPerfect provides a set of standard format settings that you can use with most documents. These standard settings are called the **default** format settings because they automatically specify a format for your document unless you purposefully change them. Figure 1-11 lists common WordPerfect default format settings. Your setup of WordPerfect may have different default settings. Some of these settings may not make sense to you now, but they will become clear as you work through the tutorials. You won't change any format settings in this tutorial.

| Default Format Settings | |
| --- | --- |
| Left Margin | 1 inch |
| Right Margin | 1 inch |
| Top Margin | 1 inch |
| Bottom Margin | 1 inch |
| Justification | Left |
| Line spacing | 1 (Single) |
| Paper Size | 8.5"x11" |
| Tabs | every 0.5" |
| Page Numbering | None |
| Hyphenation | Off |
| Repeat Value | 8 |
| Date Format | Month Day, Year |
| Widow/Orphan | Off |
| Units of Measure | " (inches) |

**Figure 1-11**
Some WordPerfect default format settings

## Using the Button Bar

As with other Windows applications, WordPerfect lets you execute commands by using the pull-down menus with the keyboard or with the mouse, by using shortcut keys, or by using buttons on a toolbar. One of the WordPerfect toolbars is the Button Bar, which usually appears just below the menu bar in the WordPerfect window, as shown in Figure 1-9.

### Executing Commands Using the Button Bar

You use the Button Bar the same way you use any Windows toolbar; you move the mouse pointer to the desired button and click the left mouse button. Let's use the Button Bar to execute the Date Text command. The Date Text command automatically inserts the current date into a document. Using the Date Text command saves you the keystrokes of typing the date and ensures that the date is accurate.

To execute the Date Text command using the Button Bar:

❶ Move the mouse pointer to [Date Text], the Date Text button on the Button Bar.

Notice that a description of this button appears in the title bar of the WordPerfect window. See Figure 1-12.

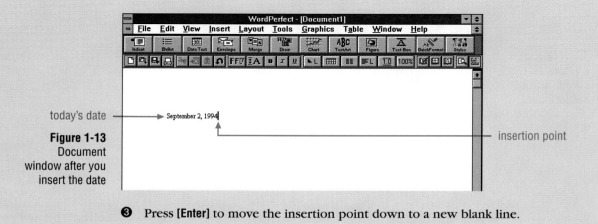

Date Text button

mouse pointer

**Figure 1-12**
Button Bar with
mouse pointer on
Date Text button

name and description
of button

**TROUBLE?**   If your screen doesn't display the Button Bar, do the following: Click View on the main menu bar, then click Button Bar. If your Button Bar doesn't show the Date Text button, try the following: move the mouse pointer to the Button Bar, click the *right* mouse button to display a menu of Button Bars, then click WordPerfect. If you still don't see the Date Text button, consult your instructor or technical support person.

❷ Click [Date Text] on the Button Bar.

WordPerfect inserts the current date into your document. See Figure 1-13. As you can see, executing a command with the Button Bar is fast and easy.

today's date ⟶ September 2, 1994

insertion point

**Figure 1-13**
Document
window after you
insert the date

❸ Press [Enter] to move the insertion point down to a new blank line.

You can execute all the commands on the Button Bar using the pull-down menus or shortcut keys. For example, you could select the Date command from the Insert menu, and then choose Date Text, or you could press [Ctrl][D].

## Moving the Button Bar

The normal location of the Button Bar is along the top of the document window, just below the menu bar, but you might prefer it in a different location. For example, positioning the Button Bar along the left edge of the screen allows more lines of text in the document window.

**REFERENCE WINDOW**

### Moving the Button Bar

- Move the mouse pointer to an edge of the Button Bar, so that the mouse pointer becomes 🖑.
- Press the left mouse button, move the mouse pointer and the outline of the Button Bar to the desired location on the screen, and release the mouse button.

Let's move the Button Bar to the left edge of the screen now.

To move the Button Bar:
❶ Move the mouse pointer to one of the edges of the Button Bar so that the mouse pointer becomes 🖑. See Figure 1-14.

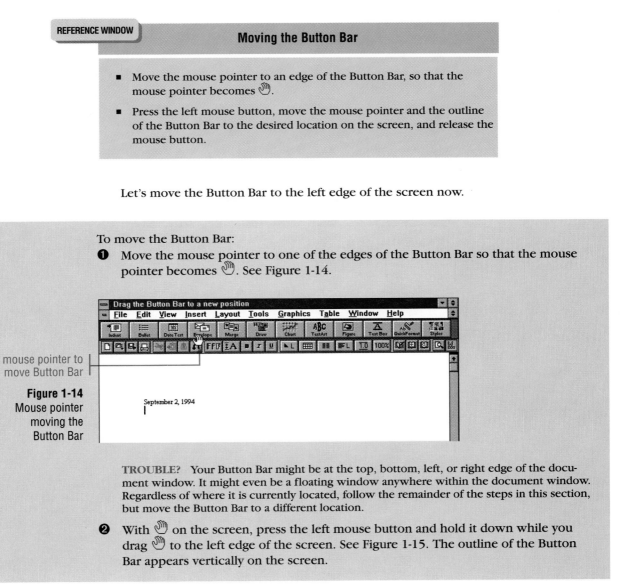

mouse pointer to
move Button Bar

**Figure 1-14**
Mouse pointer
moving the
Button Bar

**TROUBLE?**  Your Button Bar might be at the top, bottom, left, or right edge of the document window. It might even be a floating window anywhere within the document window. Regardless of where it is currently located, follow the remainder of the steps in this section, but move the Button Bar to a different location.

❷ With 🖑 on the screen, press the left mouse button and hold it down while you drag 🖑 to the left edge of the screen. See Figure 1-15. The outline of the Button Bar appears vertically on the screen.

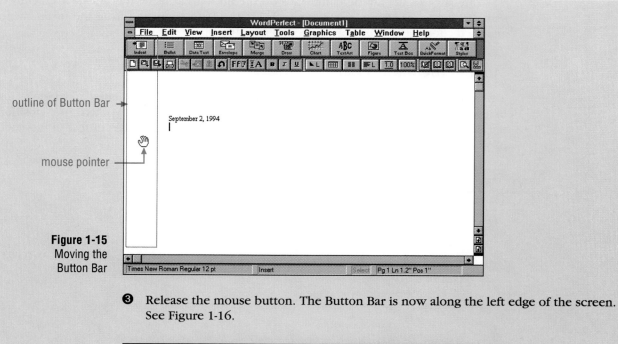

outline of Button Bar →

mouse pointer —

**Figure 1-15**
Moving the
Button Bar

❸  Release the mouse button. The Button Bar is now along the left edge of the screen. See Figure 1-16.

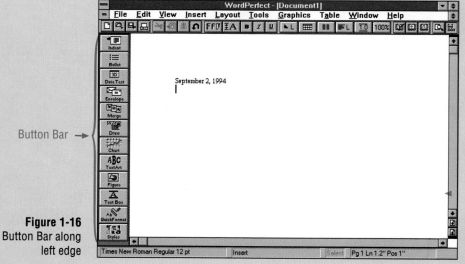

Button Bar →

**Figure 1-16**
Button Bar along
left edge

**TROUBLE?**    If you release the mouse button too soon or in the wrong place, the Button Bar might become a floating rectangular window within the document window. If this happens, move the mouse pointer to the edge of the Button Bar window until it (the mouse pointer) becomes 👋, then drag the outline of the Button Bar to the left edge of the screen and release the mouse button.

The figures in this book show the Button Bar along the top of the document window, immediately below the menu bar, so let's move it back to that location.

❹  Follow Steps 1 through 3 given above to move the Button Bar back to the top of the document window, so that it is again positioned immediately below the menu bar.

When you move the mouse pointer to execute a pull-down menu command or a Button Bar command, you will often see the mouse pointer change from ⌖ to 🖐 and back to ⌖. Don't let this bother you. As you now know, 🖐 is the mouse pointer used to move the Button Bar.

## Using the Power Bar

Just below the Button Bar along the top of the document window, WordPerfect displays another toolbar, the Power Bar, as shown in Figure 1-17.

Power Bar →

**Figure 1-17**
Power Bar

Let's use the Power Bar to change the size of the font and then insert the date in the new font size.

To change the font size using the Power Bar:

❶ With the insertion point on the blank line below the date, move the mouse pointer to 🔠, the Font Size button on the Power Bar. A description of the command appears in the title bar at the top of the screen. See Figure 1-18.

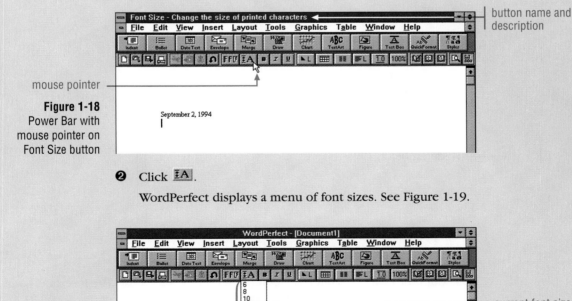

button name and description

mouse pointer —

**Figure 1-18**
Power Bar with
mouse pointer on
Font Size button

❷ Click 🔠.

WordPerfect displays a menu of font sizes. See Figure 1-19.

font size menu —

current font size

**Figure 1-19**
Menu of font sizes

❸ Click **24**.

WordPerfect closes the menu, increases the size of the insertion point, and displays the new font size in the status bar. See Figure 1-20. Now any text you type or any characters you insert into the document window will be in 24-point type.

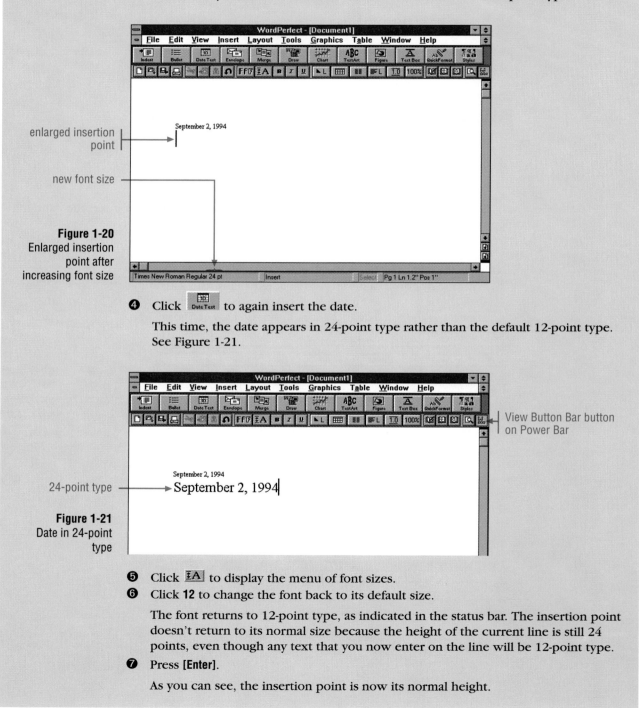

enlarged insertion
point

new font size

**Figure 1-20**
Enlarged insertion
point after
increasing font size

❹ Click [Date Text] to again insert the date.

This time, the date appears in 24-point type rather than the default 12-point type. See Figure 1-21.

View Button Bar button
on Power Bar

24-point type

**Figure 1-21**
Date in 24-point
type

September 2, 1994
September 2, 1994|

❺ Click [⬆A] to display the menu of font sizes.

❻ Click **12** to change the font back to its default size.

The font returns to 12-point type, as indicated in the status bar. The insertion point doesn't return to its normal size because the height of the current line is still 24 points, even though any text that you now enter on the line will be 12-point type.

❼ Press **[Enter]**.

As you can see, the insertion point is now its normal height.

## Displaying and Hiding the Button Bar

Because the Button Bar takes up room in the document window, there may be times when you want to hide it (turn it off). The View Button Bar button on the Power Bar is a toggle switch that alternately hides and displays the Button Bar. A **toggle switch** is like a light switch: if a feature is on, choosing the toggle switch turns it off; if the feature is off, choosing the toggle switch turns it on.

Let's use the View Button Bar button to hide the Button Bar.

To hide the Button Bar:

❶ Click [icon], the **View Button Bar button** on the Power Bar. The Button Bar disappears from the screen.

❷ Click [icon] again.

The Button Bar once again appears on the screen.

As you can see, the View Button Bar button on the Power Bar makes displaying and hiding the Button Bar quick and easy. You would use the command whenever you temporarily want more space in the document window.

## Function Keys

As with all Windows applications, WordPerfect allows you to execute many of its commands using shortcut keys. Some WordPerfect shortcut keys involve using a function key. A **function-key command** is a command you issue by pressing a function key, sometimes alone and sometimes in combination with a modifier key, that is, [Shift], [Ctrl], or [Alt]. The commands available with the function keys are listed on the function-key template (Figure 1-22). The **template** is a plastic strip that sits on the keyboard over the function keys and lists the names of the WordPerfect function-key commands, also called **WordPerfect keys**. The names of the WordPerfect keys are color-coded to indicate which modifier key, if any, you must press with the function key to issue the command. A command name in black indicates no modifier key; green indicates [Shift]; blue indicates [Alt]; and red indicates [Ctrl]. Some commands involve pressing both [Alt] and [Shift] or both [Ctrl] and [Shift] with a function key.

| WordPerfect® for Windows™ | | | F1 | F2 | F3 | F4 | | F5 | F6 | F7 | F8 | | F9 | F10 | F11 | F12 |
|---|---|---|---|---|---|---|---|---|---|---|---|---|---|---|---|---|
| | | | | | Show ¶ • | Clear • | Ctrl+Sh | | Prev Doc • | Double Indent • | | Ctrl+Sh | | | Vertical Line • | Table Data • |
| Cancel | Esc | Top of Doc | Home | | | | | | | | | | | | | |
| Undo | Z | Bottom of Doc | End | Speller | Replace | Redisplay | Close | Ctrl | Draft View | Next Doc | Hanging Indent | Margins | Ctrl | Generate | Macro Rec/Stop | Horizontal Line | Table Format |
| Cut | X | Column ←/→ | ←/→ | | | | | | | | | | | | | |
| Copy | C | Page Up | PgUp | | | Ruler Bar • | | Alt+Sh | | Prev Window • | Decimal Tab • | | Alt+Sh | | Feature Bar • | | Calculate • |
| Paste | V | Page Down | PgDn | Grammatik • | Find Previous | Reveal Codes | Exit | Alt | Page View | Next Window | Flush Right | Styles | Alt | Sort | Macro Play | Text Box Create | Table Number |
| Bold | B | Del EOL | Del | | | | | | | | | | | | | |
| Italics | I | Hard Page | Enter | Thesaurus | Find Next | Save | New | Shift | Full Page View | Prev Pane | Center | Select Cell | Shift | Merge | Repeat | Text Box Edit | Table Lines/Fill |
| Underline | U | WP Characters | W | | | | | | | | | | | | | |
| Date Text | D | Print Doc | P | Help: What Is? | | | | | | | | | | | | | |
| Version 6.0 | 74  42  4 1 | | | Help | Find | Save As | Open | | Print | Next Pane | Indent | Select | | Font | Menu | Figure | Table Create |
| © Word Perfect Corp. 1993  TMUSWWP60XID-8/93 | | | | | | | | | | | | | | | | |

**Figure1-22**
WordPerfect function-key template

For example, the function-key template lists a command called Show Symbols. This command causes WordPerfect to display special symbols that mark the spaces between words, the ends of paragraphs, the locations of tabs and indents, and so forth. These symbols are sometimes called **non-printing symbols** because they don't appear in your document when you print it. To execute the Show Symbols command, you press [Ctrl][Shift][F3].

Let's use the template and the function keys to turn on the non-printing symbols in the document window and then turn them off.

To execute the Show Symbols command using the function keys:

❶ Press **[Ctrl][Shift][F3]** (Show Symbols).

A bullet (•) appears in the spaces between the words, and a paragraph symbol (¶) appears at the end of each paragraph. See Figure 1-23. In WordPerfect, a **paragraph** is defined as a unit of text that ends when you press [Enter]. Because you pressed [Enter] at the end of each line of the current date, paragraph symbols appear there.

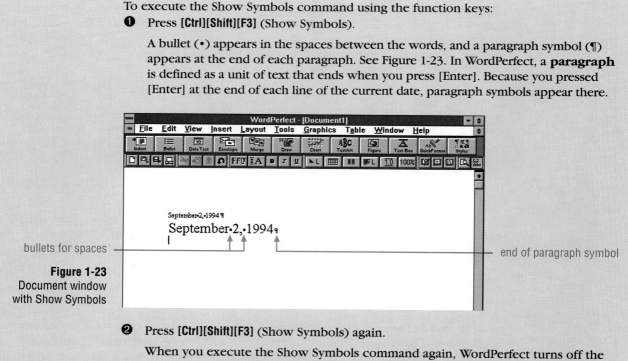

bullets for spaces

end of paragraph symbol

**Figure 1-23**
Document window
with Show Symbols

❷ Press **[Ctrl][Shift][F3]** (Show Symbols) again.

When you execute the Show Symbols command again, WordPerfect turns off the symbols in the document window.

You should feel free to turn the non-printing symbols on or off anytime you want to insert or delete spaces, tabs, or paragraphs. In this book, most of the figures illustrating the WordPerfect window will not display the non-printing symbols.

Almost all the commands listed on the function-key template have a pull-down menu equivalent. For example, to execute the Show Symbols command using a pull-down menu, you would click View, then click Show ¶.

## Choosing a Method to Execute Commands

You've seen that WordPerfect offers you several ways to execute the commands: the Button Bar, the Power Bar, pull-down menus, or shortcut keys. In most cases, you could choose two or more different methods for executing the same command.

Which method is best? The answer depends on your level of experience and your personal preference. The Button Bar or Power Bar is usually the easiest method for executing a command. In the case of the Power Bar, you have to learn the meaning of each of the icons, because, unlike the Button Bar icons, they have no text describing their function. If there is no button for a particular command, the quickest method of executing the command is to use the shortcut keys rather than the pull-down menus. However, many people find the pull-down menus easier because they can simply choose from the menu instead of memorizing the function-key commands.

In these WordPerfect tutorials, you can use whichever method you prefer or whichever method your instructor requires. In most cases, when we ask you to execute a command, we tell you the simplest method, which is usually the Button Bar or Power Bar. In some cases, we might also tell you one or more other methods, just to remind you of the power and flexibility of WordPerfect. The Task Reference at the end of these tutorials lists the various methods for executing each command.

## Closing the Document Window

Having completed this introduction to WordPerfect commands, you're ready to begin typing Steve's letter to Learning Videos. But before you can type the letter, you must be sure that the WordPerfect document window is empty. If it isn't, all the text that now appears in the window will be part of the document when you print it.

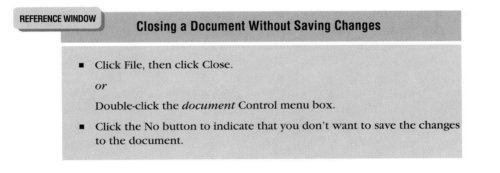

REFERENCE WINDOW

### Closing a Document Without Saving Changes

- Click File, then click Close.

  *or*

  Double-click the *document* Control menu box.

- Click the No button to indicate that you don't want to save the changes to the document.

Let's clear the screen now by closing the document window.

To close the document window:

❶ Click **File**, then click **Close.**

Remember, this instruction means to choose the File menu, then choose Close from the File menu. You could also double-click the Control menu box of the *document* window; this Control menu box is located on the left side of the menu bar. *Make sure you don't double-click the Control menu box of the WordPerfect window,* located on the left side of the title bar.

WordPerfect displays a dialog box with the prompt "Save Changes to Document1?" and then pauses for you to choose Yes, No, or Cancel. See Figure 1-24. If you executed the Close command by accident, you would choose Cancel. You could also press [Esc] if you wanted to close the dialog box without taking any action.

In this case, you want to close the document window without saving the document.

**Figure 1-24**
Dialog box for
prompt to save
document

> **WordPerfect for Windows**
>
> ? **Save changes to Document1?**
>
> [ Yes ]   [ No ]   [ Cancel ]

❷   Click the **No button.** This indicates that you want to close the current document
window without saving the document.

You have now closed the current document window without saving its contents. You
are still in WordPerfect, but now you have a new, blank document window.

## Entering Text

With a blank document window in the WordPerfect window and the insertion point at
Ln 1" Pos 1", you're ready to type Steve's letter (Figure 1-6). Let's begin by typing the date,
the inside address, and the salutation of the letter.

To type the date, the inside address, and the salutation:
❶   Press [**Enter**] six times.

This moves the insertion point down about one inch from the top margin, giving a
total of about two inches of space at the top of the page and allowing room for the
Clearwater Valve Company letterhead. The line number in the status bar should read
*Ln 2.16"* or a number close to 2.16 (such as 2.18 or 2.13), indicating that the insertion point is a little more than two inches from the top of the page. See Figure 1-25.

top margin —

six blank lines —

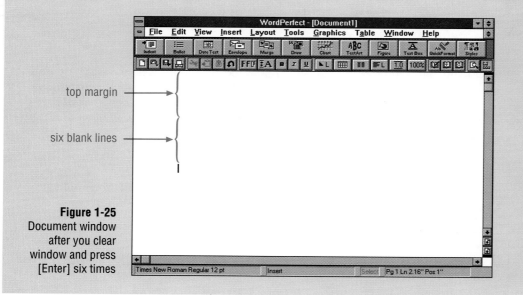

**Figure 1-25**
Document window
after you clear
window and press
[Enter] six times

**TROUBLE?**    If you pressed [Enter] too many times, just press [Backspace] to delete the extra blank lines. If the line number on your screen has a slightly different value, such as Ln 1.92" or Ln 2.26", don't worry. Different fonts and printers produce slightly different measurements when you press [Enter].

You are now ready to insert today's date.

❷ Click [Date Text] , the **Date Text button** on the Button Bar. The date appears in your document.

❸ Press **[Enter]** four times to insert three blank lines between the date and the inside address.

The status bar should now display *Ln 2.94"* (or some number close to that value).

Next, enter the inside address, shown on Andrea's note (Figure 1-5).

❹ Type **Mr. Peter Argyle** and press **[Enter]**. Type **Learning Videos, Inc.** and press **[Enter]**. Type **862 Pinewood Road, Suite #210** and press **[Enter]**. Finally, type **Pecos, TX 79772** and press **[Enter]** twice—once to end the line, once to add an extra blank line. See Figure 1-26. Don't worry if you have made typing errors. You'll be able to fix them later.

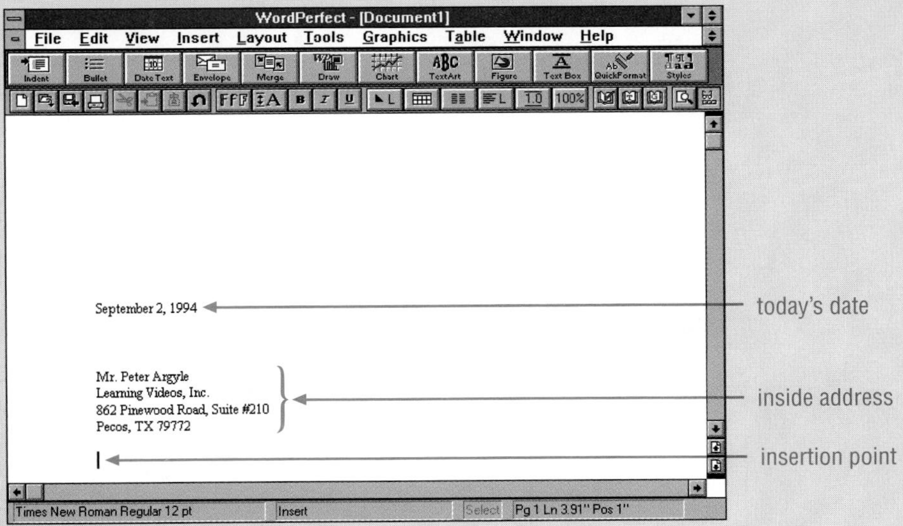

**Figure 1-26**
Document window after you insert the date and type the inside address

❺ Type **Dear Mr. Argyle:** and press **[Enter]** twice to double-space between the salutation and the body of the letter.

You have now completed the date, the inside address, and the salutation of Steve's letter, using a standard format for business letters.

## Saving a Document

The letter you're typing is currently stored in your computer's memory, but not on a disk. If you were to exit WordPerfect without saving your letter, turn off your computer, or experience an accidental power failure right now, the information you just typed would be lost. You should get in the habit of frequently saving your document to a disk. Unless a document is very short, don't wait until you've typed the whole document before saving it. As a rule, you should save your work about every 15 minutes.

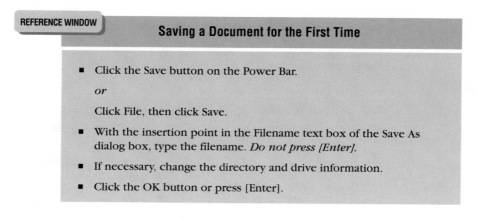

REFERENCE WINDOW

### Saving a Document for the First Time

- Click the Save button on the Power Bar.

  *or*

  Click File, then click Save.

- With the insertion point in the Filename text box of the Save As dialog box, type the filename. *Do not press [Enter].*

- If necessary, change the directory and drive information.

- Click the OK button or press [Enter].

Although Steve hasn't been working on this letter for 15 minutes yet, he decides, just to be safe, to save the document now.

To save a document:

❶ Insert the WordPerfect Student Disk into drive A.

This tutorial assumes that you have a hard disk (drive C) and at least one disk drive (drive A). In this tutorial, we will assume you are using drive A. If you are using drive B, substitute the phrase "drive B" whenever you read "drive A."

❷ Click ⌨, the **Save button** on the Power Bar (or click **File,** then click **Save**). See Figure 1-27.

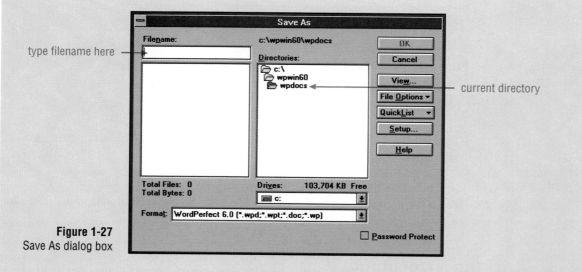

**Figure 1-27**
Save As dialog box

WordPerfect displays the Save As dialog box and waits for you to type a name for the document.

❸ Type **s1file1.dft.** *Do not press [Enter].* See Figure 1-28.

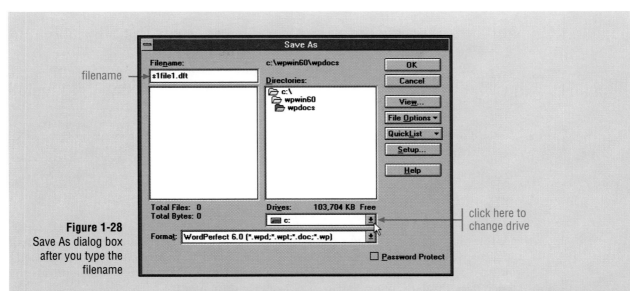

filename

**Figure 1-28**
Save As dialog box
after you type the
filename

❹ Click the **Down Arrow** on the right side of the Drives section of the dialog box. A list of available drives drops down.

❺ Click the letter of the drive in which you placed your Student Disk. This tutorial assumes that your Student Disk is in drive A, but you could be using drive B. See Figure 1-29.

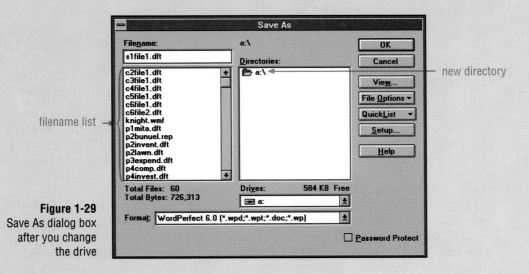

filename list

**Figure 1-29**
Save As dialog box
after you change
the drive

Notice that the Filename list and the Directories section change when you change the drive, because the new drive has different directories.

❻ Click the **OK button** or, because the *focus* (a black line around a button within a dialog box) is on the OK button, press **[Enter]**.

WordPerfect saves the document file to the disk in drive A. Pressing [Enter] will execute the button command that the focus is on, just as if you had clicked the button with the mouse pointer.

**TROUBLE?**    If the error message "Drive A not ready" appears in a dialog box, make sure the disk in drive A is positioned properly. Then click Retry. If the same message appears again, your disk is probably not formatted or your disk may be in drive B. If your disk is in drive A, remove it from the drive, insert a formatted disk, close the drive door, and select Retry. If your disk is in drive B, repeat Steps 5 and 6, but select drive B instead of drive A.

After you save the document to the disk, the path and filename of the document, "a:\s1file1.dft," appear in the title bar of the WordPerfect window (Figure 1-30). If the path of the filename in the title bar includes drive C (for example, "c:\wpwin60\wpdocs\s1file1.dft," you have accidentally saved the document to drive C instead of drive A or B. If this is the case, repeat the above procedure to save the file to drive A or B.

name of document

title bar

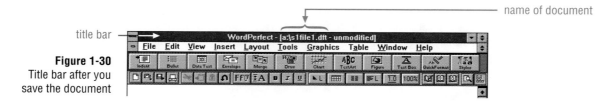

**Figure 1-30**
Title bar after you
save the document

## Document Filenames

Besides saving your documents frequently, another good habit to get into is to use descriptive filenames that help identify the contents of your files. Document filenames can be any legal DOS filename and may contain the path (such as "a:\" or "c:\wpdocs\"). The filename can contain from one to eight characters and can include a filename extension of one to three characters. In S1FILE1.DFT the filename extension .DFT stands for "draft," indicating that this is the first draft of Steve's letter.

Eight characters in the filename and an additional three in the extension often don't allow you to use complete names, but you can at least create meaningful abbreviations. For example, because Steve is writing a letter to Learning Videos, he could save the final version of his letter with the filename LVI.LET, where LVI is an abbreviation of the name of the company, and .LET reminds him that the document is a letter. If he were to write a memo to Clearwater employees about the 1994 budget, he might name the memo 94BUDGET.MEM, where the filename extension .MEM stands for memo.

In this book, the six tutorials on WordPerfect involve many files. Therefore, we use filenames that will help you and your instructor recognize the origin and content of the various documents. To name these files so you can recognize their contents, we have categorized them as follows:

| File Category | Description |
|---|---|
| Tutorial Cases | The files you use to work through each tutorial |
| Tutorial Assignments | The files that contain the documents you need to complete the Tutorial Assignments at the end of each tutorial |
| Case Problems | The files that contain the documents you need to complete the Case Problems at the end of each tutorial |
| Saved Document | Any document you have saved |

Let's take the filename S1FILE1.DFT, for example. At first glance this filename might appear to have no meaning, but it does contain meaningful abbreviations. The first character of the filename identifies the file as one of the four categories given above, as shown here:

| If the first character is: | The file category is: |
|---|---|
| C | Tutorial Case |
| T | Tutorial Assignment |
| P | Case Problem |
| S | Saved Document |

Thus, S1FILE1.DFT is a document that you have saved.

The second character of the document filename identifies the tutorial from which the file comes. Thus, S1FILE1.DFT is a file you saved from Tutorial 1. The remaining six characters of the filename identify the specific file. All documents in the tutorials are named FILE, followed by a number. Each time you save a file, you will increase the number after FILE by 1. The filename extensions also help identify the file. Although WordPerfect uses the default filename extension .WPD (for WordPerfect document), we will use our own filename extensions. In this book, a document letter has the filename extension .LET, a memo .MEM, a report .REP, and a draft document .DFT. Thus, the filename S1FILE1.DFT tells you that this is the first draft you saved in Tutorial 1.

Applying these same rules, the file T1FILE1.LET is the first document (a letter) found in the Tutorial Assignments from WordPerfect Tutorial 1, and C4FILE1.REP is the report you will use in a Tutorial Case for WordPerfect Tutorial 4. Files that you open (load from the disk into a document window) or save in the Tutorial Assignments and the Case Problems have a word or an abbreviation (other than FILE) to help identify them. For example, P1IBM.LET is the filename of the Case Problem "Letter to IBM" from Tutorial 1.

## Word Wrap

Having saved the first part of your document, you are now ready to complete the letter. As you type the body of the letter, do not press [Enter] at the end of each line. Instead, allow WordPerfect to determine where one line ends and the next one begins. When you type a word that extends into the right margin, WordPerfect automatically moves the insertion point and the word to the next line. This automatic breaking of a line of text is called **word wrap.** Word wrap ensures that each line of text fits between the left and right margins and eliminates the need for you to press [Enter] at the end of each line, as you would on a typewriter. If you happen to press [Enter] before word wrap occurs, press [Backspace] until the insertion point moves back to the previous line, then continue typing.

Let's see how word wrap works as you type the body of the letter.

To observe word wrap while you are typing a paragraph:

❶ Make sure the insertion point is at the left edge of the screen and two lines below the salutation of the letter. If it's not, press [↓] as many times as necessary.

❷ Slowly type the following sentence and observe when the insertion point automatically jumps to the next line: **I have read the catalog description of your training video number LV18427, entitled "Safety in the Work Place."** See Figure 1-31.

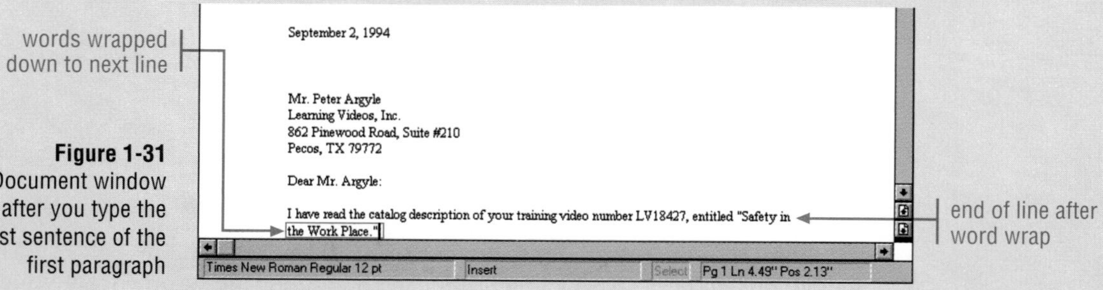

words wrapped down to next line

**Figure 1-31**
Document window after you type the first sentence of the first paragraph

```
September 2, 1994


Mr. Peter Argyle
Learning Videos, Inc.
862 Pinewood Road, Suite #210
Pecos, TX 79772

Dear Mr. Argyle:

I have read the catalog description of your training video number LV18427, entitled "Safety in
the Work Place."

Times New Roman Regular 12 pt          Insert          Select   Pg 1 Ln 4.49" Pos 2.13"
```

end of line after word wrap

**TROUBLE?**    Because different fonts have different letter widths, the word or letter at which word wrap occurs in your document might be different from our example. Moreover, the values for the line number and position number on the right side of the status bar may not be exactly the same as those in Figure 1-31. Such differences are normal. Just continue following the steps in the tutorial.

❸ Type the rest of the first paragraph of the body of the letter. See Figure 1-32.

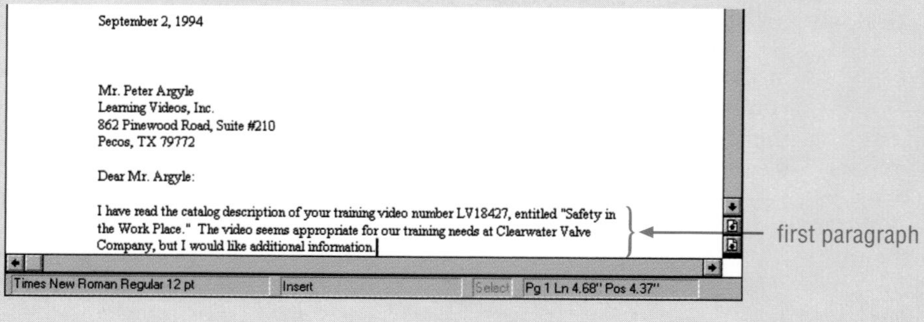

**Figure 1-32**
Document window after you type the first paragraph

```
September 2, 1994


Mr. Peter Argyle
Learning Videos, Inc.
862 Pinewood Road, Suite #210
Pecos, TX 79772

Dear Mr. Argyle:

I have read the catalog description of your training video number LV18427, entitled "Safety in
the Work Place."  The video seems appropriate for our training needs at Clearwater Valve
Company, but I would like additional information.

Times New Roman Regular 12 pt          Insert          Select   Pg 1 Ln 4.68" Pos 4.37"
```

first paragraph

❹ Press **[Enter]** to end the first paragraph, then press **[Enter]** again to double-space between the first and second paragraphs.

When you press [Enter], WordPerfect inserts an invisible code called a **hard return** into the document to mark the end of a line or the end of a paragraph. The word or punctuation mark immediately preceding a hard return always ends a line, regardless of how long or short the line is. If you want to see the location of the hard returns, click View, and then click Show ¶ (or press [Ctrl][Shift][F3]). A paragraph symbol (¶) marks the location of each hard return.

When a line ends with a word wrap, WordPerfect inserts an invisible code called a **soft return** into the document to mark the end of the line (Figure 1-33). The words before and after a soft return are not necessarily permanent—if you later add text to or delete text from the line, the word at which word wrap occurs might change.

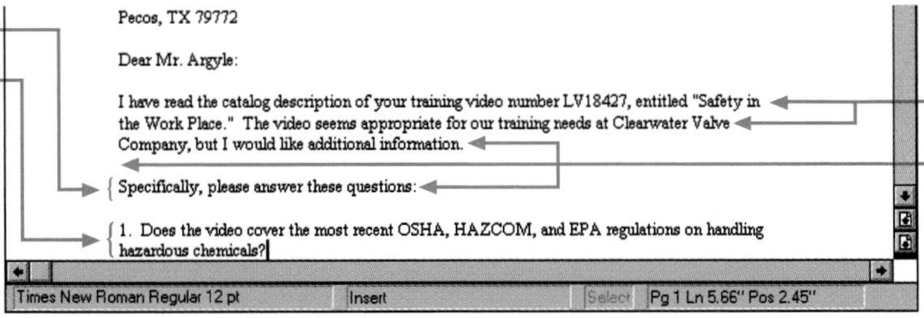

second paragraph ——
first question ——

**Figure 1-33**
Document window
after you type the
paragraph with the
first question

invisible soft returns ——
invisible hard returns ——

Remember the following rule: As you type, press [Enter] only at the end of a paragraph or where you definitely want a line to end. This allows WordPerfect to automatically insert soft returns so that each line of a paragraph fits between the left and right margins.

Let's continue with our sample letter.

To enter the rest of the body of the letter:
❶ Type the first line of the second paragraph. See Figure 1-33.
❷ Press **[Enter]** at the end of the line.
❸ Press **[Enter]** again to double-space between that line and the first question.
❹ Type **1. Does the video** and continue typing the text shown in Figure 1-33. Complete question number 1 with **hazardous chemicals?** and then stop. Don't continue typing until you're told to do so.

## Scrolling

As you can see in Figure 1-33, the insertion point is at the bottom of the document window, and the window is almost filled with text. As you continue to add text at the end of the document, the text that you typed at the beginning of the document will shift up and disappear off the top of the document window. This shifting up or down of text, called **scrolling,** allows you to see a long document one screenful at a time. The entire document is still in the computer's memory and available for editing; you just can't see it all at once (Figure 1-34). Let's watch more carefully the effect of scrolling as you insert the final text of Steve's letter.

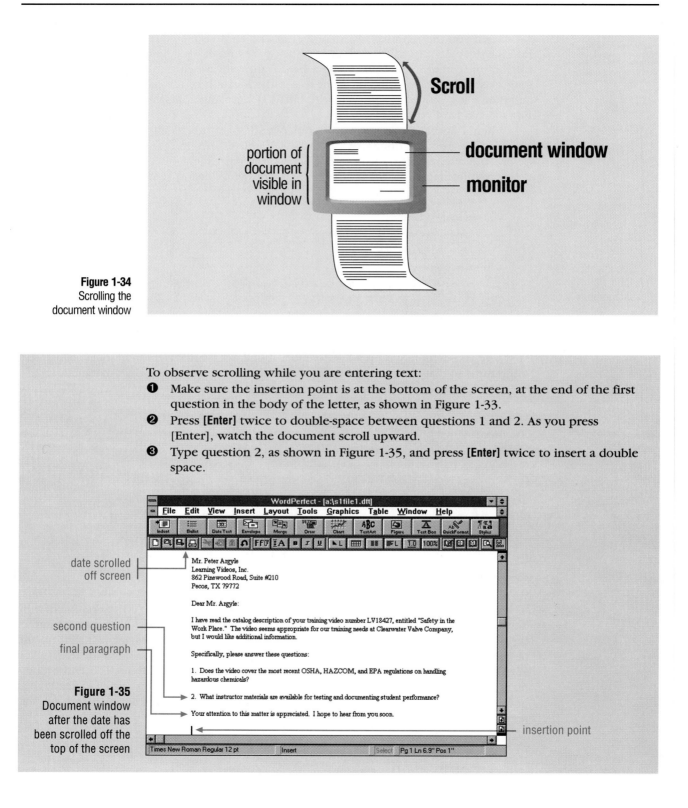

**Figure 1-34**
Scrolling the
document window

To observe scrolling while you are entering text:

❶ Make sure the insertion point is at the bottom of the screen, at the end of the first question in the body of the letter, as shown in Figure 1-33.

❷ Press **[Enter]** twice to double-space between questions 1 and 2. As you press [Enter], watch the document scroll upward.

❸ Type question 2, as shown in Figure 1-35, and press **[Enter]** twice to insert a double space.

**Figure 1-35**
Document window
after the date has
been scrolled off the
top of the screen

❹ Type the final paragraph of the body of the letter, and press **[Enter]** twice. Your screen should now look like Figure 1-35. Notice that the date has scrolled off the top of the document window.

**TROUBLE?**  Because of differences in font sizes and printers, your screen might not look exactly like Figure 1-35. These differences are normal.

Now you're ready to type the complimentary close.

❺ Type **Sincerely yours,** (including the comma).
❻ Press **[Enter]** four times to allow space for the signature. Again watch how the text scrolls up the screen as you add lines to the end of the document.
❼ Type **Steve Morgan** and press **[Enter]**, then type **Executuve Assistant, Operatiosn.** Make sure you type *"Executuve"* and *"Operatiosn"* as shown here, with the typing errors. You'll correct these errors later. See Figure 1-36.

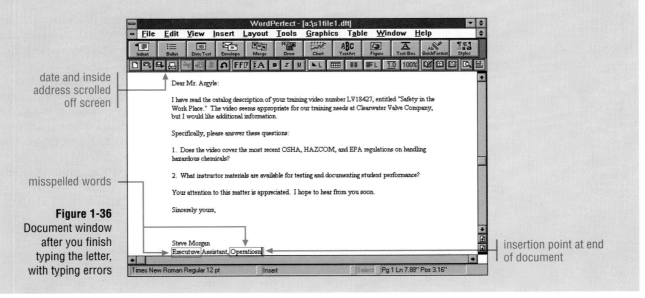

date and inside address scrolled off screen

misspelled words

**Figure 1-36**
Document window after you finish typing the letter, with typing errors

insertion point at end of document

As you can see in Figure 1-36, the date and the inside address no longer appear in the document window. When you pressed [Enter] at the bottom of the screen, the text above the insertion point scrolled up so that they are no longer in view.

To see the beginning of the letter, you can click the vertical scroll bar to scroll the text back into view.

To scroll the text using the arrow keys:
❶ Position the mouse pointer on ▲ at the top of the scroll bar and press and hold the mouse button until the text stops scrolling. You can now see the beginning of the letter.

Notice that as you press the Up Arrow on the scroll bar, the text of the letter scrolls down so that the lines at the end of the letter disappear from the screen and the lines at the beginning reappear. When the beginning of the document and the top margins are completely in view, scrolling stops because the text can't go any lower.

❷ Position the mouse pointer on ⬆ and press and hold the mouse button until the end of the letter is in view, so you can see the line "Executuve Assistant, Operatiosn."

You can also use the arrow keys to scroll the document so you can move the insertion point to any part of the document that doesn't currently appear on the screen.

## Correcting Errors

Novices and experienced WordPerfect users alike make mistakes. One of the advantages of using a word processor is that when you make a mistake, you can correct it quickly and cleanly. The following steps show you several ways to correct errors when you're entering text or executing a command.

If you discover a typing error as soon as you make it, you can press [Backspace] to erase the characters to the left of the insertion point, including the error, and then type the correct characters. The Backspace key might be a left-facing arrow. It is located in the upper-right corner of the main set of keys. You can also eliminate unwanted space. For example, if you accidentally press [Enter] or [Spacebar], you can use [Backspace] to return the insertion point to where you want it.

If you typed the last line of the letter exactly as shown, the word "Operations" is misspelled. Let's correct that error now.

To correct the typing error:
❶ Make sure the insertion point is positioned immediately after the word "Operatiosn." If it's not, click I immediately after the "n."
❷ Press **[Backspace]** twice to erase the last two letters.
❸ Type **ns**. Now "Operations" is correctly spelled. See Figure 1-37.

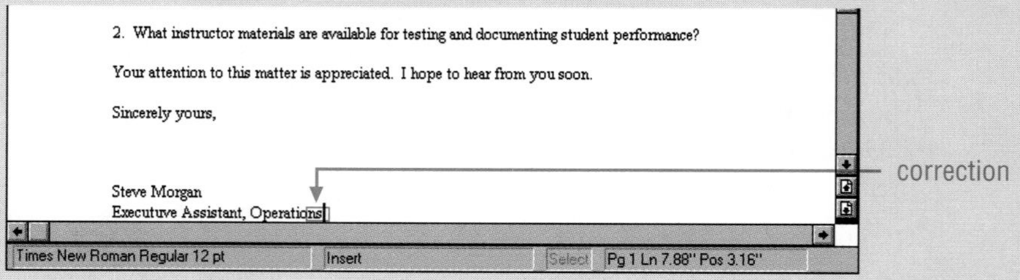

**Figure 1-37**
Document window after you type *ns* for correct spelling of *Operations*

2. What instructor materials are available for testing and documenting student performance?

Your attention to this matter is appreciated. I hope to hear from you soon.

Sincerely yours,

Steve Morgan
Executuve Assistant, Operations

— correction

Times New Roman Regular 12 pt    Insert    Select    Pg 1 Ln 7.88" Pos 3.16"

If you make an error and discover it sometime later, you can move the insertion point to the error, delete the error, and type the correct characters. The word "Executive" is also misspelled. Let's correct it now.

To correct the next typing error:

❶ Click Ị immediately to the left of the second "u" in "Executuve." See Figure 1-38.

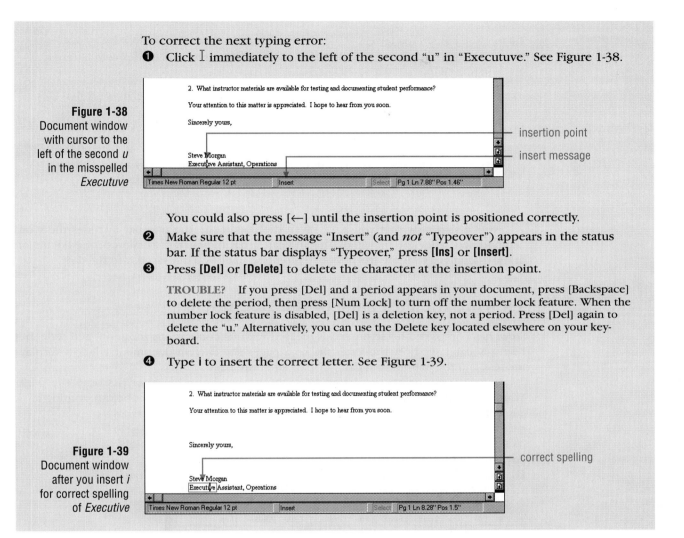

**Figure 1-38**
Document window
with cursor to the
left of the second *u*
in the misspelled
*Executuve*

You could also press [←] until the insertion point is positioned correctly.

❷ Make sure that the message "Insert" (and *not* "Typeover") appears in the status bar. If the status bar displays "Typeover," press **[Ins]** or **[Insert]**.

❸ Press **[Del]** or **[Delete]** to delete the character at the insertion point.

**TROUBLE?**    If you press [Del] and a period appears in your document, press [Backspace] to delete the period, then press [Num Lock] to turn off the number lock feature. When the number lock feature is disabled, [Del] is a deletion key, not a period. Press [Del] again to delete the "u." Alternatively, you can use the Delete key located elsewhere on your keyboard.

❹ Type **i** to insert the correct letter. See Figure 1-39.

**Figure 1-39**
Document window
after you insert *i*
for correct spelling
of *Executive*

You'll learn other methods of correcting typing errors later in this tutorial and in future tutorials.

Take a few minutes to read over the letter you've just typed. If you find any errors, move the insertion point and make the necessary corrections now.

## Saving the Completed Letter

Now that he has completed his letter, Steve wants to save the document to a disk. Although he saved the letter earlier, the version currently on his disk is incomplete. You must remember to save a document after you complete it, even if you've saved the document one or more times while you were creating it. In fact, it's a good idea to get in the habit of saving your documents before printing or checking the spelling and grammar.

Let's save the completed letter now.

To save the completed letter:

❶ Make sure the Student Disk that you used earlier to save the incomplete letter is still in drive A.

It doesn't matter where the insertion point is in the document window when you save a document.

❷ Click 🖫, the **Save button** on the Power Bar (or click **File**, then click **Save**).

Because you have saved the file previously, WordPerfect knows the filename and saves the document without prompting you for information. The mouse pointer appears as an hourglass while the file is being written to the disk.

Notice that now that you have saved the document, the title bar includes the word "unmodified" after the filename. This indicates that the current version of the document in the document window has not been modified since you last saved it to the disk.

## Viewing the Full Page of the Document

Steve has completed his letter and is pleased with its content, organization, and style, but he really can't see how the letter fits on a page. The current document window displays the text and the margins but can't display an entire page at once.

Before Steve prints the letter, he wants to see how the letter fits onto the page. WordPerfect provides a method for viewing the full page of the letter before printing it.

Let's view the full page of the letter now.

To view the full page of the document:

❶ Click 🔍, the **Page Zoom Full button** on the Power Bar. See Figure 1-40.

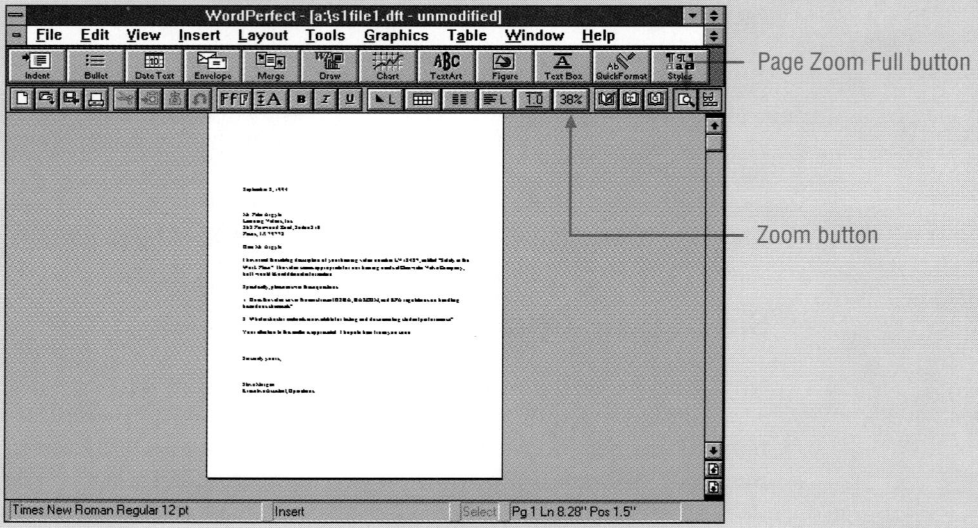

**Figure 1-40**
Document window
with Page Zoom
set to Full

Notice that the current value on the Zoom button of the Power Bar is 38%, indicating that you're viewing the document at 38% of its actual size. The words are hard to read at this zoom value, but the relationship between the text and the margins is easy to see. Notice that the Page Zoom Full icon remains depressed. If you click it again, it will pop back up.

❷ Click ⬚ again.

The button pops back up, and the document returns to its actual (100%) size.

Steve is satisfied with the format of the letter.

## Printing a Document

Having typed, saved, and viewed the full-page document, Steve is now ready to print it.

To print a document currently in a document window:

❶ Make sure your printer is turned on and the paper is properly inserted in the printer. If you have questions about setting up your printer for use with WordPerfect, see your instructor or technical support person.

❷ Click ⬚, the **Print button** on the Power Bar.

WordPerfect displays the Print dialog box. See Figure 1-41.

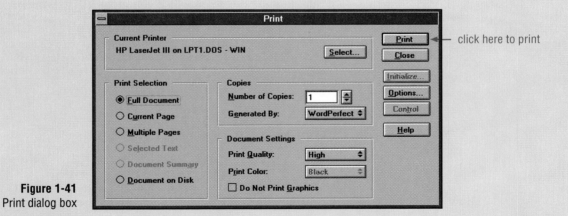

**Figure 1-41**
Print dialog box

❸ Click the **Print button** or (because the Print button has the focus) press **[Enter]** to print the document.

WordPerfect prints the letter. Your printed letter should look similar to the one shown in Figure 1-6.

## Exiting WordPerfect

Steve has now finished typing and printing his letter to Learning Videos, so he is ready to exit WordPerfect. He knows that he should never just turn off the computer without first exiting WordPerfect.

---

**REFERENCE WINDOW**

### Exiting WordPerfect

- Click File, then click Exit.

  *or*

  Double-click the WordPerfect Control menu box.

- If you are prompted to save changes to the document, click the Yes button, and then, if necessary, type a filename and pathname and click the OK button.

---

Let's see how to exit WordPerfect properly now.

To exit WordPerfect:

❶ Click **File**, then click **Exit**.

You could also double-click the Control menu box on the application window.

Because you have not modified the document since you saved it last, WordPerfect immediately exits to the Windows Program Manager.

**TROUBLE?**    WordPerfect might display a dialog box with the message "Save changes to A:\S1FILE1.DFT?" This indicates that you have modified the document since last saving it and probably need to save it again before exiting. Click the Yes button to save the current version and exit WordPerfect.

You have now exited WordPerfect. The File Manager window should now appear on the screen.

*If you want to take a break* and resume the tutorial at a later time, you can do so now. When you resume working on the tutorial, continue with the next section.

## Opening a Document

After Steve types, saves, and prints the draft version of the letter to Learning Videos, he gives the printed draft to his supervisor, Andrea Simone. Andrea reads the letter and makes a note to Steve to include a question about volume discounts (Figure 1-42). After he adds this question, Steve will print the letter again and mail it.

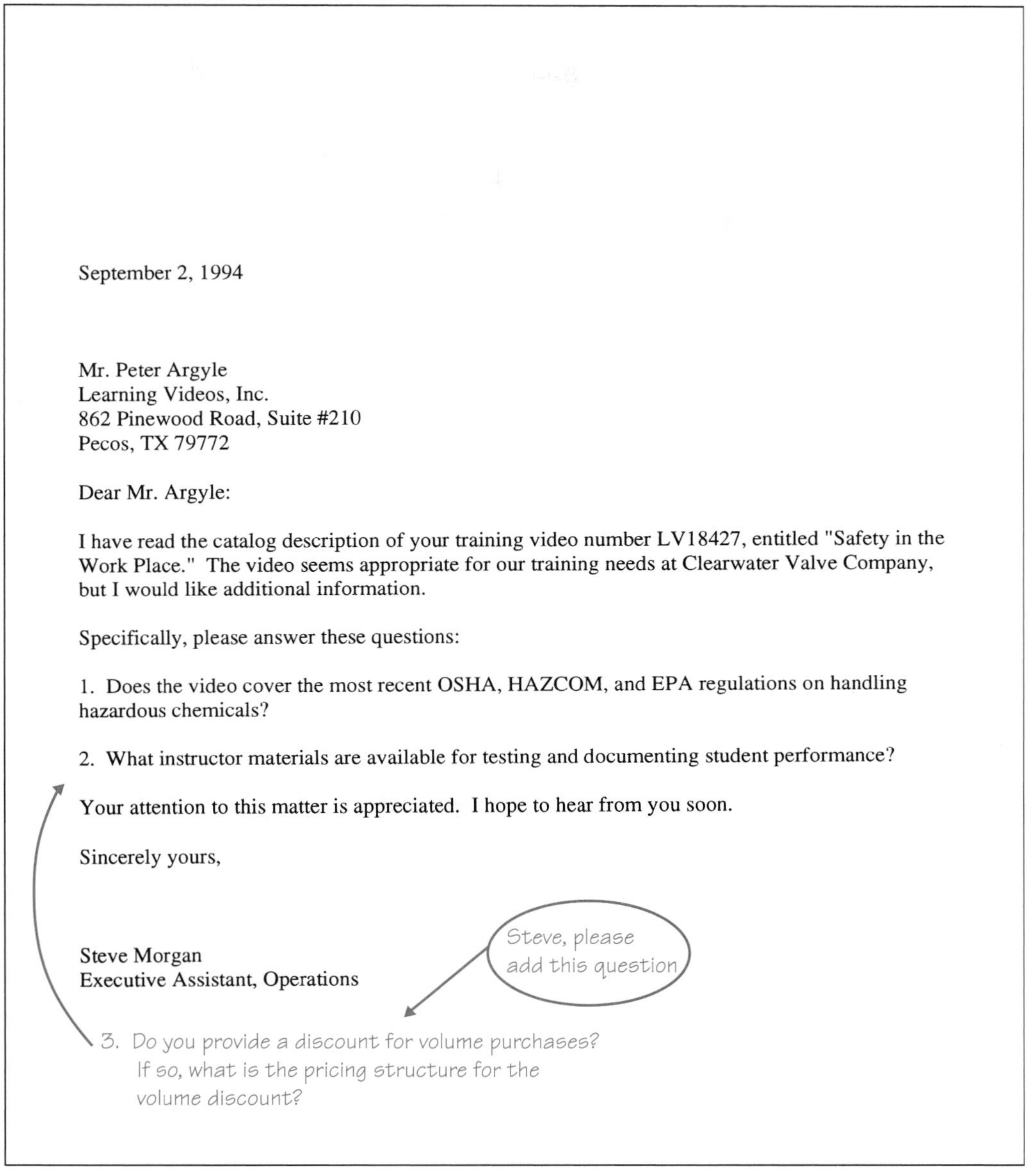

September 2, 1994


Mr. Peter Argyle
Learning Videos, Inc.
862 Pinewood Road, Suite #210
Pecos, TX 79772

Dear Mr. Argyle:

I have read the catalog description of your training video number LV18427, entitled "Safety in the Work Place." The video seems appropriate for our training needs at Clearwater Valve Company, but I would like additional information.

Specifically, please answer these questions:

1. Does the video cover the most recent OSHA, HAZCOM, and EPA regulations on handling hazardous chemicals?

2. What instructor materials are available for testing and documenting student performance?

Your attention to this matter is appreciated. I hope to hear from you soon.

Sincerely yours,



Steve Morgan
Executive Assistant, Operations

*Steve, please add this question*

3. Do you provide a discount for volume purchases? If so, what is the pricing structure for the volume discount?

**Figure 1-42**
Steve's draft with Andrea's addition

To do this, Steve must launch WordPerfect again, open the document file from the disk into computer memory, add a third question to the letter, save the revised letter, and print the final version.

REFERENCE WINDOW

**Opening a Document**

- Click the Open button on the Power Bar.
- If necessary, change the drive and directory location of the document file.
- Scroll through the Filename list until the document name appears.
- Click the name of the document in the Filename list. The filename appears in the Filename text box.
- Click the OK button or press [Enter].

Let's open the document file now.

To open a document file into a document window:

❶ Launch WordPerfect as you did earlier in this tutorial, in the section called "Launching WordPerfect."

❷ Make sure the disk on which you saved the letter is in the appropriate disk drive.

❸ Click 🖼, the **Open icon** on the Power Bar.

WordPerfect displays the Open File dialog box and waits for you to indicate the document name. See Figure 1-43.

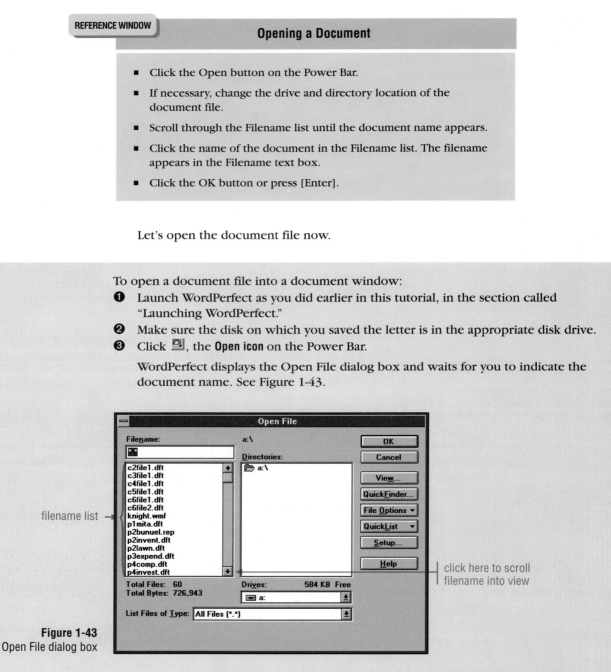

**Figure 1-43**
Open File dialog box

❹ If drive A (or B) doesn't appear in the Drives section of the dialog box, click the **Down Arrow** to the right of the Drives section, and click **a:** to choose drive A (or click the letter of the drive that your Student Disk is in).

The list of files on the student disk appears in the Filename list of the dialog box.

❺ Scroll the filename list until "s1file1.dft" appears, then click the name of the document, **s1file1.dft**, in the Filename list. The name of the document then appears in the Filename text box. See Figure 1-44.

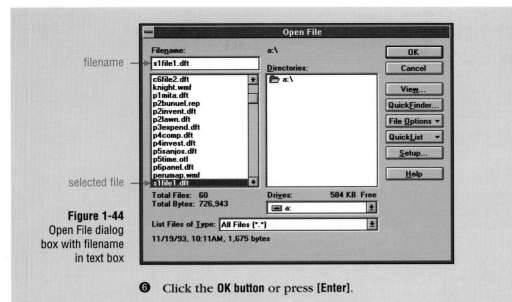

filename

selected file

**Figure 1-44**
Open File dialog
box with filename
in text box

❻   Click the **OK button** or press **[Enter]**.

WordPerfect opens the document from the disk into the document window.

Now that he has opened the file, Steve is ready to make the addition Andrea requested.

To modify the letter:
❶   Scroll the document up until you can see question 2. Click I immediately after the
phrase ". . . documenting student performance?"
❷   Make sure "Insert" appears in the status bar. If it doesn't, press **[Ins]** or **[Insert]**.
❸   Press **[Enter]** twice to insert a double space after question 2.
❹   Type **3. Do you provide a discount for volume purchases? If so, what is the pricing structure for
the volume discount?** See Figure 1-45.

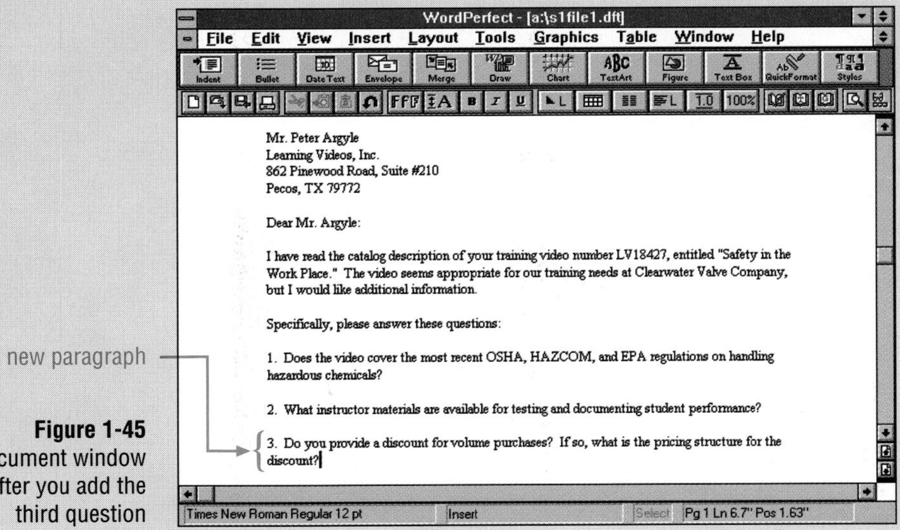

new paragraph

**Figure 1-45**
Document window
after you add the
third question

The letter is now modified the way Steve wants it. He looks over the letter one last time for any errors. He is ready to print the final version. But before he prints the letter, he has to save this new, final version because the letter on the screen is different from the one on the disk.

### Saving a Document with a New Filename

- Click File, then click Save As.
- Type the new filename. Do not press [Enter].
- If necessary, change the drive and directory location where you want to save the document.
- Click the OK button or press [Enter].

Let's save the final version now. (Under normal circumstances, you would probably save the new version over the old version, but for instructional purposes, we'll save the new version of the letter to a new document file.)

To save the final version of the letter with a new filename:

**❶** Click **File**, then click **Save As.**

WordPerfect displays the Save As dialog box. The filename of the document on the screen automatically appears in the prompt.

**❷** Type **s1file2.let.** *Do not press [Enter].*

   **TROUBLE?**    If you accidentally pressed [Enter] while the default drive was, for example, C instead of A, repeat Steps 1 and 2. This time make sure to go to the next step without pressing [Enter].

**❸** If necessary, change the drive to A (or to whichever drive holds your Student Disk) using the Drives section of the dialog box.

**❹** Click the **OK button** or press **[Enter].**

Now a copy of the final letter is saved on the disk as S1FILE2.LET.

This completes Steve Morgan's letter to Learning Videos. You can now print the final copy of the letter.

**❺** Print the document by clicking 🖳, the **Print button** on the Power Bar, then click the **Print button**. The printed letter should look like Figure 1-46.

CLEARWATER
VALVE
1555 North Technology Ave., Nutley, NJ 07110
Phone (201) 347-1628   FAX (201)374-8261

September 2, 1994

Mr. Peter Argyle
Learning Videos, Inc.
862 Pinewood Road, Suite #210
Pecos, TX 79772

Dear Mr. Argyle:

I have read the catalog description of your training video number LV18427, entitled "Safety in the Work Place." The video seems appropriate for our training needs at Clearwater Valve Company, but I would like additional information.

Specifically, please answer these questions:

1. Does the video cover the most recent OSHA, HAZCOM, and EPA regulations on handling hazardous chemicals?

2. What instructor materials are available for testing and documenting student performance?

3. Do you provide a discount for volume purchases? If so, what is the pricing structure for the discount?

Your attention to this matter is appreciated. I hope to hear from you soon.

Sincerely yours,

Steve Morgan
Executive Assistant, Operations

**Figure 1-46**
Final version of
Steve's letter

❻ Close the document window by clicking **File,** then clicking **Close.**

Satisfied with his letter, Steve mails it to Learning Videos.

## Getting Help

How do you know which button to click, which menu item to select, or which function key to press in order to change the margins, number pages, or perform any other WordPerfect command? The best way is through training and continued experience in using WordPerfect. These WordPerfect tutorials will give you the training and the experience you need to perform the most important WordPerfect operations.

But WordPerfect provides another way for you to learn what commands are available and how to execute them: the WordPerfect Help feature. Both the main menu bar and the template list the Help feature. When you click Help and then Contents or press [F1] (Help), WordPerfect displays a Help window that lets you choose various methods for getting information.

**Opening the Help Window**

- Click Help, then click Contents.

*or*

- Press [F1] (Help).

Let's open the Help Contents window now.

To open the Help window:
❶ Click **Help**, then click **Contents**; or press **[F1]** (Help). The WordPerfect Help window appears on the screen. See Figure 1-47. Your Help window might be smaller or larger than the one shown in the figure.

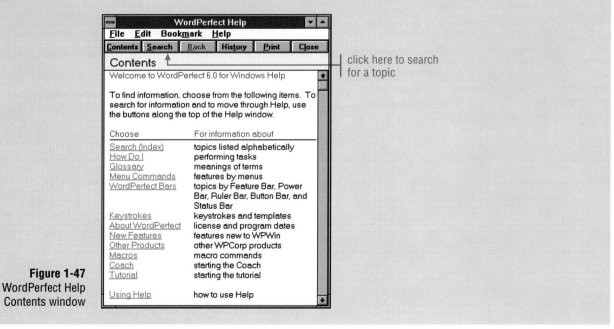

**Figure 1-47**
WordPerfect Help
Contents window

The Help window has a menu bar and a toolbar. These remain in the window as you look through different Help screens. You can click the Search button from any Help window to search for a topic. If you click the Back button, you will go back to the previous screen you were viewing. Clicking the Print button will print the current Help window, and clicking the Close button will close the Help window and return you to the main document window.

In any of the Help windows, you can click a word that is underlined and in green to get additional help on that item. As you move the mouse pointer to one of these words, the pointer becomes 🖑 with the index finger pointing at the item.

Suppose you forget how to execute the WordPerfect command for inserting the date into a document. You can use the Help feature to get information on "Date" by using the alphabetical index of features. Let's do that now.

To see an alphabetical index of features that start with the letter D:

❶ Click the **Search button** at the top of the WordPerfect Help window. WordPerfect displays a Search dialog box and waits for you to type the name (or first few letters) of a WordPerfect command. See Figure 1-48.

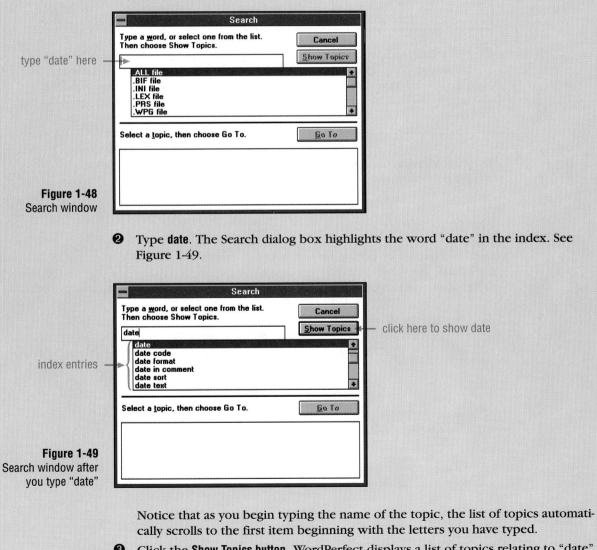

**Figure 1-48**
Search window

❷ Type **date**. The Search dialog box highlights the word "date" in the index. See Figure 1-49.

**Figure 1-49**
Search window after
you type "date"

Notice that as you begin typing the name of the topic, the list of topics automatically scrolls to the first item beginning with the letters you have typed.

❸ Click the **Show Topics button**. WordPerfect displays a list of topics relating to "date" in the box at the bottom of the dialog box. See Figure 1-50.

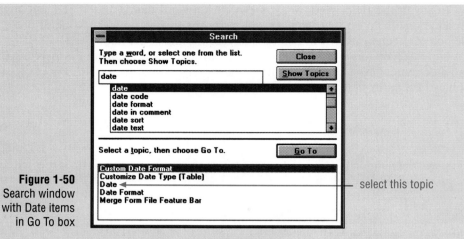

— select this topic

**Figure 1-50**
Search window
with Date items
in Go To box

❹    Click **Date**, then click the **Go To button.** The WordPerfect Help window displays
information about the Date command. Notice that WordPerfect describes the
purpose of the command and the steps required to execute the command. Also
notice that the description of the command ends with "See Also." You can click
on one of the See Also topics to get more information about the current or
related commands and features. You could also click Back to go back to the
Contents list or perform other actions to move through the Help system.

❺    After viewing the Help explanation, click the **Close button.** WordPerfect closes the
Help window and returns you to the main document window.

## Getting Help from the Coach

Another method for getting help in learning certain specialized features of WordPerfect is
the Coach. The Coach doesn't just tell you what to do and then leave you on your own, but
rather gives you instructions one step at a time as you work through an unfamiliar feature.

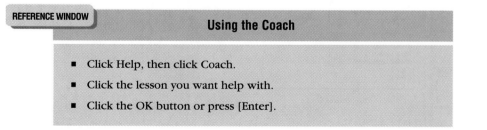

**REFERENCE WINDOW**

### Using the Coach

- Click Help, then click Coach.
- Click the lesson you want help with.
- Click the OK button or press [Enter].

For example, suppose you wanted to draw a border around a paragraph. The Coach
will help you learn this feature.

To use the Coach to draw a border around a paragraph:

❶ Type the following paragraph:

**WordPerfect is a powerful word processor. It easily performs many functions that are difficult or impossible on a normal typewriter.**

Now you're ready to draw the border around this paragraph.

❷ Click **Help**, then click **Coach**. The Coach dialog box appears on the screen with a list of the types of lessons that are available. See Figure 1-51.

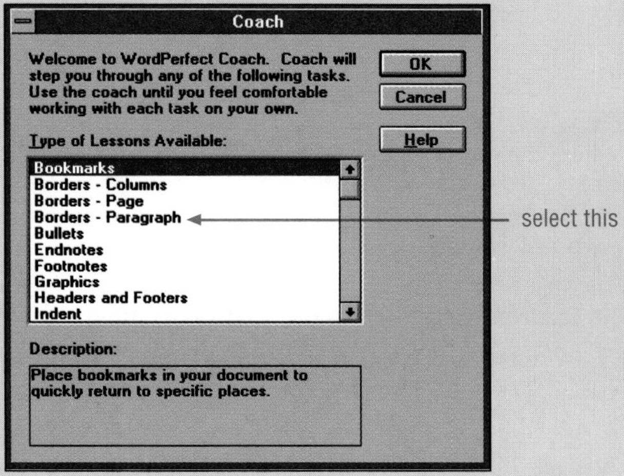

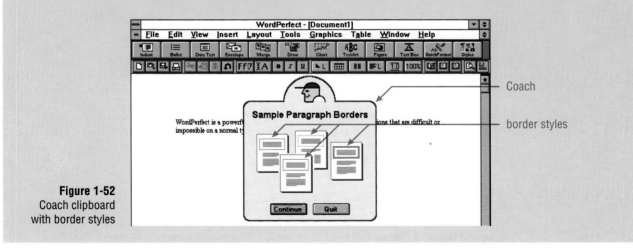

**Figure 1-51**
Coach dialog box

❸ In the Type of Lessons Available box, click **Borders - Paragraphs,** then click the **OK button** or press **[Enter]**.

A Coach "clipboard" appears on the screen with basic information about the feature you're getting help on. In this case, the Coach shows some sample paragraph borders. See Figure 1-52.

**Figure 1-52**
Coach clipboard
with border styles

Now you're ready to follow the Coach's instructions.

To use the Coach to draw a border around a paragraph:

❶  Click the **Continue button** to continue to the next Coach item. See Figure 1-53.

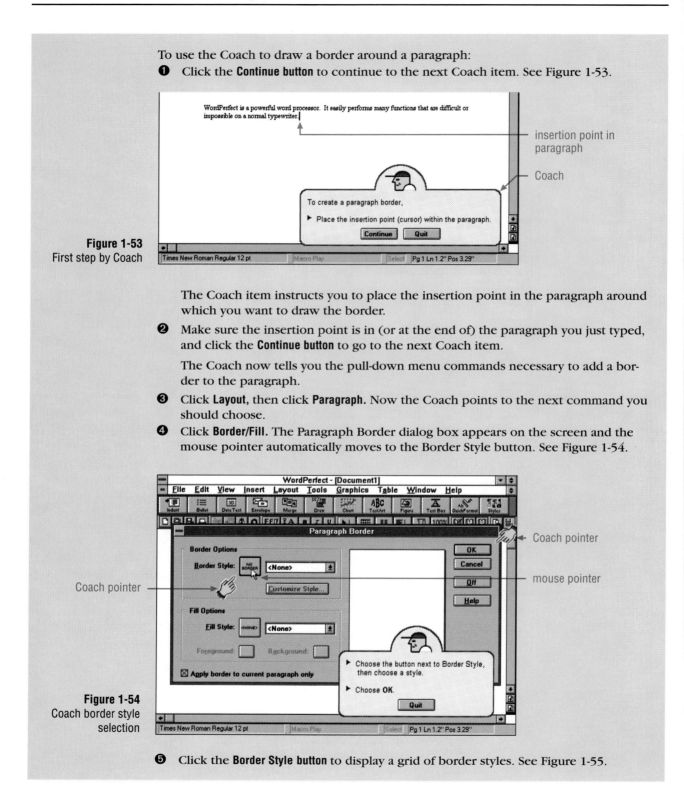

**Figure 1-53**
First step by Coach

The Coach item instructs you to place the insertion point in the paragraph around which you want to draw the border.

❷  Make sure the insertion point is in (or at the end of) the paragraph you just typed, and click the **Continue button** to go to the next Coach item.

The Coach now tells you the pull-down menu commands necessary to add a border to the paragraph.

❸  Click **Layout**, then click **Paragraph**. Now the Coach points to the next command you should choose.

❹  Click **Border/Fill**. The Paragraph Border dialog box appears on the screen and the mouse pointer automatically moves to the Border Style button. See Figure 1-54.

**Figure 1-54**
Coach border style
selection

❺  Click the **Border Style button** to display a grid of border styles. See Figure 1-55.

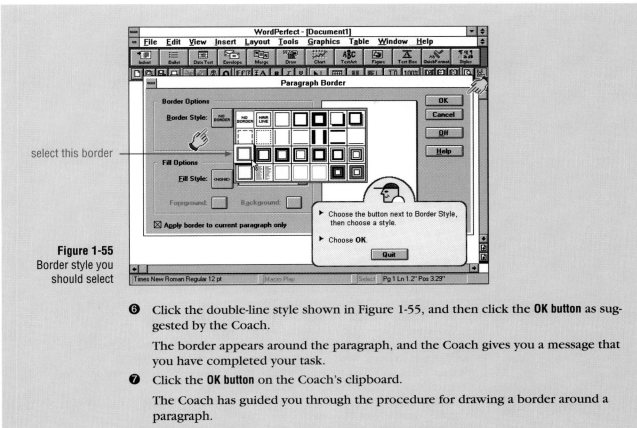

**Figure 1-55**
Border style you
should select

select this border

⑥ Click the double-line style shown in Figure 1-55, and then click the **OK button** as suggested by the Coach.

The border appears around the paragraph, and the Coach gives you a message that you have completed your task.

⑦ Click the **OK button** on the Coach's clipboard.

The Coach has guided you through the procedure for drawing a border around a paragraph.

⑧ Close the document window without saving the document.

You have now completed Tutorial 1. Remember to exit WordPerfect before turning off your computer.

# Questions

**E**

1. How do you launch WordPerfect from the Windows Program Manager?
2. What does the status bar message *Ln 4.5"* mean?
3. How can you automatically insert today's date into a WordPerfect document?
4. How would you find out information about using the Backspace key in WordPerfect?
   *Hint:* Look for the entry "Keystrokes" on the Contents screen of the Help window.
5. How would you find information about the Print command in WordPerfect?
6. What are the default margin settings in WordPerfect?
7. With the insertion point in the document window, how would you do the following?
   a. Close the current WordPerfect document window.
   b. Double-space between paragraphs.
   c. Display the WordPerfect Help window.

    d. Print the document that is in the document window.
    e. Exit WordPerfect.
8. Define the following:
    a. word wrap
    b. pull-down menu
    c. Button Bar
    d. Power Bar
    e. insertion point
    f. font
    g. open (a document)
    h. scrolling
    i. default format settings
    j. function-key template
    k. hard return
    l. soft return
    m. document window
9. Name and describe the four steps in planning a document.
10. Why should you save a document to your disk several times, even before you finish typing it?
11. What is the purpose of viewing the full page of the document before printing it?
**E** 12. Move the mouse pointer around the WordPerfect window and through the WordPerfect Help window. Describe five shapes of the mouse pointer that you see.
**E** 13. What do you think the title bar message "Document3" would mean?

Use the Help feature to answer the questions 14 through 17:
**E** 14. This tutorial covered several WordPerfect bars: the status bar, the Button Bar, the Power Bar, and so forth. What is the Ruler Bar and how do you display it?
**E** 15. Using the Coach, find out what a bulleted list is and how you would create one. List the steps given by the Coach to create a bulleted list.
**E** 16. What are the keystrokes for moving the insertion point to the beginning of the document? To the end of a document?
**E** 17. What is the difference between the Date Text command and the Date Code command?

## Tutorial Assignments

Be sure your WordPerfect Student Disk is in the disk drive and that a blank document window is on the screen. Then open the file T1FILE1.DFT and do the following:
1. Delete the date at the beginning of the letter, then use WordPerfect's Date Text command to insert today's date into the document.
2. Save the letter as S1FILE3.LET.
3. View the document in full-page zoom to see what it will look like on the page before you print it.
4. Print the document.

Clear the document window, open the letter T1FILE2.DFT from your Student Disk, and do the following:
5. In the body of the memo, insert a space between "Work" and "place" in the word "Workplace."
6. Delete the lowercase "p" in "place" and type an uppercase letter, so that the phrase reads "Work Place."
7. Correct the error in the word "Valev" to make it "Valve."
8. Correct the error in the word "traiming" (in the first paragraph) to make it "training."
9. Save the document as S1FILE4.MEM.
10. Print the document.

```
MEMORANDUM — Clearwater Valve Company

Date: February 17, 1995

To:  Andrea Simone, Executive Assistant, Operations

From:  Megan Lui, Human Resources Manager

Re: Safety Training


Thanks, Andrea, for the great job you did in setting up safety
training for our employees.  Everyone I talked to thought the
training was great.  That's a real compliment given the
fundamentally boring nature of the subject matter!

Keep up the good work.




cc:    Steve Morgan, Operations Manager
```

**Figure 1-56**

Clear the document window, then use Figure 1-56 to complete Assignments 11 through 15.

11. Type the memo, pressing [Spacebar] twice after "Date:," "To:," "From:," and "Re:."
12. Use WordPerfect's Date Text feature to insert today's date.
13. After completing the memo, save it as S1FILE5.MEM.
14. View the memo in full-page zoom before printing it.
15. Print the memo.

**E**

16. One of the shortcut key commands is [Shift][F1] (Help: What Is?).
   a. Press [Shift][F1] (Help: What Is?).
   b. Describe the appearance of the What Is? mouse pointer after you press [Shift][F1].
   c. With the What Is? mouse pointer, click View on the main menu bar.
   d. With the View Menu help window on the screen, click Zoom.
   e. Print the information on the Zoom command.
   f. Close the Help window.

# Case Problems

### 1. Letter to Request Information About Copier Machines

Ivan Janetski is the equipment manager for the public accounting firm of Hofstetter, Inouye & Pilling. One of his responsibilities is to purchase office copiers for the company. After reading an advertisement for Mita copiers, he decides to write for more information on copier models and prices. He has already written the body of the letter and now needs only to insert the date, the inside address, the salutation, the complimentary close, and his name and title.

Open the document P1MITA.DFT from your WordPerfect Student Disk into a document window, and do the following:

1. Move the insertion point to the beginning of the document and press [Enter] six times to insert sufficient space for a letterhead.
2. Use WordPerfect's Date Text command to insert today's date.
3. Insert four blank lines after the date and, using the proper business letter format, type the inside address: Mita Copystar America, Inc., P.O. Box 3900, Peoria, IL 61614.
4. Insert a blank line after the inside address, type the salutation "Dear Sales Representative:," then insert another blank line.
5. Move the insertion point to the end of the document, insert a blank line, and type the complimentary close "Sincerely," (including the comma).
6. Add four blank lines to leave room for the signature and then type the name and title: Ivan Janetski, Office Equipment Manager.
7. Move the insertion point to the beginning of the document, then use ⫯A⫯, the Font Size button on the Power Bar, to change the font size to 14-point.

**E**

8. With the insertion point still at the beginning of the document, click ⫯FF⫯, the Font Face button on the Power Bar. Then click the font named Courier New.
9. Save the letter as S1MITA.LET.
10. Preview the letter using the Page Zoom Full button on the Power Bar.
11. Print the letter.

## 2. Memo to Congratulate the Head of a Sales Team

One of your co-workers at Clearwater Valve Company, Leslie Homen, is head of a sales team. Her team recently received a company award for having the highest sales for the quarter.

Do the following:

1. Write a memo to Leslie Homen congratulating her on receiving the award. Remember to use the four-part planning process. You should plan the content, organization, and style of the memo, and use a standard memo format similar to the one shown in Figure 1-56.
2. Save the document as S1HOMEN.MEM.
3. Print this version of the memo.

**E**

4. Move the insertion point to the beginning of the document, then click ⫯FF⫯, the Font Face button on the Power Bar. Then click the font named Courier (or some other font name) to change the font in your document.
5. With the insertion point still at the beginning of the document, click ⫯A⫯, the Font Size button on the Power Bar, to change the font size to 14-point.
6. Save the document as S1HOMEN2.MEM.
7. Preview the memo using the Page Zoom Full button on the Power Bar.
8. Print the memo.

## 3. Letter of Introduction to a Distributor

Suppose you're a sales representative for Clearwater Valve Company. You have a list of distributors through whom you would like to sell your product. One of the distributors is Mr. Dale Chow of Energy Ventures, 891 Second Street, Los Altos, CA 94002, a company that distributes equipment for oil rigs.

Do the following:

1. Write a letter introducing yourself to Mr. Chow and requesting the opportunity to visit him to discuss the possibility of having Energy Ventures distribute Clearwater Valve Company products.

**E**

2. Use WordPerfect's Help feature to learn how to use the pull-down menus to change the font, then move the insertion point to the beginning of your letter and change the font. You may choose any font you like other than Times New Roman.

**E**

3. Use the Coach to help you draw a border around the entire page of the letter.
4. Save the letter as S1ENERGY.LET.
5. Preview the letter using the Page Zoom Full button on the Power Bar.
6. Print the letter.

*Read*

# Formatting and Editing a Document

## Writing a Product Information Memo for an Ad Launch

**Decision Development Corporation**   David Truong is an assistant product manager at Decision Development Corporation (DDC), a company that specializes in software tools for business. David reports to Liz Escobar, the product manager. One of David's responsibilities is to write product description memos to the DDC advertising group to explain the key features and benefits of new products. The advertising group uses these memos to help them prepare for launch meetings, at which they plan the advertising campaigns for new products.

Liz has just stopped by David's office and asked him to write a product description memo to the ad group about DDC's newest product, InTrack, an investment tracking program. Liz reminds David that she wants him to submit his first draft to her for comments and corrections. After she returns the draft to him, he should make the necessary changes and print three copies of the memo—one for the advertising group, one for her, and one for the InTrack product file.

In this tutorial you'll plan, write, and edit David's memo to DDC's advertising group.

# Planning the Document

First, David plans the four components of the document. He considers content, organization, style, and format.

### Content

David has kept notes on the key features of InTrack and has a copy of the program specifications produced by DDC's software design team. He distills this information so the advertising group will understand the product and still have the necessary details to write the text of the advertisements, commonly called ad copy. He knows that the ad group is familiar with computer software, so he feels free to use technical terminology.

### Organization

Because the product description is a memo, David knows that his document will begin with the standard memo heading. He decides that the body of the memo will be a numbered list of the key features of InTrack.

### Style

David assumes that the ad group will adapt and edit his information to a style that suits the needs of the ad campaign. His style, therefore, will be clear and straightforward.

### Format

David decides that in his first draft he will use WordPerfect's default format settings, which include one-inch margins and text aligned along the left margin but ragged along the right margin. Liz might suggest format changes, but for now he'll use the defaults.

Having planned the document, David uses WordPerfect to write the rough draft. He submits it to Liz, who later returns the draft with her editing marks and notes (Figure 2-1). David looks over her comments and is ready to create the final draft of the InTrack product description memo.

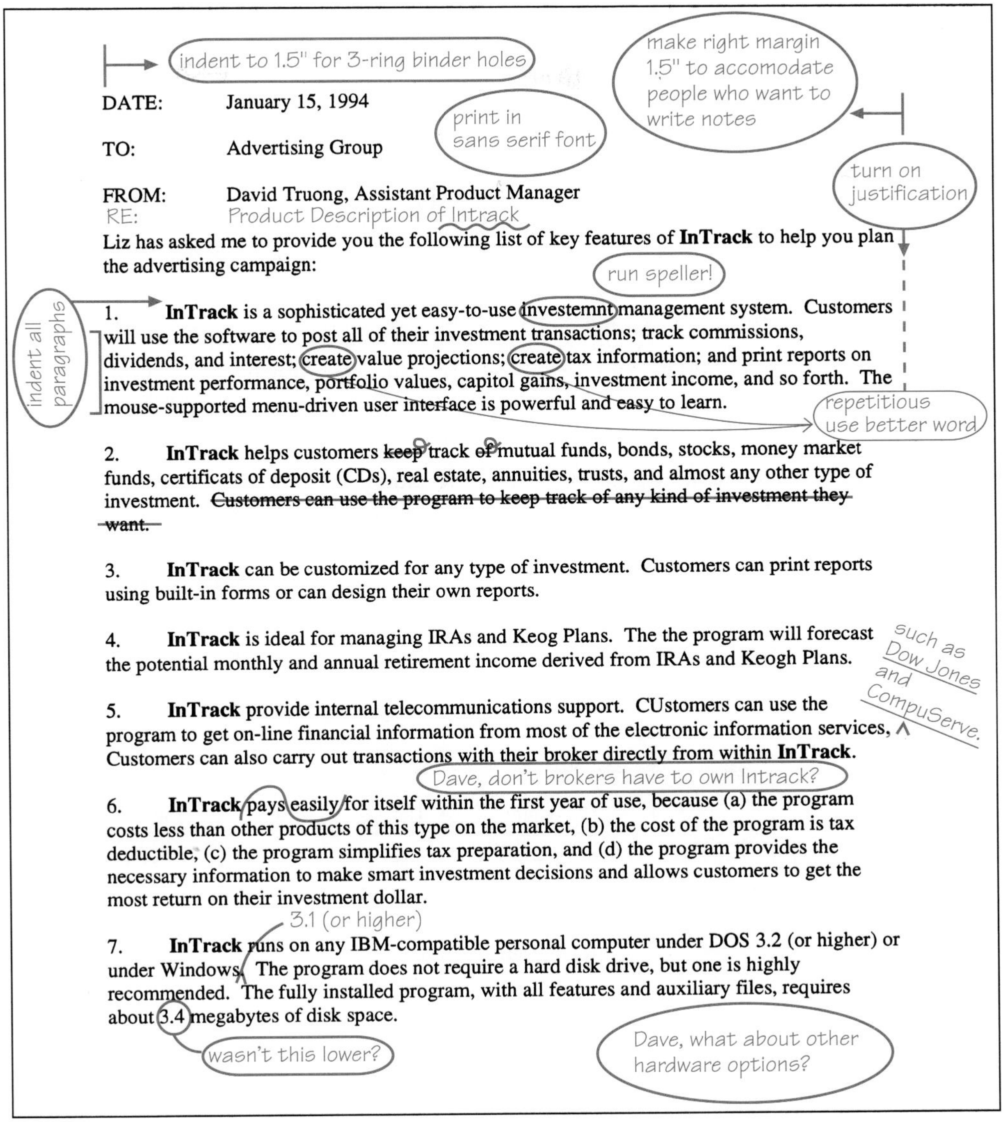

DATE: January 15, 1994

TO: Advertising Group

FROM: David Truong, Assistant Product Manager

Liz has asked me to provide you the following list of key features of **InTrack** to help you plan the advertising campaign:

1. **InTrack** is a sophisticated yet easy-to-use investemnt management system. Customers will use the software to post all of their investment transactions; track commissions, dividends, and interest; create value projections; create tax information; and print reports on investment performance, portfolio values, capitol gains, investment income, and so forth. The mouse-supported menu-driven user interface is powerful and easy to learn.

2. **InTrack** helps customers keep track of mutual funds, bonds, stocks, money market funds, certificats of deposit (CDs), real estate, annuities, trusts, and almost any other type of investment. ~~Customers can use the program to keep track of any kind of investment they want.~~

3. **InTrack** can be customized for any type of investment. Customers can print reports using built-in forms or can design their own reports.

4. **InTrack** is ideal for managing IRAs and Keog Plans. The the program will forecast the potential monthly and annual retirement income derived from IRAs and Keogh Plans.

5. **InTrack** provide internal telecommunications support. CUstomers can use the program to get on-line financial information from most of the electronic information services. Customers can also carry out transactions with their broker directly from within **InTrack**.

6. **InTrack** pays easily for itself within the first year of use, because (a) the program costs less than other products of this type on the market, (b) the cost of the program is tax deductible, (c) the program simplifies tax preparation, and (d) the program provides the necessary information to make smart investment decisions and allows customers to get the most return on their investment dollar.

7. **InTrack** runs on any IBM-compatible personal computer under DOS 3.2 (or higher) or under Windows. The program does not require a hard disk drive, but one is highly recommended. The fully installed program, with all features and auxiliary files, requires about 3.4 megabytes of disk space.



**Figure 2-1**
Memo with Liz Escobar's suggested changes

In the instructions on editing the memo, you'll be given a choice, when appropriate, of whether to use pull-down menus (with the keyboard or with the mouse), the function-key template and the function keys, or the Button Bar to execute WordPerfect commands.

## Opening the Document

David begins by opening the first draft of his memo, which has the filename C2FILE1.DFT. Remember, the filename extension .DFT stands for "draft."

To open the document:

❶ Launch WordPerfect (if you haven't done so already) and make sure a blank document window is on the screen. If necessary, refer to Tutorial 1 to see how to clear the document window.

❷ Insert your WordPerfect Student Disk into drive A.

TROUBLE?   If your Student Disk doesn't fit in drive A, use drive B. Then, whenever this tutorial refers to drive A, use drive B instead.

❸ Click 🖻, the **Open button** on the Power Bar. The Open File dialog box appears on the screen.

❹ Click the **Down Arrow** to the right of the Drives section, then click **a:** to choose drive A.

The list of files on the Student Disk appears in the Open File dialog box.

❺ Click the filename **c2file1.dft**, then click the **OK button** or press **[Enter]**. The rough draft of David Truong's memo appears on the screen.

To avoid the problem of accidentally overwriting the disk file C2FILE1.DFT, let's save your document back to the disk using another filename. That way, you'll always have the original tutorial file on disk.

❻ Click **File**, then click **Save As** to display the Save As dialog box.

❼ Type the new filename **s2file1.dft**.

Your WordPerfect window should now look like Figure 2-2.

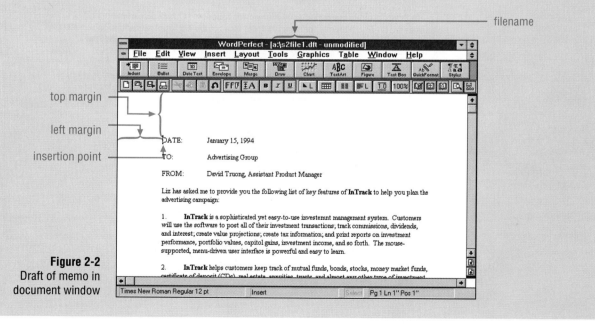

Figure 2-2
Draft of memo in
document window

## Making Large-Scale Insertion Point Moves

You already know how to use the arrow keys ([→], [←], [↑], [↓]) to move the insertion point one character to the right or left or one line up or down. Now you'll see how to use the keyboard to move the insertion point more than one character or one line at a time.

These large-scale insertion point moves will save you considerable time and energy when you have to move the insertion point around to different parts of your documents.

As you work through the following steps, you may notice several typographical and spelling errors in David's memo. Leave them for now. They appear in the document to help you learn various ways of editing the text and correcting the spelling—two skills we'll cover later in this tutorial.

To make large-scale insertion point moves:

❶ Press **[Ctrl][End]**.

Pressing this key combination moves the insertion point to the end of the document. See Figure 2-3.

**Figure 2-3**
Document window after moving insertion point to end of document

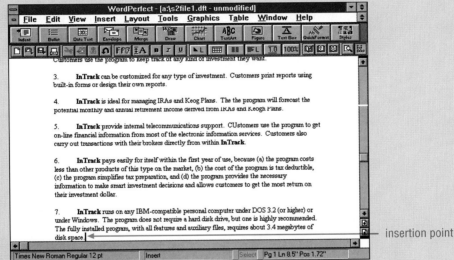

insertion point

❷ Press **[Ctrl][Home]** to move the insertion point to the beginning of the document.

❸ Position Ⅰ immediately to the left of the "1" in the first numbered paragraph of the memo and click the left mouse button, or press **[↓]** enough times to move the insertion point there.

❹ Press **[End]** to move the insertion point to the end of the current line.

❺ Press **[Home]** to move the insertion point to the beginning of the current line.

❻ Press **[Ctrl][→]** (Word Right) three times to move the insertion point to the word "a," then press **[Ctrl][←]** (Word Left) three times to move the insertion point back to the "1."

As you can see, [Ctrl][→] moves the insertion point one word to the right, and [Ctrl][←] moves the insertion point one word to the left.

❼ Press **[Page Down]** (or **[PgDn]** with Num Lock off) to move the insertion point to the bottom of the document window. Press it again to move the insertion point down another window. See Figure 2-4. (Because of differences in fonts and printers, your screen may look slightly different from Figure 2-4.)

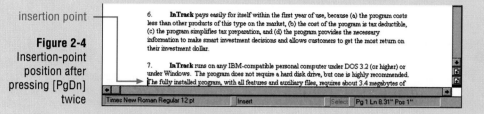

insertion point

**Figure 2-4**
Insertion-point
position after
pressing [PgDn]
twice

Pressing [Page Down] or [PgDn] moves the insertion point to the bottom of the current document window. When you press it again, the insertion point moves to the bottom of the next screenful of text.

❽ Press **[Page Up]** (or **[PgUp]** with Num Lock off) twice.

Pressing [Page Down] or [PgDn] once moves the insertion point to the top of the current window. Pressing it again moves the insertion point up another screenful of text. See Figure 2-5. Your insertion point might be in a slightly different position due to differences in fonts and printers.

insertion point

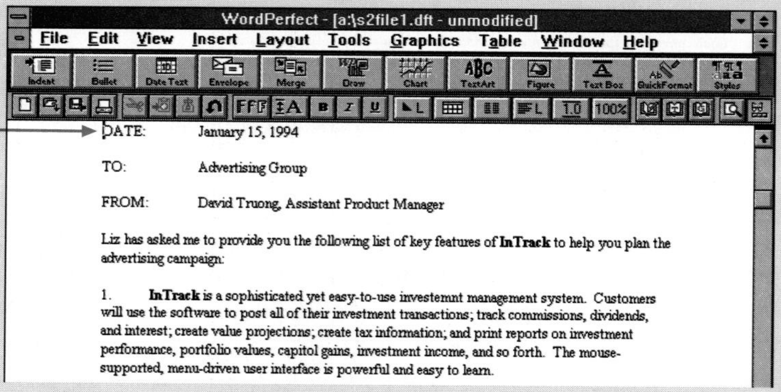

**Figure 2-5**
Insertion-point
position after
pressing [PgUp]
twice

The insertion-point movement keys demonstrated in the preceding steps are only a few of the many ways you can move the insertion point in WordPerfect. Figure 2-6 lists most of the WordPerfect insertion-point movement commands. You'll use some of the other methods in later tutorials.

| Insertion-Point Movement Keys | |
|---|---|
| **Key** | **Movement** |
| [←] | Left one character |
| [→] | Right one character |
| [↑] | Up one line |
| [↓] | Down one line |
| [Ctrl][←] | Left one word |
| [Ctrl][→] | Right one word |
| [Home] | Beginning of line |
| [End] | End of line |
| [PgUp] | Top of screen, then up one screen at a time |
| [PgDn] | Bottom of screen, then down one screen at a time |
| [Ctrl][Home] | Beginning of document (after initial formatting codes) |
| [Ctrl][Home] twice | Beginning of document (before initial formatting codes) |
| [Ctrl][End] | End of document |

**Figure 2-6**
Insertion-point
movement keys

Of course, you can also move the insertion point to any location in the document window simply by clicking I on that location. In some cases, you might find it easier to use the mouse than the keyboard, and in other cases you might find it easier to use the keyboard than the mouse. Your own experiences and preferences will dictate which method you use in a given situation. Throughout these tutorials, when we give instructions to move the insertion point to different places in a document, we usually won't specify how you should move the insertion point; that decision is up to you.

As you move the insertion point through a document, you'll discover that the insertion point won't move to any region of the screen unoccupied by text. If the insertion point is at the end of a document, for example, and you press [PgDn], the insertion point won't move, since it can't go lower than the end of the document. Similarly, if the insertion point is at the end of a short line of text and you press [→], the insertion point won't go any farther to the right. Instead, it will move to the first character of the next line.

Sometimes as you move the insertion point through a document, you'll see WordPerfect reformat the screen by shifting text left or right, wrapping words from one line to another, and so forth. This happens because some format changes don't actually appear on the screen until you move the insertion point through the affected text.

## Changing Fonts

David's first task in editing the memo is to change the font from Times Roman to a sans serif font, such as Arial, Swiss, Dutch, or Helvetica. A **serif** is a small embellishment at the end of a character, as shown in Figure 2-7. Because "sans" is French for "without," a sans serif font is a font without the embellishments. Sans serif fonts are usually reserved for titles and headings, because in long lines of text, serif fonts are easier to read. However, Liz wants the memo to have a distinctive, slightly artistic look, so she asks David to use a sans serif font.

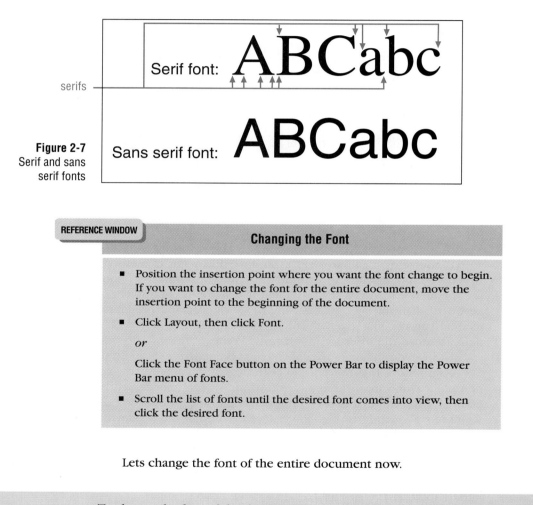

serifs

**Figure 2-7**
Serif and sans
serif fonts

Serif font: ABCabc

Sans serif font: ABCabc

Lets change the font of the entire document now.

To change the font of the document:

❶ Press **[Ctrl][Home]** to move the insertion point to the beginning of the document (or click I just to the left of the "D" in "Date").

As with almost all WordPerfect formatting commands, a font change in a document takes effect from the location of the insertion point to the end of the document. Since David wants the font change to affect the entire document, he moves the insertion point to the beginning of the document. Format changes stay in effect until another format change is made.

❷ Click **Layout,** then click **Font.**

WordPerfect displays the Font dialog box, as shown in Figure 2-8. Notice that a list of available fonts in alphabetical order, with the name of the current font highlighted, appears in the Font Face section. Your list of fonts might be different from those shown in the figure. You could also click **FFF**, the Font Face button on the Power Bar. The Font dialog box, however, allows you to choose not only the font face, but the size, style, and appearance of the font. The Font dialog box also displays an example of the selected font in the lower-left corner above the words "Resulting font." This is helpful if you're not sure which font to choose.

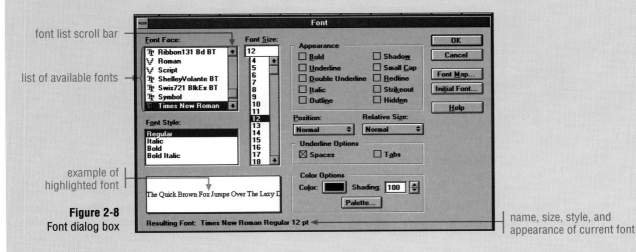

font list scroll bar

list of available fonts

example of highlighted font

**Figure 2-8**
Font dialog box

name, size, style, and appearance of current font

❸ If necessary, click the **Up Arrow** on the scroll bar of the Font Face section until Arial (or some other sans serif font) comes into view.

**TROUBLE?**   If Arial doesn't appear in the list, use some other sans serif font such as Swiss or Helvetica or Humanst521 Lt BT. If you're not sure if a font is serif or sans serif, click its name and look at the example in the lower-left corner of the dialog box. If you're still not sure which font to select, consult your instructor or technical support person.

❹ Highlight the desired font by clicking its name.

❺ Make sure that "12" is highlighted in the Font Size list to ensure that the font size is 12 points.

One point equals 1/72 inch; hence, a 12-point font is 12/72 or 1/6 inch in height. Six lines of a 12-point font equals approximately one vertical inch in your document.

❻ Click the **OK button** or press **[Enter].**

The insertion point returns to the main document window.

The document window displays the new font, as shown in Figure 2-9. Because of differences in fonts, the appearance of the characters and the number of words per line may look different in your document window.

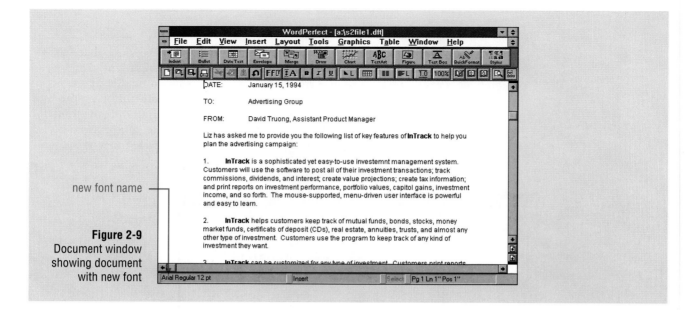

new font name —

**Figure 2-9**
Document window
showing document
with new font

## Changing Margins

David's next task in editing the memo is to change the left and right margins. You can change margins by using the Ruler Bar or the Margins command on the Layout menu.

The **Ruler Bar** is a bar at the top of the document window that displays grid marks at every 1/8 inch (if the default measurement is inches) and marks the location of the left and right margins, the tab stops, the column positions (if any), and so forth. You can use the Ruler Bar to modify any of these formatting elements in your document.

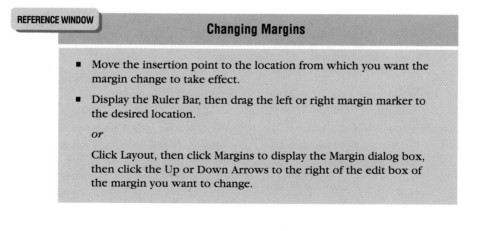

**REFERENCE WINDOW**

### Changing Margins

- Move the insertion point to the location from which you want the margin change to take effect.

- Display the Ruler Bar, then drag the left or right margin marker to the desired location.

  *or*

  Click Layout, then click Margins to display the Margin dialog box, then click the Up or Down Arrows to the right of the edit box of the margin you want to change.

## Changing Margins Using the Ruler Bar

Let's use the Ruler Bar to change the left margin of David's memo.

To display the Ruler Bar and change the margin:

❶ Make sure the insertion point is at the beginning of the document, before any text.

Remember, format changes take effect from the location of the insertion point to the end of the document, so if you want to change the margin for an entire document, you must move the insertion point to the beginning of the document before you set the new margin value.

❷ Click **View**. If Ruler Bar has no checkmark next to it, then click **Ruler Bar**. If there is no checkmark next to Ruler Bar, do not click it. The Ruler Bar should appear at the top of the document window. See Figure 2-10.

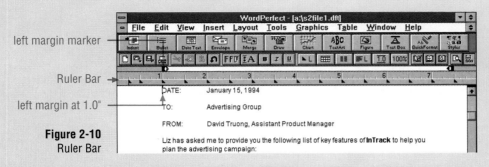

left margin marker

Ruler Bar →

left margin at 1.0"

**Figure 2-10**
Ruler Bar

❸ Position the mouse pointer on the **left margin marker** and press (and hold down) the left mouse button. See Figure 2-11. WordPerfect turns the margin marker blue and displays a vertical dotted line to mark the left margin position in the document. The status bar displays the current left margin value.

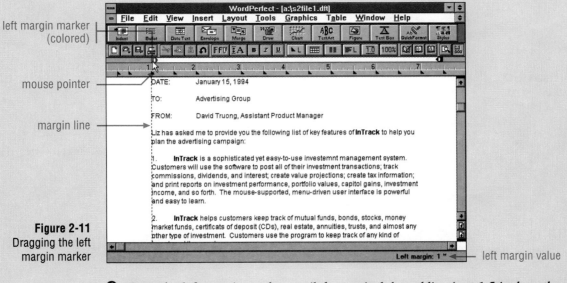

left margin marker
(colored)

mouse pointer

margin line →

**Figure 2-11**
Dragging the left
margin marker

left margin value

❹ Drag the left margin marker until the vertical dotted line is at 1.5 inches, then release the left mouse button. WordPerfect reformats the document with the new left margin.

You'll keep the Ruler Bar on the screen for now, but later in this tutorial you'll learn how to hide it from view.

### Changing the Margins Using the Layout Menu

The second method for changing margins is with the Margins command on the Layout menu.

To change the right margin using the Margins command:
❶ Make sure the insertion point is at the beginning of the document.
❷ Click **Layout**, then click **Margins** to display the Margin dialog box. See Figure 2-12.

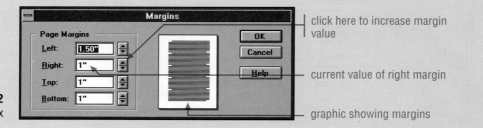

**Figure 2-12**
Margins dialog box

The current left, right, top, and bottom margin settings appear in the dialog box. David's task is to make the right margin 1.5 inches, as suggested by Liz in Figure 2-1.

❸ Click the **Up Arrow** to the right of the Right input box five times so that the right margin value becomes 1.50". As you click, watch how the document graphic in the Margins dialog box changes. See Figure 2-13.

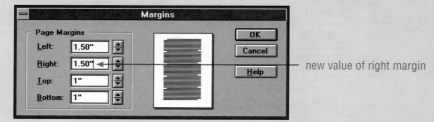

**Figure 2-13**
Margins dialog box
with right margin
change

❹ Click the **OK button** or press **[Enter]**. The right margin of the document changes from 1 inch to 1.50 inches. See Figure 2-14.

**Figure 2-14**
New, wider right
margins

If you want to change *any* of the margins—left, right, top, or bottom—you can follow this same procedure except that in Step 3, you double-click the margin value you want to change, then type the new value.

## Justifying Text

**Justification** usually means adjusting the spacing between characters in any given line so that text is aligned along the right margin as well as along the left. Modern word processors and desktop-publishing software, however, define justification more broadly. Specifically, WordPerfect supports five types of justified text: Left, Right, Center, Full, and All (Figure 2-15).

---

**Left Justification:**
This paragraph is an example of *Left* justification. The lines of text are aligned along the left margin but ragged along the right margin. This gives a less ordered look to the document but is generally easier to read than fully justified text. Left justification is the initial default setting in WordPerfect.

**Right Justification:**
This paragraph is an example of *Right* justification. The lines of text are aligned along the right margin but ragged along the left margin. You would never use right justification in the body of a normal document, but you might use it for special effects.

**Center Justification:**
This paragraph is an example of *Center* justification. The lines of text are centered between the left and right margins. You would never use center justification in the body of a normal document, but you would frequently use it in creating title pages.

**Full Justification:**
This paragraph is an example of *Full* justification. The lines of text are aligned along the left and the right margins. This gives an ordered look to the document but is generally more difficult to read than left justified text. Short lines at the end of paragraphs are not aligned along the right margin.

**All Justification:**
This paragraph is an example of *All* justification. The lines of text, including short lines at the ends of paragraphs, are aligned    along    the    left    and    the    right    margins.

---

**Figure 2-15**
The five types of justification

The WordPerfect default format setting is left justification, and that is how David formatted the first draft of his product description memo, as shown in Figure 2-1. But Liz has suggested that he change the format setting to full justification to make the memo appear more formal. David does this by using the Justification button on the Power Bar.

To change justification:

❶ Make sure the insertion point is at the beginning of the document.

Remember that because you want to change justification for the entire document, you must move the insertion point to the beginning of the document.

❷ Click ▤L, the **Justification button** on the Power Bar, and hold down the left mouse button while you drag the highlight bar to **Full** (see Figure 2-16), then release the mouse button.

**Figure 2-16**
Full justification command on the Power Bar

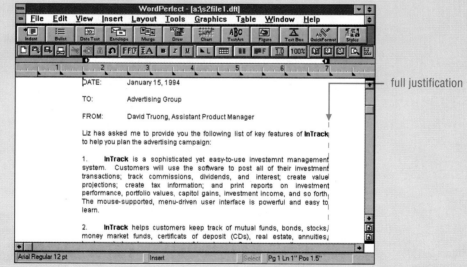

Some menus appear and remain on the screen with a single click of the button, but others, like the Justification button on the Power Bar, require that you drag a highlight to the desired command and then release the mouse button to choose that command.

The Justification button now shows that the current Justification is Full, and the entire document is fully justified, as shown in Figure 2-17. If the change in justification doesn't show up on your screen, execute the Redisplay command given in the following step.

**Figure 2-17**
Document window with full justification

❸ Press **[Ctrl][F3]** (Redisplay). This command has no Button Bar, Power Bar, or pull-down menu equivalent.

As with most WordPerfect commands, you can also change the justification using a pull-down menu or the keyboard. You could click Layout, then click Justification, and finally Full; or you could press [Ctrl][J]. The method you choose to justify text is a matter of personal taste.

## Using Tabs

As Figure 2-1 shows, David's next task in revising the memo is to insert the "RE," or reference line, below the "FROM" line. In the following steps you'll use [Enter] to insert new lines, and then press [Tab] to insert space between the word "RE:" and the word "Product," as was already done between "TO:" and "Advertising" (Figure 2-18).

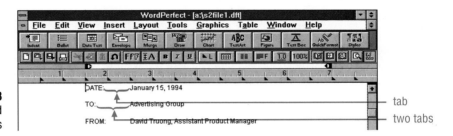

**Figure 2-18**
Space created
by tabs

The Tab key indents text by inserting space from the current insertion-point location to the next tab stop. **Tab stops** are precise locations on the text lines; WordPerfect's default tab settings are every one-half inch from the left margin, as shown on the Ruler Bar in Figure 2-19. Tabs are useful in aligning text vertically in your documents. In the case of David's memo, the tab stops after "DATE:," "TO:," and "FROM:" keep the text precisely aligned (Figure 2-19). You should never use the Spacebar to align text. If you do, the text might appear aligned in the document window, but it might not be aligned when you print the document.

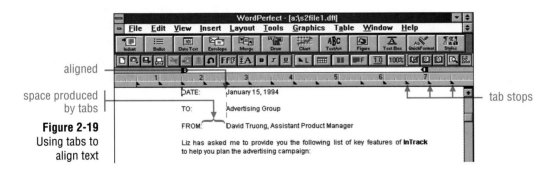

**Figure 2-19**
Using tabs to
align text

To use [Tab] to insert space:
- ❶ Move the insertion point to the end of the line that begins with the word "FROM:." The insertion point should be immediately to the right of the "r" in Manager.
- ❷ Press **[Enter]** twice to double-space after the "FROM" line.
- ❸ Type **RE:** and press **[Tab]** twice.

Pressing [Tab] twice inserts space between "RE:" and the tab stop at Pos 2.5". The insertion point is now directly beneath the word "David."

❹ Type **Product Description of** and press **[Spacebar]**.

You're now ready to type the word "InTrack" in boldface text.

## Creating Boldface Text

One way to highlight a word in your document is to use boldfacing. **Boldface text** is text with thicker characters than normal text.

REFERENCE WINDOW

### Typing Text in Bold, Underlined, or Italic Font

- Make sure the insertion point is where you want to type the bold, underlined, or italic text.
- Click the Bold Font, Underline Font, or Italic Font button on the Power Bar.
- Type in your text.
- To turn off the font, again click the Bold Font, Underline Font, or Italic Font button on the Power Bar.

Let's type the word "InTrack" in boldface in David's memo.

To create boldface text:

❶ Make sure the insertion point is to the right of the space after the phrase "Product Description of" that you typed in the previous section.

❷ Click 🅱, the **Bold Font button** on the Power Bar.

Notice that the name of the font on the left side of the status bar appears in boldface and that the Bold Font button on the Power Bar is depressed. See Figure 2-20. With Bold turned on, whatever new text you type will appear in boldface on the screen and in your printed document.

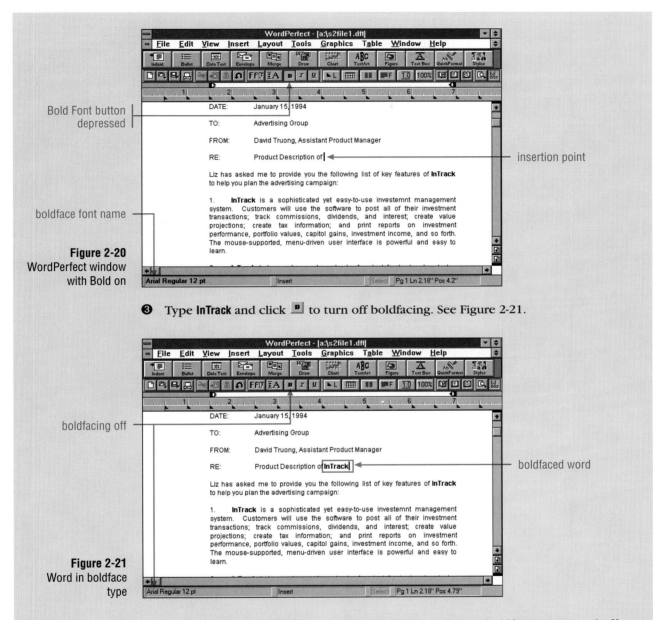

Bold Font button depressed

insertion point

boldface font name

**Figure 2-20**
WordPerfect window
with Bold on

❸ Type **InTrack** and click 🅱 to turn off boldfacing. See Figure 2-21.

boldfacing off

boldfaced word

**Figure 2-21**
Word in boldface
type

When you execute the Bold command the second time, boldfacing is turned off. The font name on the status bar returns to normal text, and the Bold Font button on the Power Bar pops up.

As you can see from these steps, the Bold command is a toggle switch. Remember that a toggle switch is any key or command that alternates between "on" and "off."

## Underlining Text

David next wants to address Liz's question at the end of paragraph 5 in the memo. David decides to insert a note explaining that the brokers mentioned in the memo must also have InTrack. He wants the note to be in parentheses, with the word "Note" underlined.

To underline text:

❶ Move the insertion point to the end of the paragraph numbered 5, after the phrase ". . . directly from within InTrack."

❷ Press **[Spacebar]** twice to insert two spaces at the end of the sentence and type ( (left parenthesis).

❸ Click 🔲, the **Underline Font button** on the Power Bar.

This depresses the Underline Font button and underlines the font name on the status bar. See Figure 2-22. With underline turned on, whatever text you type will be underlined in your printed document. The Underline command, like the Bold command, is a toggle switch.

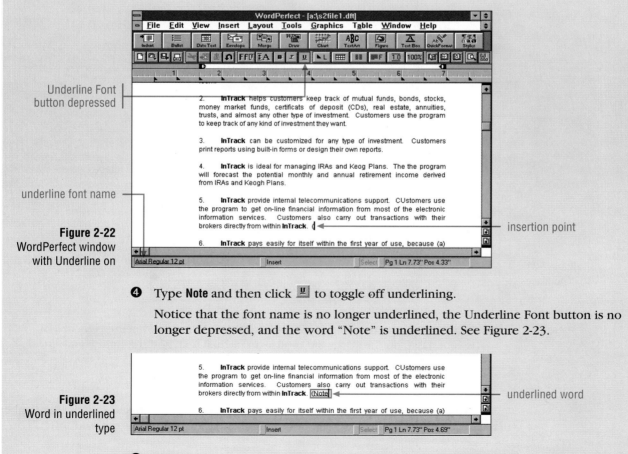

Underline Font button depressed

underline font name

**Figure 2-22**
WordPerfect window with Underline on

insertion point

❹ Type **Note** and then click 🔲 to toggle off underlining.

Notice that the font name is no longer underlined, the Underline Font button is no longer depressed, and the word "Note" is underlined. See Figure 2-23.

**Figure 2-23**
Word in underlined type

underlined word

❺ Type : (a colon), press **[Spacebar]** twice, then type **Their brokers must also have** and press **[Spacebar]**.

❻ Click 🅱 to turn on Bold, and then type **InTrack**.

❼ Click 🅱 to toggle off boldfacing.

❽ Press **[Spacebar]** and type **to use this option.).** See Figure 2-24.

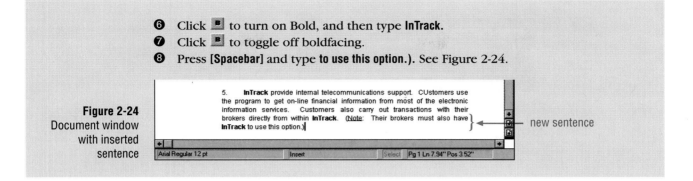

**Figure 2-24**
Document window
with inserted
sentence

## Italicizing Text

Also in paragraph 5, Liz has asked David to list, in italics, the names of two on-line information services, *Dow Jones* and *CompuServe*.

To italicize text:

❶ Move the insertion point to the right of the period following the phrase "electronic information services."

❷ Press **[Backspace]** to delete the period, type **,** (a comma) and press **[Spacebar]**, and then type **such as** and press **[Spacebar]**.

You're now ready to type the first italicized words, *Dow Jones*.

❸ Click 𝐼, the **Italic Font button** on the Power Bar.

The font name on the status bar appears in italics and the Italic Font button becomes depressed. The Italics command, like the Bold and Underline commands, is a toggle switch.

❹ Type **Dow Jones** and click 𝐼.

The Italics command toggles off.

❺ Press **[Spacebar]** after the word *Jones,* type **and** and then press **[Spacebar]** again.

❻ Turn on italics, type **CompuServe,** turn off italics, and type **.** (a period).

You have added the phrase with the italicized text. Your document window should now look like Figure 2-25.

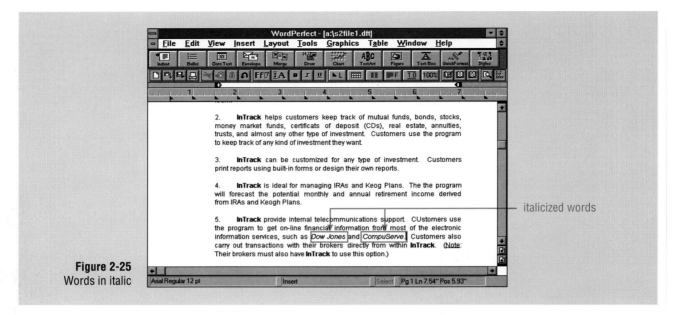

**Figure 2-25**
Words in italic

<hr/>

## Saving an Intermediate Version of the Document

David has now worked on the document for more than 15 minutes and feels that it's time to save his changes.

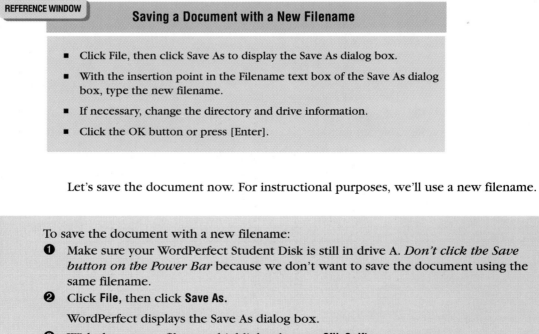

**REFERENCE WINDOW**

### Saving a Document with a New Filename

- Click File, then click Save As to display the Save As dialog box.
- With the insertion point in the Filename text box of the Save As dialog box, type the new filename.
- If necessary, change the directory and drive information.
- Click the OK button or press [Enter].

Let's save the document now. For instructional purposes, we'll use a new filename.

To save the document with a new filename:

❶ Make sure your WordPerfect Student Disk is still in drive A. *Don't click the Save button on the Power Bar* because we don't want to save the document using the same filename.

❷ Click **File**, then click **Save As**.

WordPerfect displays the Save As dialog box.

❸ With the current filename highlighted, type **s2file2.dft**.

❹ If necessary, change the Drives setting to drive A (or to drive B if that's the location of your Student Disk).

❺ Click the **OK button** or press **[Enter]**.

WordPerfect saves the edited memo to your Student Disk using the filename S2FILE2.DFT. The new filename appears on the title bar at the top of the document window.

Because we're through using the Ruler Bar, let's hide it to make more space in the document window.

❻ Click **View**, then click **Ruler Bar** to hide the Ruler Bar.

*If you want to take a break* and resume the tutorial at a later time, you can exit WordPerfect. When you resume, launch WordPerfect and open S2FILE2.DFT into a document window.

## Revealing Format Codes

Whenever you execute a WordPerfect format command, WordPerfect inserts invisible format codes into your document. These codes tell WordPerfect how to format the document on the screen and how to print the document.

When you're typing a document, you usually don't need to see these format codes. But every once in a while—for instance, when you've pressed the wrong key or you want to change one of the format codes—you need to reveal them.

To reveal the hidden format codes:

❶ Move the insertion point to the beginning of the document.

❷ Click **View**, then click **Reveal Codes**.

The document window is now divided into two parts. The top is the main document window and the bottom is the Reveal Codes window. See Figure 2-26.

main insertion point

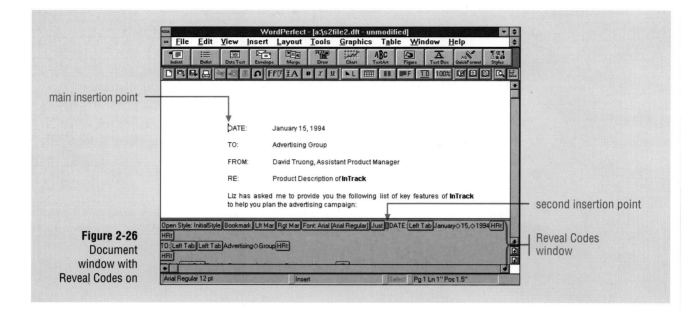

second insertion point

Reveal Codes
window

**Figure 2-26**
Document
window with
Reveal Codes on

The location of the insertion point in the Reveal Codes window is marked with a red rectangle. For example, in Figure 2-26 the insertion point is to the left of the "D" in "DATE." Because both the document window and the Reveal Codes window have an insertion point, the screen actually shows two insertion points. Let's move the insertion point using the keyboard to demonstrate how they move together.

To move the insertion point with Reveal Codes on:

❶ Press [↓] several times until the insertion point is to the left of the "3" at the beginning of paragraph 3 in the memo.

As you press [↓], the text in the document window and the information in the Reveal Codes window scroll up.

❷ Press and hold down [→] for a few seconds to watch how the two insertion points move across the screen. As you can see, the two insertion points always move together through the document.

❸ Press **[Ctrl][Home]** to move the insertion point back to the beginning of the document.

Note that you can't scroll the Reveal Codes window. If you use the scroll bar to scroll the document window, the Reveal Codes window doesn't change. The text in the Reveal Codes window scrolls only if the insertion point moves.

In the Reveal Codes window, the words on the buttons are the format codes. Notice that the first code is Open Style:InitialStyle. This is the code that sets the default format codes in every document. The second code is Bookmark, which we will discuss in a later tutorial. The next codes, Lft Mar (the left margin code) and Rgt Mar (the right margin code), were inserted into the document when you changed the margin settings earlier in this tutorial. The Just code was inserted when you changed the justification.

You can see the settings of these format codes by moving the insertion point to the left of the codes. Let's move the insertion point to the Lft Mar code to see what the left margin setting actually is.

To view the left margin setting associated with the format code:
❶ Click the **Lft Mar code button** or press [←] until the insertion point in the Reveal Codes window is immediately to the left of the left margin code.

The code now appears as *Lft Mar: 1.5"*. See Figure 2-27.

insertion point

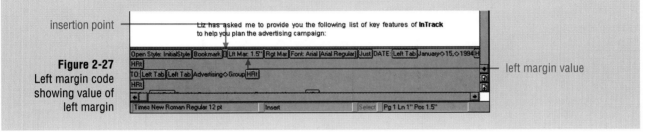

**Figure 2-27**
Left margin code
showing value of
left margin

left margin value

Other format codes in your document, some of which you can see now and some of which you can't, include Left Tab to mark where you pressed [Tab], HRt for hard return, SRt for soft return, and the paired codes Bold (with the button in the shape of a bullet, and the bullet pointing right) to mark the beginning of boldface text and Bold (with the bullet pointing left) to mark the end of boldface text. You can view these various codes by moving the insertion point down through the document.

Figure 2-28 is a list of common WordPerfect format codes. Some of these codes won't make sense to you now, but their meanings will become clear as you work through this and later tutorials.

Keep Reveal Codes on, because in the next section you'll use the Reveal Codes window to help you edit the document.

| WordPerfect Format Codes | |
|---|---|
| **Codes** | **Meaning** |
| Bold | Bold |
| Bookmark | Bookmark |
| Hd Cnt on Marg | Center line between margins |
| Dec Tab | Decimal align in Tab |
| Hd Flsh Rgt | Flush right |
| HSpace | Hard space |
| - | Hard hyphen |
| Hpg | Hard page break |
| HRt | Hard return |
| -Hyphen | Hyphen |
| Hyph | Hyphenation on or off |
| Hd Left Ind | Indent |
| Italc | Italics |
| Just | Justification |
| Lft Mar or Rgt Mar | Left or right margin set |
| HdLeft/Right Indent | Double indent |
| Ln Spacing | Line spacing |
| Select | Select begin |
| SPg | Soft page break |
| SRt | Soft return |
| Subscpt | Subscript |
| Suprscpt | Superscript |
| Left Tab | Tab (move to next tab stop) |
| Top Mar or Bot Mar | Top or Bottom margin values |
| Und | Underline |
| Wid/Orph | Widow/Orphan protection |

**Figure 2-28**
Common
WordPerfect
format codes

# Indenting a Paragraph

The Reveal Codes window will help David perform his next task. One of Liz's suggestions for the product description memo is to indent the numbered paragraphs, aligning all the text under the first letter following the number. David doesn't want to use tabs to do this because a tab inserts space only on one line at a time. Instead, he uses the Indent command, which indents not just the first line of the paragraph, but all subsequent lines until the end of the paragraph, which is marked by a hard return. David's task, therefore, is to change the Left Tab format code to the Hd Left Ind (Hard Left Indent) format code at the beginning of each numbered paragraph.

To change Left Tab codes to Hd Left Ind codes:

❶ Make sure the Reveal Codes window appears on the screen. If necessary, click **View**, then click **Reveal Codes**.

❷ Move the insertion point to the "1" of the first numbered paragraph. You can now see a Left Tab code to the right of the 1 in the Reveal Codes window.

❸ Click the **Left Tab code button** or press [→] twice to put the insertion point immediately to the left of the Left Tab code. See Figure 2-29.

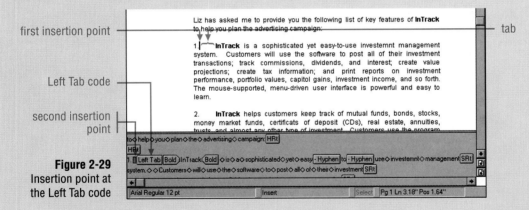

first insertion point

Left Tab code

second insertion point

tab

**Figure 2-29**
Insertion point at
the Left Tab code

❹ Press **[Del]** to delete the Left Tab code. (Remember, if you use the Del key on the numeric keypad, Num Lock must be off.) With Reveal Codes turned on, [Del] deletes the code to the right of the second insertion point, and [Backspace] deletes the code to the left of the second insertion point.

The Left Tab code disappears and the text beginning with "InTrack is a . . ." moves next to the "1."

❺ Click 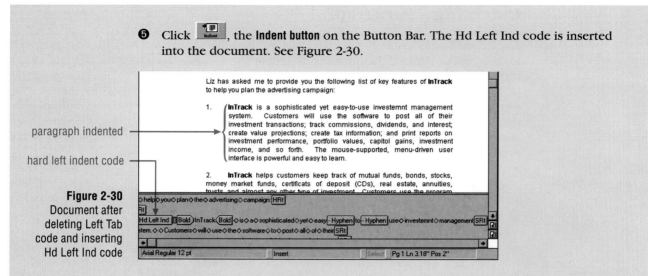, the **Indent button** on the Button Bar. The Hd Left Ind code is inserted into the document. See Figure 2-30.

paragraph indented ——————————→

hard left indent code ——————————

**Figure 2-30**
Document after
deleting Left Tab
code and inserting
Hd Left Ind code

As you can see, when Hd Left Ind appears in the Reveal Codes window, the paragraph in the document window is indented. If the entire paragraph isn't indented on your screen, press [Ctrl][F3] (Redisplay) to have WordPerfect reformat the screen.

The amount of space the text is indented depends on the location of the tab stops. Since WordPerfect's default format settings have a tab stop every 0.5 inch, executing the Indent command once normally indents a paragraph 0.5 inch from the left margin. Therefore, in this case, where the left margin is 1.5 inches, the paragraph is indented 2.0 inches from the left edge of the page.

❻ Move the insertion point to the Left Tab code at the beginning of the next numbered paragraph, delete the code, and click 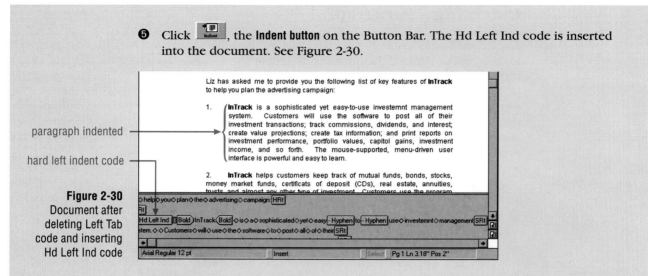 to insert the Hd Left Ind code at that location. Repeat this step until you have indented all seven paragraphs. Remember, if you scroll the text in the main document window using the scroll bar, you need to click I at the new position in the document window to scroll the text in the Reveal Codes window.

**TROUBLE?**   If you see a large space and double line somewhere between paragraphs 6 and 7, don't worry. The space represents the bottom margin of the first page and the top margin of the second page, and the double line represents a soft page break, explained below.

❼ Click **View,** then click **Reveal Codes** to close the Reveal Codes window and display a full-screen document window.

The document window should now look similar to Figure 2-31. As you can see, Reveal Codes is a toggle command: Choosing it once opens the Reveal Codes window, and choosing it again closes it.

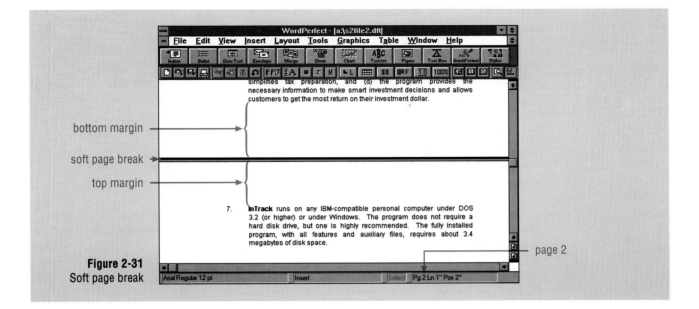

**Figure 2-31**
Soft page break

As you made these changes, WordPerfect automatically inserted a **soft page break,** a code that indicates where one page ends and another begins. A soft page break is shown as a double horizontal line across the document window (Figure 2-31). It is called a soft page break because if you add or delete text before the break, the page break might change. Your page break might be at a different location.

In this section, you've learned how to reveal the format codes, delete the codes, and insert other codes. You can use these same methods to change any format code. For example, if you decide that you want to change some boldface text back to regular type, you could turn on Reveal Codes, move the insertion point to the code that marks the beginning or the end of the boldface text, and delete the code. When you delete one of a pair of codes, WordPerfect automatically deletes the other.

## Deleting Words and Lines of Text

You're already familiar with using [Backspace] to delete a character or a code to the left of the insertion point and with using [Del] to delete a character or a code at the insertion point. WordPerfect also provides ways for you to delete larger chunks of text.

For example, in the first line of paragraph 2 in the product description memo, Liz suggests that the phrase "keep track" of be simplified to "track." David will use [Ctrl][Backspace] (Delete Word) to delete the word "keep." He will use the mouse to highlight the word "of" before deleting it. Let's make these changes in your document.

To delete a word from the text:

❶ Move the insertion point to the first letter of the word "keep" in the first line of paragraph 2.

To use the [Ctrl][Backspace] (Delete Word) command, you can move the insertion point anywhere within the word or immediately to the right of the word you want to delete.

❷ Press **[Ctrl][Backspace]** (Delete Word). The word and the space after it disappear from the document.

Now we'll use the mouse to highlight the word for deletion.

❸ Double-click the word **of**.

WordPerfect highlights the entire word and the space following it.

❹ Press **[Del]** or **[Backspace]**. The word and the space after it disappear from the document. See Figure 2-32.

position of
deleted words

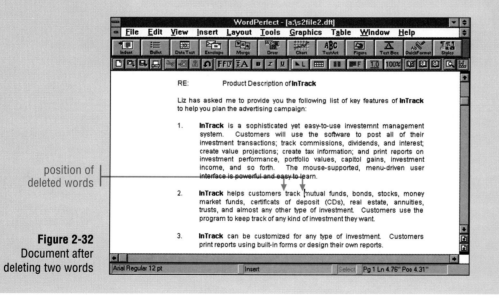

**Figure 2-32**
Document after
deleting two words

Another valuable deletion command is [Ctrl][Del] (Del to EOL), which instructs WordPerfect to "delete all characters from the insertion point to the end of the current line." You can use this command to delete a complete or partial line of text. In the product description memo, Liz wants David to delete the last sentence of paragraph 2. Let's use [Ctrl][Del] (Del to EOL) to delete this sentence.

To delete from the insertion point to the end of a line:

❶ Move the insertion point to the left of the "C" in "Customers" in the second sentence of paragraph 2. See Figure 2-33.

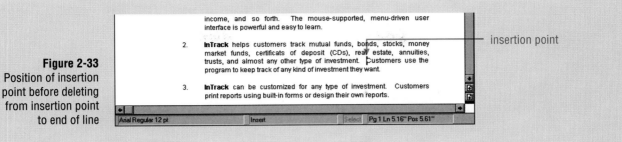

insertion point

**Figure 2-33**
Position of insertion
point before deleting
from insertion point
to end of line

❷   Press **[Ctrl][Del]** (Del to EOL).

WordPerfect deletes the text from the insertion point to the end of the line, and the remaining text in the sentence moves into the place of the deleted text. See Figure 2-34.

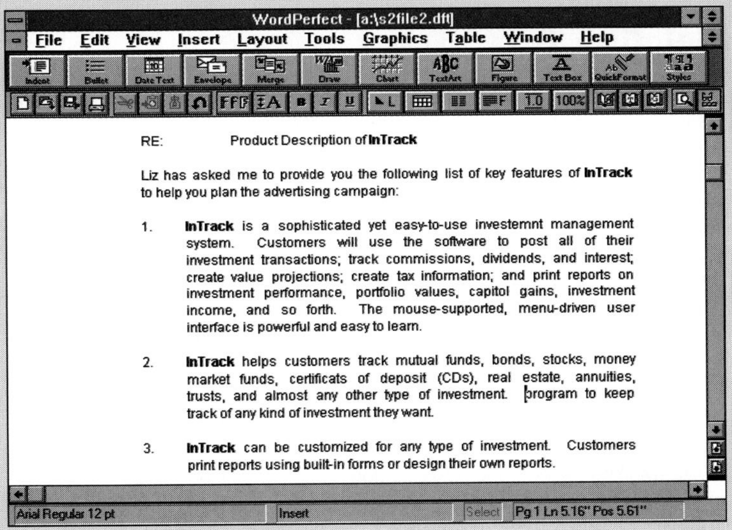

**Figure 2-34**
Document after
deleting from
insertion point to
end of line

**TROUBLE?**   Because of differences in printers and fonts, the exact location of the sentence that you're deleting might not be the same on your screen as it is in the figure. For this reason, the amount of text deleted when you press [Ctrl][Del] in this case may be different.

❸   Press **[Ctrl][Del]** (Del to EOL) as many times as necessary until you have deleted the entire sentence.

❹   Press **[Backspace]** twice to delete the spaces after the period at the end of the first sentence.

In addition to [Ctrl][Backspace] (Delete Word) and [Ctrl][Del] (Del to EOL), you can use the other keystrokes shown in Figure 2-35 to delete text. As you become more familiar with WordPerfect, you'll be able to use these other delete commands in your own documents.

| WordPerfect Deletion Keys | |
| --- | --- |
| **Keys** | **Deletion** |
| [Del] | Character to right of insertion point |
| [Backspace] | Character to left of insertion point |
| [Ctrl][Backspace] | Word at insertion point |
| [Ctrl][Del] | From insertion point to end of line |
| [Ctrl][Shift][Del] | From insertion point to end of page |

**Figure 2-35**
Common
WordPerfect
deletion
keystrokes

## Undeleting Text

Whenever you delete text from a document, WordPerfect temporarily saves the deleted text, just in case you want to undelete (restore) it later. WordPerfect doesn't store all your deletions, only the last three.

REFERENCE WINDOW

**Undeleting Text**

- Move the insertion point to the place in the document where you want to undelete one of the three most recent deletions.

- Click Edit, then click Undelete. The most recently deleted text appears in the document window at the insertion point.

- If you want to restore other deleted text, click Next or Previous button.

- With the desired text restored into the document window, click the Restore button.

Let's use WordPerfect's Undelete capability to delete and then restore the word "investment."

To undelete text:

❶ Double-click the word "investment" at the end of paragraph 2. The word becomes highlighted.

❷ Press **[Del]** to delete the word "investment" and the period following it.

Let's suppose that now you want the word and the period back in your document.

❸ Click **Edit**, then click **Undelete**.

WordPerfect immediately restores the most recent deletion to the screen, highlights it, and displays the Undelete dialog box. To see the next-to-the-last deletion, click the Previous button; to see the deletion before that, click the Previous button again.

TROUBLE?    If the Undelete dialog box obscures the restored text, drag the dialog box to another location on the screen.

❹ Click the **Restore button.** The deleted word "investment" and the accompanying period are restored to the document.

After deleting text, you can type new text, move the insertion point, or execute other commands before you undelete the deleted text. Let's say you have moved the insertion point to a new location in the document, and then clicked Edit, then Undelete, and then the Restore button. WordPerfect restores the deleted text at the *current* location of the insertion point, not where the deleted text originally appeared. David can, therefore, use Undelete to move a word or a phrase from one location to another. Let's try this by deleting the word "pays" in paragraph 6 and restoring it after the word "easily" to switch the order of the words, as Liz suggests.

To use Undelete to move a word:
❶ Double-click the word **pays** in the first line in paragraph 6.
❷ Press **[Del]** to delete the word.
❸ Move the insertion point past "easily" to the "f" in the word "for."
❹ Click **Edit**, click **Undelete**, then click the **Restore button.** See Figure 2-36.

switched words

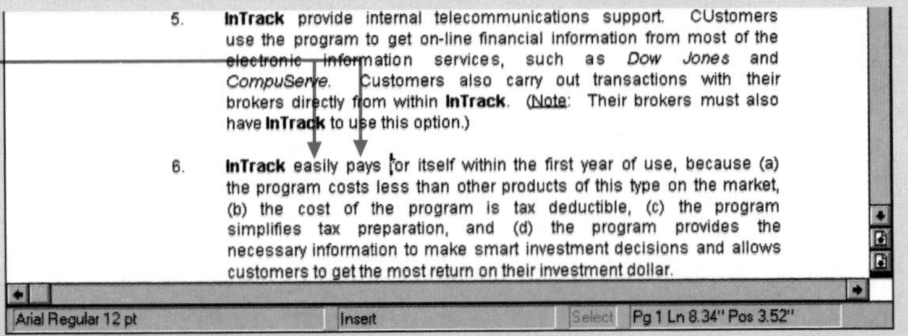

**Figure 2-36**
Document after switching words by deleting, moving insertion point, and undeleting

5.  InTrack provide internal telecommunications support. CUstomers use the program to get on-line financial information from most of the electronic information services, such as *Dow Jones* and *CompuServe*. Customers also carry out transactions with their brokers directly from within **InTrack**. (Note: Their brokers must also have **InTrack** to use this option.)

6.  **InTrack** easily pays for itself within the first year of use, because (a) the program costs less than other products of this type on the market, (b) the cost of the program is tax deductible, (c) the program simplifies tax preparation, and (d) the program provides the necessary information to make smart investment decisions and allows customers to get the most return on their investment dollar.

Arial Regular 12 pt       Insert       Select  Pg 1 Ln 8.34" Pos 3.52"

Now the phrase reads "InTrack easily pays for itself," as Liz suggests.

You'll learn other ways to move text in a later tutorial.

## Using the Undo Command

WordPerfect's Undo command lets you undo (reverse) your last editing action. It works similarly to Undelete, except
• Undo doesn't display a prompt, but immediately reverses the action.
• Undo reverses any kind of action, not just deletions.
• Undo can only undo the most recent editing action.
Let's use Undo in an example. Suppose David decides to add the phrase "several times over" following the phrase "easily pays for itself." Then, after adding the new phrase, he realizes it's an overstatement and wants to "undo" it, that is, reverse the operation of adding the phrase.

To use the Undo command:

❶ Move the insertion point to left of the "w" in "within" after the phrase "easily pays for itself" in paragraph 6.

As you type the phrase given in Step 2, resist the temptation to correct any typographical errors you might make. Because the Undo command reverses the most recent editing action, it will undo the entire phrase *only* if you have not taken any other editing action, such as [Backspace] or [Del].

❷ Type **several times over** and press **[Spacebar]** so that the line appears as shown in Figure 2-37.

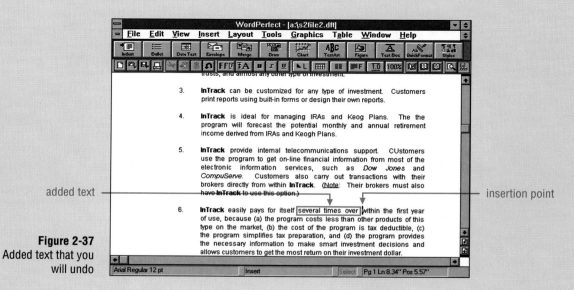

added text —————— insertion point

**Figure 2-37**
Added text that you
will undo

Now you decide that you really don't like the phrase. Rather than executing several commands (such as [Backspace]) to delete the phrase, you can execute one command to undo it.

❸ Click 🔄, the **Undo button** on the Power bar.

The most recently typed text disappears from the document window.

**TROUBLE?**   If the entire phrase does not disappear from the screen, delete it now using familiar deletion keys, such as [Backspace] and [Del].

The important point to understand about Undo is that it has the ability to undo only the most recent editing action. If you make a serious editing mistake for example, you accidentally delete a large block of text and then move the insertion point to a new location and you catch the mistake immediately, you can undo the action. When you undo a deletion, the text will reappear in your document in its original position, not necessarily at the current location of the insertion point. If you undo an action but decide that you shouldn't have, you can undo the undo! (To correct simple typos, don't use Undo. Instead, use common insertion-point movement and deletion keys.)

# Using Typeover Mode

When you start WordPerfect, the document window starts out in **insert mode,** which means that the characters you type are inserted into the document at the insertion point, and existing characters (if any) move to the right. In insert mode, the word "Insert" appears in the center of the status bar at the bottom of the document window.

If you press [Ins] (Insert), the document window toggles from insert mode to **type-over mode,** which means that the characters you type *replace* existing text at the insertion point. When typeover mode is on, the word "Typeover" appears on the status bar in place of "Insert."

As shown in Figure 2-1, Liz wants David to add "3.1 (or higher)" to the second line of paragraph 7. Let's use insert mode to insert this text and then use typeover mode to change "3.4" to "2.5" later in that same paragraph.

To use insert mode:
1. Move the insertion point between "Windows" and the period (.) at the end of the first sentence in paragraph 7.
2. Make sure "Insert" appears on the status bar. If it doesn't, press [Ins] to return to insert mode.
3. Press [Spacebar] and type **3.1 (or higher).**

When you type this phrase, watch as the sentence "The program does not require . . ." is pushed to the right and one or more of the words is wrapped to the next line.

Next let's use typeover mode to change "3.4" to "2.5."

To use typeover mode:
1. Move the insertion point to the left of "3" in "about 3.4 megabytes" in the last line of paragraph 7.
2. Press [Ins]. The word "Typeover" appears in the center of the status bar at the bottom of the document window.
3. Type **2.5.** With typeover mode on, the new characters replace, or type over, the original characters at the insertion point. See Figure 2-38.

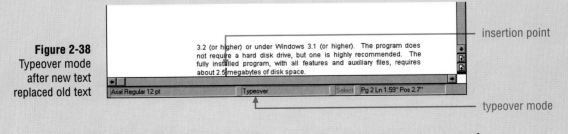

**Figure 2-38**
Typeover mode after new text replaced old text

4. Press [Ins] to turn off typeover mode and return to insert mode.

## Inserting a Hard Page Break

Look at Liz's question at the bottom of Figure 2-1: "Dave, what about other hardware options?" In response to this question, David decides to add a paragraph at the end of the product description.

To add a paragraph to the memo:

❶ Move the insertion point to the end of the document.

❷ Press **[Enter]** twice to double-space between paragraph 7 and the new paragraph you're about to type.

❸ Type paragraph number 8, as shown in Figure 2-39. Don't forget to indent after the paragraph number and to make the word "InTrack" boldface. When you're finished, your screen should look like Figure 2-39.

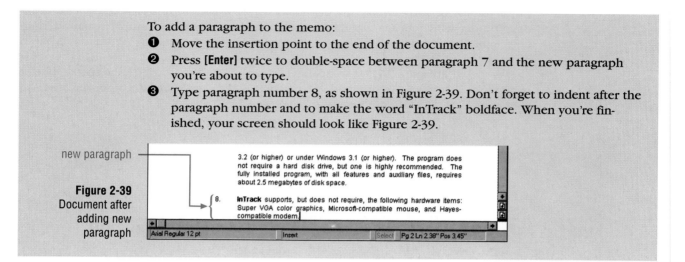

new paragraph

**Figure 2-39**
Document after
adding new
paragraph

This last paragraph completes the text of the memo. But notice that some or all of paragraph 7 is split between page 1 and page 2. (On your screen, paragraph 7 might not be split between the two pages because of differences in font sizes. Even if it is not split, continue reading and follow the next set of steps.) David doesn't want a page break within a numbered paragraph, so he decides to use what is called a hard page break just before paragraph 7. A **hard page break** is a format code that forces the text following it onto the next page. Even if a page had only one line of text in it before a hard page break, the text on the page would end at that point, and the text that followed would go onto the next page. WordPerfect marks the location of a hard page break with a double horizontal line that extends across the width of the screen.

Let's insert a hard page break to force paragraph 7 and the text that follows it onto the next page.

To insert a hard page break:

❶ Move the insertion point to the "7" at the beginning of paragraph 7.

**TROUBLE?**   If all of paragraph 7 is on page 2, move the insertion point to the 6 at the beginning of paragraph 6. In the following discussion about the location of the page break, note that your screen and document will be different.

❷ Click **Insert,** then click **Page Break** to force paragraph 7 onto the next page. The hard page break appears on the screen below paragraph 6 and above paragraph 7. See Figure 2-40.

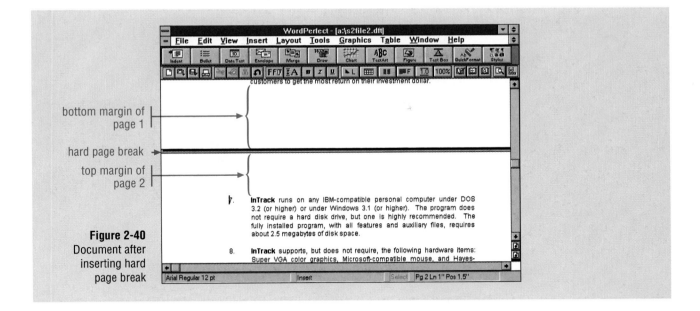

bottom margin of page 1

hard page break

top margin of page 2

**Figure 2-40**
Document after inserting hard page break

The format code for a hard page break is HPg. You can treat this code as you have the other codes you've already learned about. For example, to delete a hard page break, you would move the insertion point to the location of the page break and press [Backspace]. If you desire, you could turn on Reveal Codes so you could see the HPg code and delete it using [Backspace] or [Del].

***If you want to take a break*** and resume the tutorial at a later time, you can save the document by clicking the Save button on the Power Bar, then exit WordPerfect. When you resume, launch WordPerfect and open the file S2FILE2.DFT into a document window.

## Checking the Spelling in a Document

David's memo still contains misspelled words and other typographical errors, commonly called "typos." You can catch most misspellings and typos by running the speller, a WordPerfect feature that checks the spelling within a document as Liz suggested to David in the first paragraph of the memo. When you run the speller, WordPerfect checks each word in your document against the WordPerfect dictionary, which is a file on your hard disk.

REFERENCE WINDOW

### Using the Speller

- With the insertion point anywhere within the document, click the Speller button on the Power Bar.

- At the Speller dialog box, click the Start button.

- When the speller stops at a word that isn't in its dictionary, click the Replace button to replace the misspelled word with a suggested word; click the Skip Once button to skip the misspelled word this time; click the Skip Always button to tell WordPerfect to skip that spelling for the remainder of the document; or make other choices presented by the Speller dialog box.

## Running the Speller

Let's correct the spelling errors in David's memo by using the speller.

To run the speller:

❶ Click 🖺, the **Speller button** on the Power Bar. WordPerfect displays the Speller dialog box. A message in the upper-left corner of the dialog box should say "Spell-check: Document." See Figure 2-41.

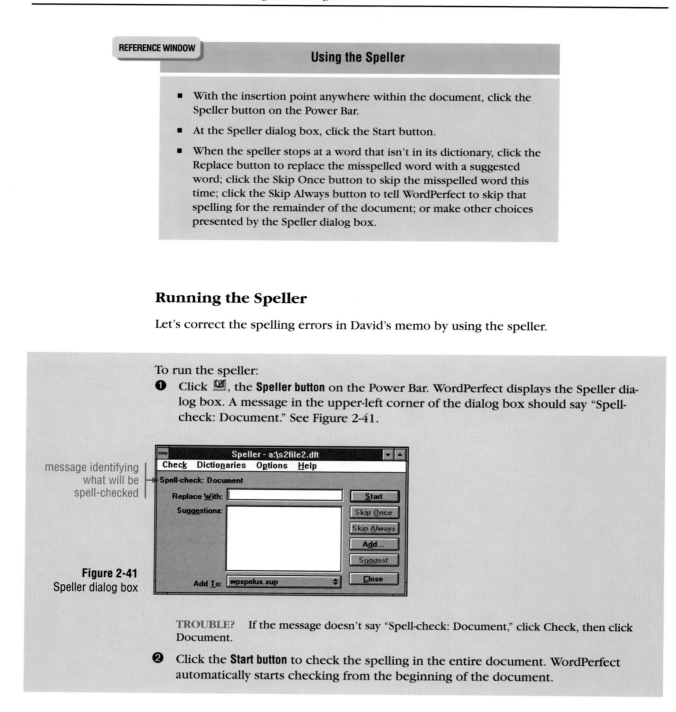

message identifying what will be spell-checked

**Figure 2-41**
Speller dialog box

**TROUBLE?**    If the message doesn't say "Spell-check: Document," click Check, then click Document.

❷ Click the **Start button** to check the spelling in the entire document. WordPerfect automatically starts checking from the beginning of the document.

## Skipping a Word Not Found in the Dictionary

The first "misspelled" word detected by WordPerfect is "Truong" (Figure 2-42). Although "Truong" is spelled correctly, it is not in WordPerfect's dictionary. WordPerfect highlights the word to flag it as a potential error. A list of suggested spellings appear in the Speller dialog box. Because we don't want to change "Truong" to any of the suggested spellings, let's tell WordPerfect to skip this word from now on.

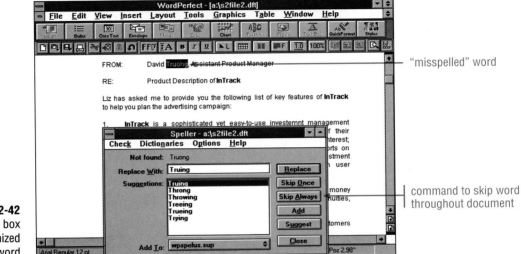

"misspelled" word

command to skip word throughout document

**Figure 2-42**
Speller dialog box with unrecognized word

To skip a word not found in WordPerfect's dictionary:

❶ Click the **Skip Always button.** This option tells WordPerfect to skip all occurrences of the word "Truong" in the remainder of the document.

WordPerfect next stops at "InTrack." This is another example of a correctly spelled word that isn't in WordPerfect's dictionary.

❷ Click the **Skip Always button** to skip this and all future occurrences of "InTrack" in this document.

WordPerfect continues checking words in the document against words in the dictionary until it comes to the next word not found in the dictionary.

## Selecting a Suggested Spelling

The first word that David actually misspelled is "investemnt." WordPerfect highlights the word and gives only one suggested spelling ("investment"), as shown in Figure 2-43.

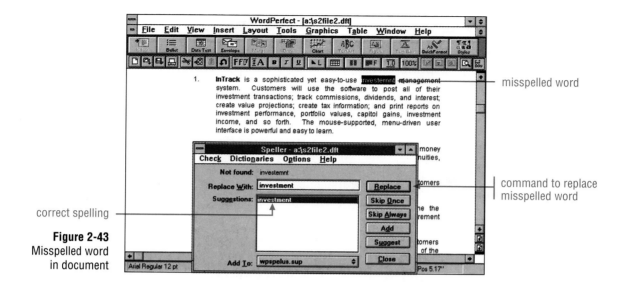

**Figure 2-43**
Misspelled word
in document

In the following steps, you'll select a replacement word from the Suggestions box. WordPerfect will then replace the misspelled word in the document with the word you select.

To select a suggested spelling from the Suggestions box:

❶ Make sure the correctly spelled word is highlighted, then click the **Replace button.** WordPerfect replaces the misspelled word with the correctly spelled word, "investment."

The next misspelled word is "certificats." WordPerfect displays two suggested words in the Speller dialog box, as shown in Figure 2-44.

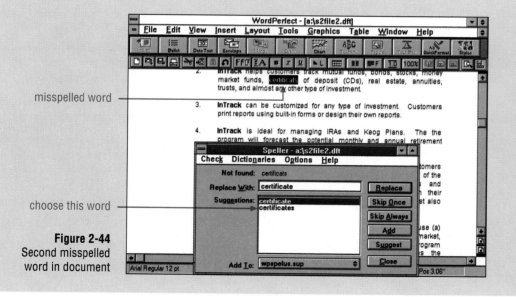

**Figure 2-44**
Second misspelled
word in document

❷  Click **certificates** in the Suggestions box. The word "certificates" now appears in the Replace With box.

❸  Click the **Replace button** or press **[Enter]** to replace the misspelled word.

You can press [Enter] here because Replace is the default option. To choose "certificates" as the replacement word, you can also double-click the word.

## Skipping a Word Once

WordPerfect next stops at the word "CDs," an abbreviation for "certificates of deposit," and presents a list of possible words in the Speller dialog box. (Because of different release dates of versions of WordPerfect for Windows or because of customization of the speller, your list of suggested words might be different from that shown in the figure. Don't worry about this.) Because none of these words is correct, let's tell WordPerfect to skip this word once but flag any later occurrence of "CDs" or "cds" that might occur in the document.

To skip a word once:

❶  Click the **Skip Once button.** This option tells WordPerfect that you want to skip the word this time, but stop at any future occurrences.

The next "misspelled" word is "IRAs."

❷  Click the **Skip Always button** to skip this and all future occurrences of "IRAs" in the document.

As a general rule, you should click Skip Once if there's a chance that the flagged word might actually be a misspelling later in the document. Click the Skip Always button if you know that the word will appear again later in the document but you don't want the speller to flag it.

## Editing a Misspelled Word

WordPerfect next stops at the word "Keog" and displays several suggested words in the Speller window (Figure 2-45). The correct word is "Keogh," which is the name of a retirement investment plan. In this case, "Keog" is not a correct spelling, nor is the correct spelling found in the WordPerfect dictionary. Thus, you need to edit the word so that it is spelled correctly.

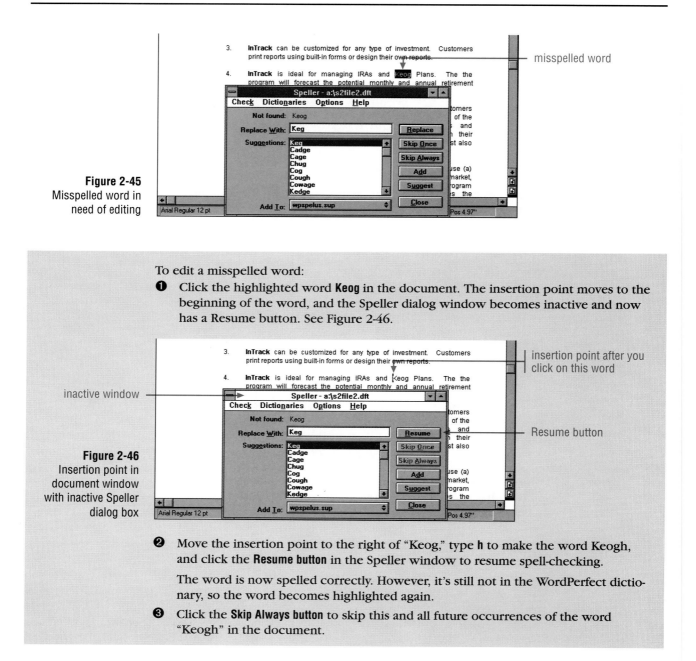

**Figure 2-45**
Misspelled word in
need of editing

To edit a misspelled word:

❶ Click the highlighted word **Keog** in the document. The insertion point moves to the beginning of the word, and the Speller dialog window becomes inactive and now has a Resume button. See Figure 2-46.

**Figure 2-46**
Insertion point in
document window
with inactive Speller
dialog box

❷ Move the insertion point to the right of "Keog," type **h** to make the word Keogh, and click the **Resume button** in the Speller window to resume spell-checking.

The word is now spelled correctly. However, it's still not in the WordPerfect dictionary, so the word becomes highlighted again.

❸ Click the **Skip Always button** to skip this and all future occurrences of the word "Keogh" in the document.

## Correcting Duplicate Words

WordPerfect next stops at the duplicate words "The the" and displays just one of the words in the Replace With box in the Speller dialog box (Figure 2-47).

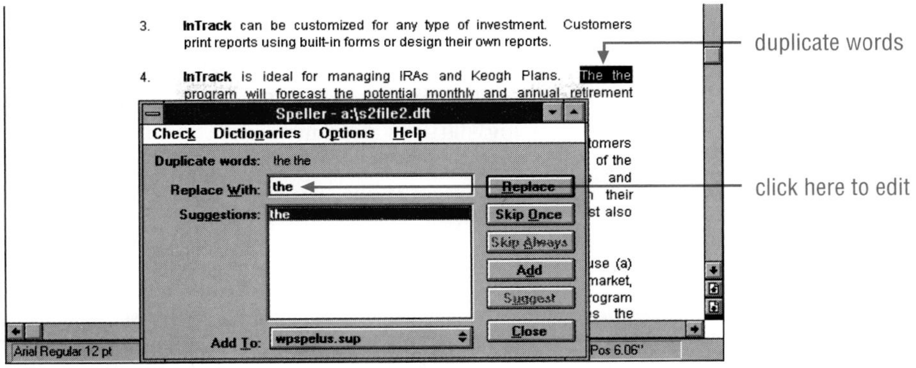

**Figure 2-47**
Duplicate word
found by speller

To correct duplicate words:
❶ Click I in the Replace With box and edit the word "the" to make "The," because this is the first word of the sentence.
❷ Click the **Replace button.**

Your document now has only "The" instead of "The the" in paragraph 4 of the document.

## Correcting Irregular Case

The next typo that WordPerfect encounters is an irregular case error. An irregular case error is a word that has some lowercase letters and one or more uppercase letters after the initial letter. When David typed the rough draft of the memo, he accidentally held the Shift key down too long and typed "CUstomer" instead of "Customer." When such an error occurs, WordPerfect highlights the affected word and displays a list of suggested corrections in the Speller dialog box.

To correct irregular case:
❶ Click **Customers** in the Suggestions box and then click the **Replace button.**

WordPerfect replaces the irregular case error with the selected word.

❷ Continue through the spell-check. When the speller stops at any other word not found in the dictionary (such as "CompuServe," "VGA," or "Microsoft"), click the **Skip Always button.** Repeat this step until the speller reaches the end of the document.

TROUBLE?    If the speller stops at a word that is obscured by the Speller dialog box, drag the Speller dialog box out of the way. To drag the dialog box, move ⬚ to the Speller title bar, press and hold down the left mouse button, and drag the box to a new location on the screen.

When spell-checking is complete, a dialog box appears asking you if it's OK to close the Speller.

❸ Click the **Yes button.**

You have now completed spell-checking the document.

### Checking for Misused Words

Keep in mind that the WordPerfect speller checks only spelling, not meaning or usage. For example, in paragraph 1 of his memo, David used the word "capitol," which means a building in which a legislature convenes, instead of "capital," which means assets or wealth. WordPerfect can't help you catch this type of error, so you must carefully proofread your document for correct usage. Let's correct the error now.

To correct a misused word:

❶ Move the insertion point to the left of "o" in "capitol" in paragraph 1 of the memo.

❷ Press [Ins] to turn on typeover mode.

❸ Type **a** to change "capitol" to "capital."

❹ Press [Ins] to toggle back to insert mode.

## Using the Thesaurus

David is now ready to address Liz's last suggestion. In paragraph 1, David used the verb "create" twice in the same series of items. Liz thinks this is repetitious and suggests he choose better words. He agrees but isn't sure what words to use instead, so he decides to use WordPerfect's thesaurus to help him. The **thesaurus** is a WordPerfect program that contains a list of words and their synonyms and antonyms.

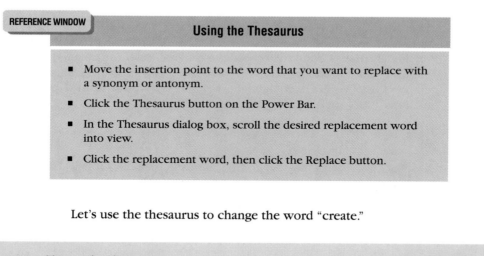

**REFERENCE WINDOW**

**Using the Thesaurus**

- Move the insertion point to the word that you want to replace with a synonym or antonym.

- Click the Thesaurus button on the Power Bar.

- In the Thesaurus dialog box, scroll the desired replacement word into view.

- Click the replacement word, then click the Replace button.

Let's use the thesaurus to change the word "create."

To use the thesaurus:

❶ Move the insertion point to the first occurrence of "create" on the third or fourth line of the first numbered paragraph.

The insertion point can be anywhere in the word or at the space just after the word.

❷ Click 📖, the **Thesaurus button** on the Power Bar. WordPerfect highlights "create" and then displays the Thesaurus dialog box, which contains a list of the synonyms and antonyms of "create." See Figure 2-48. You will see only a partial list; you must scroll the list to see all the synonyms and antonyms.

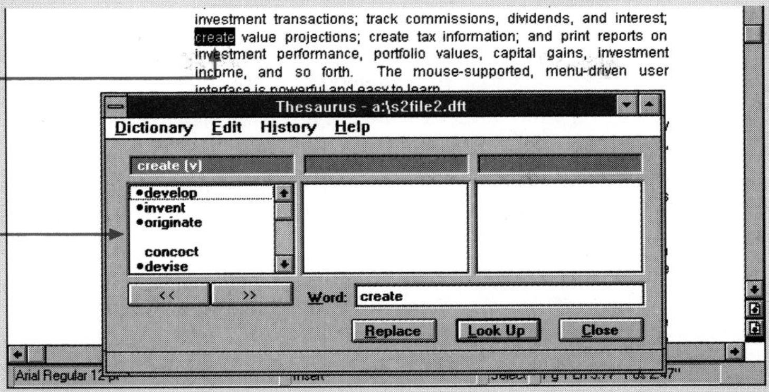

**Figure 2-48**
Thesaurus dialog
box for "create"

**TROUBLE?**    If the Thesaurus dialog box obscures the highlighted word "create" in the document window, drag it out of the way.

❸ Scroll through the list of words until the antonym "destroy" appears at the bottom of the list. See Figure 2-49.

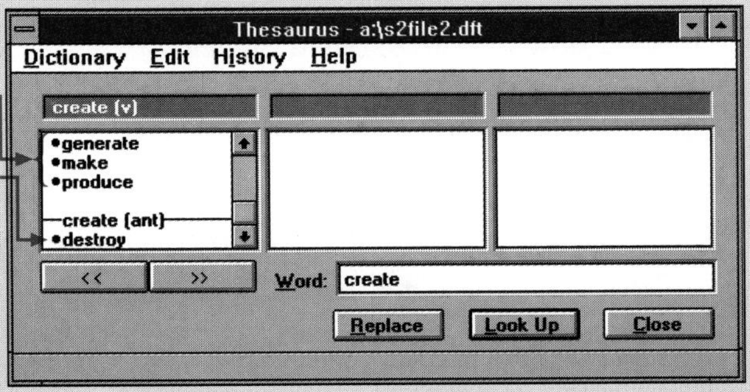

**Figure 2-49**
List of synonyms
and antonyms
after scrolling to
bottom of list

David looks over the synonyms and decides that the word "make" is the best choice to replace "create."

❹ Click the synonym **make** to highlight it, and then click the **Replace button.**
WordPerfect closes the Thesaurus dialog box and replaces "create" with "make."

David decides to replace the second occurrence of "create" as well. Because WordPerfect closes the Thesaurus window after an option is chosen from the Thesaurus dialog box, David has to reissue the Thesaurus command.

❺ Move the insertion point to the second occurrence of "create" in the same paragraph and click 🔳.

David looks at the list again and decides to use "generate" this time.

❻ Scroll through the list of words in the Thesaurus dialog box until "generate" appears, then click **generate,** and click the **Replace button.**

As you can see, the thesaurus can help you increase your word power as you write.

## Using the Grammar Checker

Just to make sure his document is as polished as possible, David decides to run Grammatik. (Grammatik is pronounced so that it rhymes with "dramatic" not "technique.") **Grammatik** is WordPerfect's grammar checker and style analysis program. Grammatik is an aid, but by no means a cure-all, for grammatical and stylistic problems. In fact, Grammatik works best for writers who are already familiar with the basic rules of grammar and style. As you'll see, Grammatik makes many suggestions that may or may not be appropriate for your document.

**REFERENCE WINDOW**

### Checking the Grammar in a Document

- With the insertion point anywhere in the document, click the Grammatik button on the Power Bar.

- At the Grammatik dialog box, click the Start button.

- Follow the instructions given in the Grammatik dialog box to correct any grammatical or stylistic errors in your document.

Let's execute Grammatik now to analyze David's memo.

To execute Grammatik:

❶ Click 🖼, the Grammatik button on the Power Bar.

The Grammatik dialog box appears on the screen. See Figure 2-50. The menu bar at the top of the dialog box provides various commands, including Check (to let you check all or part of your document), Options (to let you specify the writing style and other options), and Help (to give you help on using Grammatik). Normally, you would leave all the options set to their defaults.

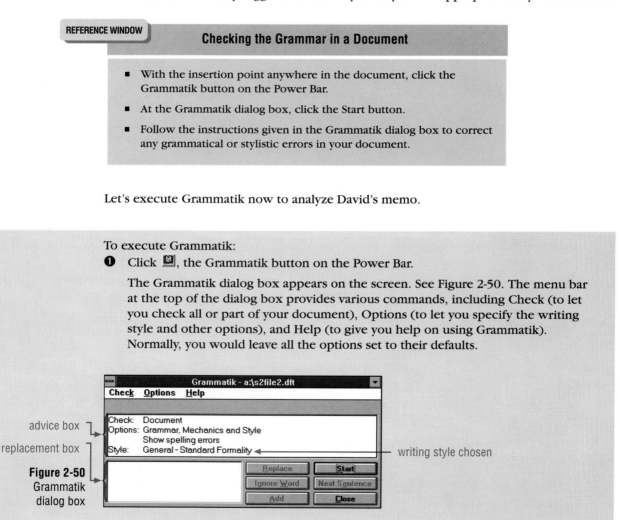

advice box
replacement box

**Figure 2-50**
Grammatik
dialog box

writing style chosen

The Writing Style command on the Options menu allows you to select the writing style that is appropriate to the type of document you are working on. These styles include General (standard formality), Advertising, Business Letter, Documentation, Fiction, Journalism, Memo, Proposal, Report, and so forth. The main difference in how Grammatik checks your document in these writing styles is in the level of formality. For example, in the formal writing style of a business letter or a report, Grammatik flags any contractions ("can't," "won't"), jargon, and colloquial language. In the informal writing style of advertising, on the other hand,

Grammatik doesn't flag these constructions. For most documents, you can accept the default writing style, General, as shown in Figure 2-50.

Because David doesn't want to change any of the default settings in Grammatik, he proceeds to checking his document.

To begin checking a document with Grammatik:

❶ Click the **Start button.** Grammatik begins checking through the document.

The first potential problem encountered by Grammatik is the misspelled word "Truong." The dialog box lists the potential problem in the Rule Class: Spelling. See Figure 2-51.

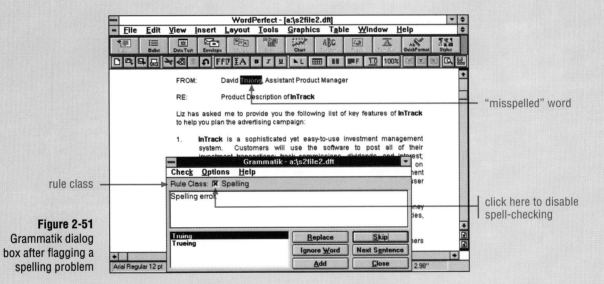

**Figure 2-51**
Grammatik dialog box after flagging a spelling problem

Grammatik uses numerous rule classes to detect potential grammatical and stylistic problems in your documents. A rule class is a grouping of rules for such things as subject/verb agreement, possessive form, split infinitive, capitalization, spelling, punctuation, passive voice, wordiness, and clichés. The Advice box lists the rule class for the current problem Grammatik has detected.

As you can see in Figure 2-51, the current rule class is Spelling. Because you have already checked the spelling in this memo, you can disable this rule class so Grammatik doesn't flag potential spelling errors.

❷ Click the checkbox next to the Rule Class: Spelling. The checkbox is no longer checked.

Grammatik displays a message warning that you are turning off this rule class. Once you've turned off one rule class, you can turn off others without getting this warning.

❸ Click the **OK button** or press **[Enter]** to turn off the Spelling rule class.

Although you've turned off the Spelling rule class, the word "Truong" remains highlighted.

❹ Click the **Ignore Word button** in the Grammatik dialog box to tell Grammatik to ignore the highlighted word "Truong."

Grammatik now scans for the next problem and stops at a potential subject-verb disagreement. See Figure 2-52. The program has incorrectly interpreted "easy-to-use" as the verb "use." Grammatik proposes that the phrase "InTrack use" should be "InTrack uses," but of course that's not what David wants in the memo. Since this is a false error, you can ignore it by skipping the problem.

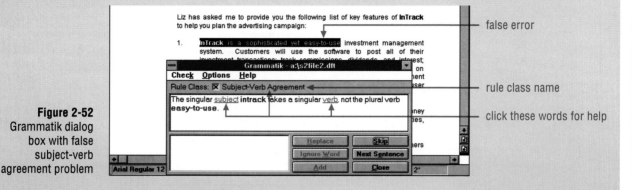

**Figure 2-52**
Grammatik dialog
box with false
subject-verb
agreement problem

false error

rule class name

click these words for help

**TROUBLE?**   If you don't understand a grammar rule that Grammatik is using, click 🖑 on any underlined green word or the rule class name in the Grammatik dialog box. You will then get help on the meaning of those words.

❺  Click the **Skip button** to skip this false error.

The next potential error is the use of the semicolon after the phrase "make value projections." Grammatik suggests that you check to see if the clauses are independent. Because they are, you can skip this false error.

❻  Click the **Skip button.**

Now Grammatik stops at the word "and" after the last semicolon. This too is a false error.

❼  Click the **Skip button.**

Now Grammatik finds the problem of a paragraph with only one sentence (paragraph 2). This is normally not a good practice, but in this case, because each paragraph is an item in a numbered list, we want to ignore this occurrence here and throughout the document.

❽  Click the checkbox next to the Paragraph Problem rule class to disable the rule class, then click the **Skip button.**

Next, Grammatik finds a serious grammatical error—the disagreement between subject and verb in "InTrack provide." See Figure 2-53.

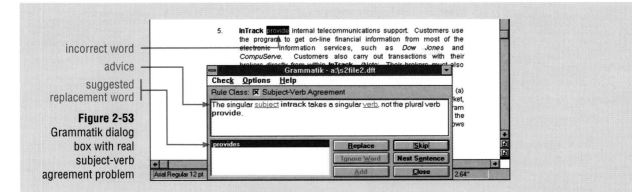

incorrect word

advice

suggested
replacement word

**Figure 2-53**
Grammatik dialog
box with real
subject-verb
agreement problem

⑨ Click the **Replace button** to replace "provide" with "provides" and go to the next problem.

Grammatik continues checking the document and flagging several more potential errors. All of the remaining problems that Grammatik flags are false errors, so you should choose Skip for each of them.

To finish checking the document and close Grammatik:
❶ Click the **Skip button** for all the remaining problems that Grammatik flags.

TROUBLE? If Grammatik stops at a potential problem, but you can't see the highlighted text in the document window, drag the Grammatik dialog box out of the way.

After checking the entire document, Grammatik displays a message informing you that the grammar check is complete and asking you if it's OK to close Grammatik.
❷ Click the **Yes button** to close Grammatik.

WordPerfect now displays a dialog box informing you that you have turned off some rule classes and asking if you want to save those changes. The changes you made, however, were temporary. You do not want to make it a permanent feature of the General writing style.
❸ Click the **No button** to close the dialog box and return to the document window without changing the rule class settings.

You should now read paragraph **5** to verify that Grammatik changed the word "provide" to "provides."

# Saving the Final Version of the Document

David has now completed all the changes that Liz suggested. Your sample memo should look like Figure 2-54.

DATE:        January 15, 1994

TO:          Advertising Group

FROM:        David Truong, Assistant Product Manager

RE:          Product Description of **InTrack**

Liz has asked me to provide you the following list of key features of **InTrack** to help you plan the advertising campaign:

1.   **InTrack** is a sophisticated yet easy-to-use investment management system.  Customers will use the software to post all of their investment transactions; track commissions, dividends, and interest; make value projections; generate tax information; and print reports on investment performance, portfolio values, capital gains, investment income, and so forth.  The mouse-supported, menu-driven user interface is powerful and easy to learn.

2.   **InTrack** helps customers track mutual funds, bonds, stocks, money market funds, certificates of deposit (CDs), real estate, annuities, trusts, and almost any other type of investment.

3.   **InTrack** can be customized for any type of investment.  Customers print reports using built-in forms or design their own reports.

4.   **InTrack** is ideal for managing IRAs and Keogh Plans.  The program will forecast the potential monthly and annual retirement income derived from IRAs and Keogh Plans.

5.   **InTrack** provides internal telecommunications support.  Customers use the program to get on-line financial information from most of the electronic information services, such as *Dow Jones* and *CompuServe*.  Customers also carry out transactions with their brokers directly from within **InTrack**. (Note:  Their brokers must also have **InTrack** to use this option.)

6.   **InTrack** easily pays for itself within the first year of use, because (a) the program costs less than other products of this type on the market, (b) the cost of the program is tax deductible, (c) the program simplifies tax preparation, and (d) the program provides the necessary information to make smart investment decisions and allows customers to get the most return on their investment dollar.

**Figure 2-54**
Final printout of David's memo (page one)

**Figure 2-54**
Final printout of
David's memo
(page two)

7.    **InTrack** runs on any IBM-compatible personal computer under DOS 3.2 (or higher) or under Windows 3.1 (or higher). The program does not require a hard disk drive, but one is highly recommended. The fully installed program, with all features and auxiliary files, requires about 2.5 megabytes of disk space.

8.    **InTrack** supports, but does not require, the following hardware items: Super VGA color graphics, Microsoft-compatible mouse, and Hayes-compatible modem.

After editing any document, you should save it to your disk; otherwise, the disk copy of the document will still be the previous version, without any of the corrections you made since your last save. In this case, let's assume David wants to keep a record of the most recently saved version (S2FILE2.DFT). Therefore, he saves the final version of the memo as S2FILE3.MEM.

To save the final version of the document:
❶  Make sure your Student Disk is still in the disk drive.
❷  Click **File**, then click **Save As.**

WordPerfect displays the Save As dialog box.

❸  Type the new filename **s2file3.mem** and click the **OK button** or press **[Enter].**

WordPerfect saves the final version of the memo to your disk using the filename S2FILE3.MEM.

## Printing Multiple Copies of a Document

David's final task is to print three copies of the memo. He could simply execute the Print command three times, but there is an easier way. Let's use WordPerfect's Number of Copies feature to print three copies of the memo.

To print multiple copies of a document:
❶  Click 🖳, the **Print button** on the Power Bar.

WordPerfect displays the Print dialog box.

❷  Click the **Up Arrow** to the right of Number of Copies in the Copies section of the dialog box until the number of copies is 3. Alternatively, you could double-click the current value and type a new number.
❸  Click the **Print button.**

This completes Tutorial 2. If you want to exit WordPerfect, click File, then click Exit. Because you've already saved the final version of the memo, WordPerfect should close immediately and take you to the Windows Program Manager.

■            ■            ■

# Questions

1. Which key(s) do you press to move the insertion point
   a. to the beginning of the document?
   b. to the end of the document?
   c. one word to the left?
   d. one word to the right?
   e. to the end of a line?
   f. to the beginning of a line?
2. Describe what you would do to change the right margin of a document to 1.5 inches.
3. Write a list of steps required to do the following:
   a. Turn on underlining for text that you are about to type
   b. Turn off underlining after you have typed some underlined text
   c. Change the font
   d. Change the margins
   e. Reveal the format codes
4. Why would you delete a format code, such as Bold On, and how would you delete it?
5. What would you do to see the format code that marks the location where you changed the margins within a document?
6. What is the WordPerfect code for each of the following?
   a. Soft return
   b. Hard return
   c. Soft page break
   d. Hard page break
   e. Tab (normal left tab)
   f. Indent (hard left indent)
   g. Change in the left margin
7. Explain the meaning of the following WordPerfect terms:
   a. Full justification
   b. Left justification
   c. Center justification
   d. Right justification
   e. All justification
8. Explain the difference between a tab and an indent.
9. What is the difference between a soft return and a hard return?
10. Explain the difference between insert mode and typeover mode. What key do you press to change from one mode to the other?
11. What is the command to force a page break. Why would you want to do this?
12. What key(s) do you press to delete the following portions of a document? *Hint:* See Figure 2-35.
    a. The word at the insertion point
    b. From the insertion point to the end of the line
    c. From the insertion point to the beginning of a word
    d. From the insertion point to the end of a word
13. After you've carried out an editing action in WordPerfect, how do you undo it?

14. After you've deleted a word or a phrase, how do you undelete, or restore, the word or phrase?
15. After you've deleted a word or a phrase, how can you restore it to another location in your document?
16. How many instances of deleted text does WordPerfect save for future undelete operations?
17. Name at least three types of errors that WordPerfect's speller can find.
18. If you type the sentence "That is just to bad!" and then run the speller, why won't the speller detect the incorrect usage of the word "to"?
19. What WordPerfect feature can you use to detect errors of the type given in the previous question?
20. Besides synonyms, what does the WordPerfect thesaurus list?
21. What procedure would you follow to print five copies of a memo?
22. Define the word toggle as it applies to WordPerfect commands.

**E** 23. Execute the Grammatik command. Then under Options, list the various writing styles, and then, as required, go into Write Style Edit to do the following:
   a. List the ten writing styles
   b. List at least five rule classes allowed in the Fiction writing style that are not allowed in the General writing style.

**E** 24. Using the Thesaurus to help you, list at least ten synonyms of the word "product."

## Tutorial Assignments

In the following Tutorial Assignments, make sure you clear the document window before opening each file.
   Open the file T2FILE1.DFT and do the following:
1. Change the justification from left to full for the entire document.
2. Change the spaces after "MEMO TO:," "FROM:," and "SUBJECT:," to tabs, so that the text opposite these words is vertically aligned.
3. In the numbered paragraphs, change the tabs to indents.
4. Use the WordPerfect speller to correct misspelled words, duplicate words, and irregular case words.
5. Use Grammatik to check the grammar and style of the document. Make changes to the document in response to grammatical errors, but ignore the suggested problems with style.
6. Carefully read the document and make a list of the words that are misspelled or incorrectly used but that the speller and Grammatik failed to flag. Edit the document to correct these words.
7. Save the document as S2FILE4.MEM.
8. Print the document.
   Open the file T2FILE2.DFT and do the following:
9. Change the font to a serif Times-type font, such as CG Times, Roman, or Times New Roman.
10. Use the thesaurus to substitute another word for the word "obtuse." Use a more common word that has approximately the same meaning.
11. Use the thesaurus to list the antonym(s) of the word "truculent," then reword the sentence using an antonym.
12. Save the document as S2FILE5.MEM.
13. Print three copies of the document by changing the Number of Copies option in the Print dialog box.
   Open the file T2FILE3.DOC and do the following:
14. Change the font in the document to a sans serif font, such as Arial, Helvetica, or Dutch.
**E** 15. Change the font size to 14-point.

16. Insert a hard page break after the date (March 1994), so that the first several lines, down to the date, become a title page and the rest of the document is on a separate page.
17. At the beginning of the second page, just after the page break, change the justification to full.
**E**  18. Set the title page to center justification.
19. Save the document as S2FILE6.DOC.
20. Print one copy of the document.

Open the file T2FILE4.DFT and do the following:
21. Change the space after the "Date:," "To:," "From:," and "Subject:," to one or two tabs, so that the information to the right of these words is aligned.
22. Change the margins of the memo to 1.5" on the right and left.
23. After the first paragraph to the right of the colon, type "I'm impressed! InTrack helped me dramatically improve the earnings on my investments." Make InTrack boldface.
24. Use typeover mode to change the number "6,438.15" to "5,892.46."
25. Run the speller to correct the typos in the document.
26. Save the document as S2FILE7.MEM.
27. Print one copy of the document.

Open the file T2FILE5.DOC and do the following *in the order given:*
28. Turn on Reveal Codes and make a handwritten list of all the format codes you can see in the document.
29. Clear the document window, then type the list of format codes you found. Type only one code per line.
30. Number each code in the list and indent ([F7]) after each number.
**E**  31. After each format code, type a colon (:), then type what you think is the meaning of the code, based on its name and its function in the document.
32. Save the document as S2CODES.DOC.
33. Print the document.

# Case Problems

## 1. Intelligent Inventions, Inc.

Roger Plunkett has always wanted to market one of his inventions. He sees an advertisement in the newspaper from Intelligent Inventions, Inc. offering help in marketing new inventions. He decides to write a letter to find out more about the company and about marketing new products.

Open the file P2INVENT.DFT and do the following:
1. Set the entire document to full justification.
2. Change the font to Century or Courier or some other serif font besides Times or Times Roman.
3. Change the left margin to 0.75 inch.
4. Change the right margin to 0.75 inch.
5. Change the date in the document to the current date.
6. Number the three paragraphs that ask a question. Indent all the lines of the paragraph after the paragraph number.
7. After the third numbered question in the letter, add a fourth numbered paragraph with the following question: "Does the inventor retain the patent (if any) for the new invention?"
8. In the second question, use the thesaurus to pick a better word for "promulgate."
9. Run the speller to correct any typos and spelling errors.
10. Run Grammatik to correct any grammatical errors.

11. Proofread the document for errors that the speller and Grammatik might have missed.
12. Save the document as S2INVENT.LET.
13. Use WordPerfect's number of copies feature to print two copies of the letter.

## 2. LawnTools, Inc.

Sujat Jahmiel works as a product manager for LawnTools, Inc. He would like to begin marketing a line of low-cost, environmentally safe push-mowers. He feels that the product has significant market potential, but he must get approval from the members of the Corporate Products group. He decides to send them each a memo extolling the virtues of his proposed push-mower.

Open the file P2LAWN.DFT and do the following:

1. Set the font to a sans serif font such as Helvetica, Swiss, or Arial.
2. Change the left margin to 1.5 inches.
3. Change the right margin to 0.75 inch.
4. Change the justification to full.
5. Change the date of the document to the current date.
6. Insert tabs between "FROM:" and "Sujat Jahmiel" so that the name is aligned above the SUBJECT information.
7. After the SUBJECT information (following the comma at the end of the line), insert the name of the product in boldface type: **SwiftBlade.**
8. In the numbered paragraphs, change the Left Tab codes to Hd Left Ind codes.
9. At the beginning of numbered paragraph 2, insert the phrase "According to *Consumer Reports.*" Type the name of the magazine in italics. Type a comma after the name of the magazine and change the "T" in "Today" to lowercase.
10. Using typeover mode, change the value in paragraph 2 from $139 to $150.
11. If necessary, insert a hard page break before the paragraph to ensure that the final paragraph of the document is not split between two pages.
12. Run the speller to correct any typographical and spelling errors.
13. Run Grammatik to correct any grammatical errors.
14. Save the memo as S2LAWN.MEM.
15. Print the memo.

## 3. Buñuelos

Luz Reyes is the chief executive officer for Buñuelos, a successful Puerto Rican restaurant chain of eight stores. She has arranged a meeting with the members of the board of directors to discuss company growth and set goals for the future. She prepares a short report describing company performance over the past fiscal year.

Open the file P2BUNUEL.REP and do the following:

1. Change the justification to center, so that the title and the author's name at the beginning of the report will be centered.
2. After the author's name, change the justification back to left, so that the remainder of the report will be left-justified.
3. Below the title, set the left and right margins to 2.0 inches.
4. Change the font in your report to any other font of your choosing.
5. Save the report as S2BUNUEL.REP.
6. Print the report.

# Using Additional Editing Features

## Writing an Inventory Observation Memo

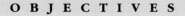

### O B J E C T I V E S

In this tutorial you will:

- Align text flush right
- Center a line of text between the left and right margins
- Find and replace text
- Use Select operations to change the appearance of existing text
- Use Select operations to move, delete, and copy text
- Drag and drop text to move or copy it

**Sorority Designs, Inc.** Melissa Walborsky graduated last June with a degree in accounting and has earned her C.P.A. certificate. She recently began work on the auditing staff at McDermott & Eston, an accounting firm in Syracuse, New York. One of Melissa's first assignments is an audit of Sorority Designs, Inc. (SDI), a clothing company that markets stylish apparel designed for college-age women. As a member of the audit team, she observed the inventory at SDI's warehouse in Syracuse. Susan Guttmann, Melissa's manager, has asked her to write the inventory observation memo for the audit working papers (documents that verify the nature of an audit and the results). Melissa will write a first draft of the memo. Then, based upon her own proofreading, she will revise the memo. Finally, she will submit her draft to Susan for approval, in accordance with the established policy for all McDermott & Eston documents.

# Planning the Document

Before writing the memo, Melissa looks at her own notes, the audit working papers, and several other inventory observation memos to help her determine the content, organization, style, and format of her document.

## Content

Melissa decides to base the content of her memo primarily on her notes (Figure 3-1) and her personal recollection of the inventory.

**Figure 3-1**
Melissa's handwritten notes from the inventory observation

Inventory Observation, Syracuse Warehouse, September 15, 1994

— Arrived 7:20 a.m.
— No merchandise shipped that day.
— Slow-moving and damaged merchandise: shipped to Ithaca outlet.
— Periodic test counts on 31% of inventory.
— Cutoff controls: noted apparel received on September 13 and noted no merchandise shipped on September 14.

## Organization

Melissa's document will follow the standard organizational structure of an inventory observation memo, with the headings "Observation of Inventory Taking," "Slow-Moving and Damaged Merchandise," "Test Counts," "Cutoff Controls," and "Conclusions." She determines that the memo needs only one or two paragraphs under each heading.

## Style

Melissa decides to use a straightforward writing style. She will also use auditing terminology because her audience will be other accountants at McDermott & Eston.

## Format

Melissa decides not to change any of WordPerfect's default format settings. She leaves the margins at one inch on the left, right, top, and bottom and keeps the (default) left justification. Melissa will modify the format of the heading, however, so that the document follows the standard McDermott & Eston format for inventory observation memos.

# Opening the Document

Let's begin by opening Melissa's rough draft.

To open the document:

❶ If you haven't done so already, launch WordPerfect.

❷ Insert your WordPerfect Student Disk into drive A.

**TROUBLE?**   If your Student Disk doesn't fit in drive A, use drive B. Then, whenever this tutorial refers to drive A, use drive B instead.

❸ Click 🖼, the **Open button** on the Power Bar. The Open File dialog box appears on the screen.

❹ Click the **Down Arrow** to the right of the Drives section, then click **a:** to choose drive A.

The list of files on the Student Disk appears in the Open File dialog box.

❺ Click the filename **c3file1.dft**, then click the **OK button** or press **[Enter]**. The rough draft of Melissa's memo appears in the document window.

To avoid accidentally overwriting the disk file C3FILE1.DFT, let's save your document back to the disk using another filename.

❻ Click **File**, then click **Save As** to display the Save As dialog box.

❼ Type the new filename **s3file1.dft**, then click the **OK button**

Your WordPerfect window should now look like Figure 3-2.

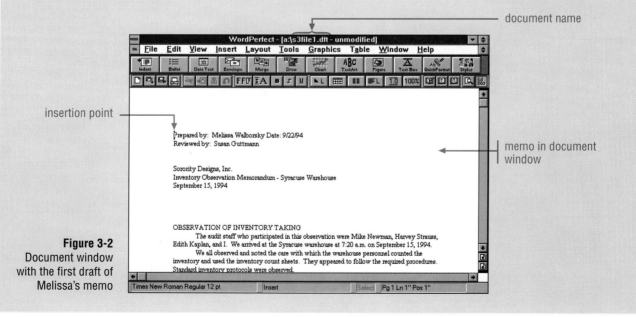

**Figure 3-2**
Document window
with the first draft of
Melissa's memo

Remember that this is Melissa's rough draft, which she has not yet revised. It contains formatting, spelling, and other errors. In the following section, Melissa will revise the memo before she submits it to Susan. Take time now to read through the entire document and familiarize yourself with its content and some of its problems. Don't make any revisions at this time.

## Using Flush Right

Melissa begins by observing that in most of the other company memos, the date on the top line of the document appears flush against the right margin. She decides, therefore, to use WordPerfect's Flush Right feature to move the date in her memo. Let's use Flush Right to position the date at the right margin.

To move existing text flush right:

❶ Move the insertion point to the left of the "D" in "Date" on the first line of the document.

Whenever you use Flush Right, you must position the insertion point to the left of the first letter of the word or group of words you want to move.

❷ Click **Layout**, click **Line**, then click **Flush Right.**

The date text moves to the right margin. See Figure 3-3.

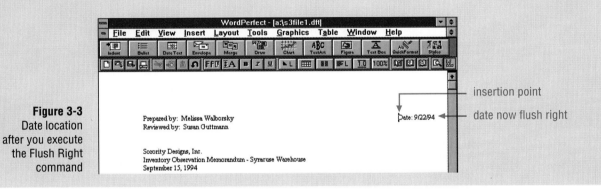

**Figure 3-3**
Date location
after you execute
the Flush Right
command

Melissa next adds the date that Susan Guttmann presumably will review the memo.

To type flush-right text:

❶ Move the insertion point to the end of the second line, after "Susan Guttmann."
❷ Click **Layout**, click **Line**, then click **Flush Right.** The insertion point is now at the right margin of the document.
❸ Type **Date: 9/26/94**.

Notice that as you type, the insertion point stays in the same place rather than moving from left to right. The characters move from right to left, away from the right margin.

## Centering Text

Melissa realizes that the three title lines in the inventory observation memo—starting with Sorority Designs, Inc. and ending with the date of the audit, "September 15, 1994"— should be centered between the left and right margins. Let's use WordPerfect's Center command to format these three lines of text.

To center text:

❶ Move the insertion point immediately to the left of "S" in "Sorority," at the beginning of the third line of text in the document window.

To center any line of existing text, you first place the insertion point at the beginning of that line.

❷ Click **Layout**, click **Line**, then click **Center**. As soon as you execute the Center command, WordPerfect centers the line of text between the margins. See Figure 3-4.

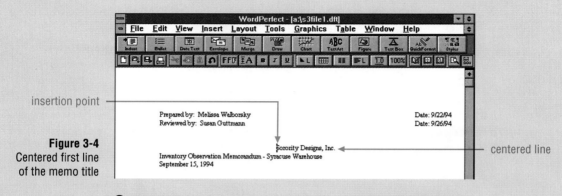

**Figure 3-4**
Centered first line
of the memo title

insertion point

centered line

❸ Move the insertion point to the beginning of the next line.
❹ Click **Layout**, click **Line**, then click **Center.**
❺ Use the same procedure to center the last line of the title.
❻ Turn on Reveal Codes to see the Hd Flush Right and Hd Center on Marg format codes that WordPerfect inserted into the document in this and the previous set of steps. (You will have to move the insertion point to the beginning of the document to see the Hd Flush Right codes.) After you have viewed the codes, turn off Reveal Codes.

As a general rule, when you want to center many lines of text, such as all the lines on a title page of a report, use the Center Justification command on the Justification button of the Power Bar, as you learned in Tutorial 2. When you want to center only a few lines of text, use the Layout, Line, Center command.

## Finding Text

When you're working with a short document—a half page in length, for example—you can find a specific word or phrase or move the insertion point to a specific location just by using the insertion-point movement keys. But when you're working with a longer document, the best way to find a specific word or phrase or move to a specific location is usually with the Find command, which carries out a search operation. A **search** is an operation you use to position the insertion point at a specified sequence of characters or codes, called the **find string** or **search string.** The find string may include a single character, such as "T" or "4"; a format code, such as Hd Left Ind or HRt; a word or group of words, such as "inventory" or "shipping log"; or any combination of characters, codes, or words.

**Finding Text**

- Move the insertion point to the beginning of the document if you want to find the first occurrence of the find string, or leave the insertion point where it is if you want to find the next occurrence of the find string.
- Click Edit, then click Find.
- With the insertion point in the Find text box or with the current find string highlighted, type the (new) find string.
- Click Find to initiate the search.

Let's look at an example of how you would use the Find command. Melissa notices that in her memo she left out the word "of" after "31%" in the first line under "TEST COUNTS." She decides to use WordPerfect's Find command to move the insertion point quickly to that location in the memo.

To find text:

❶ Move the insertion point to the beginning of the document.

Unless you specify otherwise, WordPerfect will search forward from the insertion point to the end of the document. Positioning the insertion point at the beginning of the document ensures that you will find the specified find string, no matter where it is in your document.

❷ Click **Edit**, then click **Find**.

WordPerfect displays the Find Text dialog box and waits for you to type the find string. See Figure 3-5.

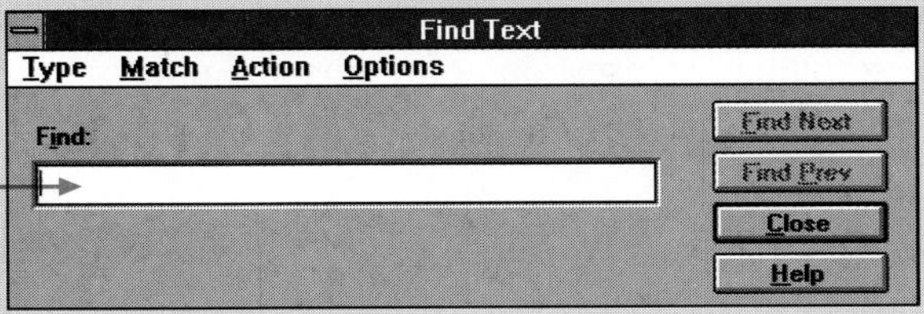

type find string here ⟶

**Figure 3-5**
Find Text dialog box

❸   Type **31%** into the Find text box and click the **Find Next button** or press **[Enter]**.

WordPerfect searches through the document until it finds the find string—
"31%"—and then highlights it. The Find Text dialog box remains active. See
Figure 3-6.

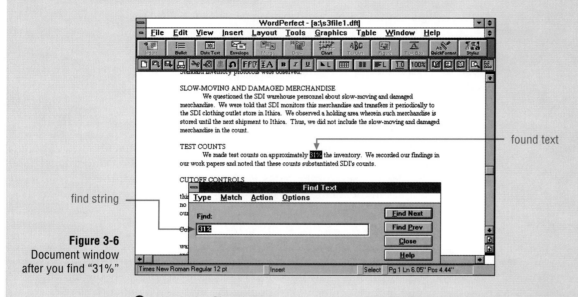

**Figure 3-6**
Document window
after you find "31%"

❹   Click the **Close button** on the Find Text dialog box. The insertion point appears
immediately to the right of the find string in the document window. You are now
ready to insert "of" after "31%."

❺   Press **[Spacebar]** and type **of** to add the missing word.

After you have had some practice, you'll find that using the Find command to move
the insertion point to specific locations within longer documents is usually much faster
than using the the scroll bar or insertion-point movement keys.

## Finding and Replacing Text

**Find and replace**, sometimes simply called **replace**, is an operation that searches
through a document for a **find string** and then replaces one or more occurrences of that
find string with another specified string, called the replacement string. The **replacement
string**, like the find string, can be any combination of characters, codes, or words. You
can use find and replace to change one word to another word, one phrase to another
phrase, one set of format codes to another set of format codes, and so forth, throughout
your document.

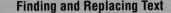

**REFERENCE WINDOW**

**Finding and Replacing Text**

- Move the insertion point to the beginning of the document if you want to find the first occurrence of the find string, or leave the insertion point where it is if you want to find the next occurrence of the find string.

- Click Edit, then click Replace.

- With the insertion point in the Find text box or with the current find string highlighted, type the (new) find string.

- Press [Tab] to move the insertion point to the Replace With text box, or click the mouse pointer in that text box.

- Type the replacement string.

- Click the Find, Replace, or Replace All button to initiate the search. If you know you want to replace all occurrences of the find string with the replacement string, use the Replace All button. If you want to find each occurrence one at a time and then decide whether or not to replace it, use the Find button to initiate or continue a search, and the Replace button to make any desired replacements.

Let's use replace to change an incorrect word in the inventory observation memo to the correct word. For example, Melissa notices that she misspelled "Ithaca" throughout the document. She can't use WordPerfect's speller to make the correction, because "Ithaca," a proper noun, is not in the speller dictionary. She decides, therefore, to use WordPerfect's Replace feature to find all occurrences of "Ithica" and replace them with "Ithaca."

To find and replace a string of text:

**❶** Move the insertion point to the beginning of the document.

The Replace feature works from the position of the insertion point to the end of the document for a forward search. Thus, to perform the operation for an entire document, you need to move the insertion point to the beginning of the document.

**❷** Click **Edit,** then click **Replace.** WordPerfect displays the Find and Replace Text dialog box. See Figure 3-7.

previous find string ───►

**Figure 3-7**
Find and Replace
Text dialog box

```
┌─────────────────────────────────────────────────┐
│ ─              Find and Replace Text              │
│ Type  Match  Replace  Direction  Options          │
│                                                   │
│ Find:                              ┌──────────┐   │
│ ┌──────────────────────────────┐   │   Find   │   │
│ │81▓                           │   └──────────┘   │
│ └──────────────────────────────┘   ┌──────────┐   │
│                                    │ Replace  │   │
│ Replace With:                      └──────────┘   │
│ ┌──────────────────────────────┐   ┌──────────┐   │
│ │                              │   │Replace All│  │
│ └──────────────────────────────┘   └──────────┘   │
│                                    ┌──────────┐   │
│                                    │  Close   │   │
│                                    └──────────┘   │
│                                    ┌──────────┐   │
│                                    │  Help    │   │
│                                    └──────────┘   │
└─────────────────────────────────────────────────┘
```

The contents of the Find text box (your previous find string) is highlighted. The next thing you type will automatically replace the highlighted text.

❸ In the Find text box, type **Ithica**, then press **[Tab]** to move the insertion point to the Replace With text box. You can also click I in the Replace With text box. Notice that in a dialog box pressing [Tab] moves the insertion point (or the focus) from one field or one text box to another, whereas in the document window pressing [Tab] advances the text and the insertion point to the next tab stop.

TROUBLE?    If you accidentally pressed [Enter] after typing "Ithica," WordPerfect found the first occurrence of the find string, highlighted it, and left the Find and Replace Text dialog box on the screen. Click I in the Replace With text box, type "Ithaca," and click the Replace button. Then skip to Step 5.

❹ Type **Ithaca.** See Figure 3-8.

**Figure 3-8**
Find string and replacement string in the Find and Replace Text dialog box

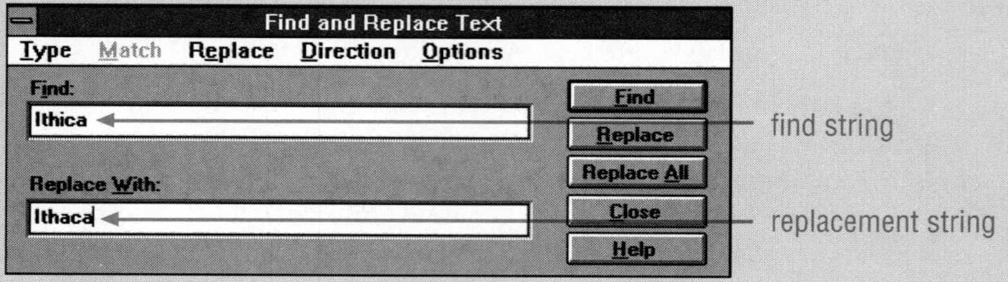

"Ithica" becomes the new find string, and "Ithaca," the correct spelling of the city name, becomes the replacement string.

❺ Click the **Replace All button.**

WordPerfect changes all occurrences of "Ithica" to "Ithaca." The Find and Replace Text dialog box remains on the screen. The insertion point is now located at the last occurrence of the find string. Because there are no other occurrences in the document, the Replace operation terminates.

TROUBLE?    If you pressed [Enter] or clicked the Find button, WordPerfect stopped at the first occurrence of "Ithica" and highlighted the word. Click the Replace All button and proceed to the next step.

❻ Click the **Close button** to close the dialog box and return to the main document window.

As Melissa reads through her draft of the memo, she realizes that she has used the word "merchandise" excessively. She decides that in some places she could use the word "apparel" instead, since apparel is the only type of merchandise SDI sells. To avoid the repetitive use of "merchandise," she performs a find and replace using the Replace command instead of the Replace All command. This means that at each occurrence of "merchandise" in the document, WordPerfect will stop and ask her if she wants to replace "merchandise" with "apparel."

Let's use the Replace command this time instead of Replace All so we can change some (but not all) of the occurrences of "merchandise" to "apparel." In the following steps, the choice of when to change a word and when to leave it unchanged is based on whatever seems better to Melissa, not on any rules.

To replace some occurrences of the find string with the replacement string:

**❶** Move the insertion point to the beginning of the document and click **Edit,** then click **Replace.**

**❷** Type **merchandise** in the Find text box and press **[Tab]** or click I in the Replace With text box. The word "merchandise" becomes the find string.

**❸** Type **apparel** in the Replace With text box.

The word "apparel" becomes the replacement string.

**❹** Click the **Find button** or press **[Enter]** to tell WordPerfect to search for the next occurrence of the find string.

WordPerfect finds and highlights the first occurrence of "merchandise," located in the second heading.

**❺** Click the **Replace button** to replace "merchandise" with "apparel" in the second heading.

WordPerfect continues to the next occurrence of "merchandise," highlights the word, and stops for you to accept or decline the replacement. When you want to accept the replacement, click the Replace button. When you want to decline the replacement, click the Find button, which tells WordPerfect to skip that occurrence and find the next occurrence of the find string. The word "merchandise" occurs four times in the paragraph following the second heading.

**❻** Click the **Replace button** to accept the replacement in the first sentence of the paragraph, click the **Find button** to decline replacement in the second sentence, click the **Find button** again in the third sentence, and click the **Replace button** in the last sentence of the paragraph.

**❼** Click the **Find button** twice to decline replacement of both occurrences of merchandise in the paragraph under "CUTOFF CONTROLS." Click the **Replace button** for the first occurrence in the final paragraph, then click the **Find button** for the last occurrence.

The find and replace operation is now complete. WordPerfect displays the Find and Replace message: "merchandise" Not Found.

**❽** Click the **OK button** to close the dialog box containing the message, then click the **Close button** to close the Find and Replace Text dialog box.

Your document will now look similar to Figure 3-9. The word "Apparel" in the second heading isn't in all uppercase letters as it should be, but you'll fix that later. The first letter of "Apparel" is uppercase because, in a find and replace, WordPerfect automatically capitalizes the first letter of the *replacement* word when the first letter of the *replaced* word is uppercase.

Prepared by:  Melissa Walborsky                          Date: 9/22/94
Reviewed by:  Susan Guttmann                             Date: 9/26/94

Sorority Designs, Inc.
Inventory Observation Memorandum - Syracuse Warehouse
September 15, 1994

OBSERVATION OF INVENTORY TAKING
    The audit staff who participated in this observation were Mike Newman, Harvey Strauss, Edith Kaplan, and I.  We arrived at the Syracuse warehouse at 7:20 a.m. on September 15, 1994.
    We all observed and noted the care with which the warehouse personnel counted the inventory and used the inventory count sheets.  They appeared to follow the required procedures. Standard inventory protocols were observed.

SLOW-MOVING AND DAMAGED Apparel
    We questioned the SDI warehouse personnel about slow-moving and damaged apparel. We were told that SDI monitors this merchandise and transfers it periodically to the SDI clothing outlet store in Ithaca.  We observed a holding area wherein such merchandise is stored until the next shipment to Ithaca.  Thus, we did not include the slow-moving and damaged apparel in the count.

TEST COUNTS
    We made test counts on approximately 31% of the inventory.  We recorded our findings in our work papers and noted that these counts substantiated SDI's counts.

CUTOFF CONTROLS
    We took time to gain access to and examine the Receipt Log and the Shipping Log for this warehouse.  We noted the merchandise received on September 13, 1994; we also noted that no merchandise was shipped on September 14, 1994.  We used the September 13 numbers for our subsequent purchases and sales cutoff tests.

Conclusions
    I believe we made an accurate count of all saleable apparel in the Syracuse warehouse on September 15, 1994, because the SDI personnel followed all required procedures and because the merchandise held for delivery to the Ithaca outlet store was not counted.

**Figure 3-9**
Printed memo after
first round of editing

# Saving and Printing the Document

Melissa feels that the inventory observation memo is now ready to save to the disk and to print for review by her manager, Susan. The document is still in draft form, but Melissa needs Susan's feedback before she edits, saves, and prints the final version.

To save and print the draft document:
❶  Make sure your Student Disk is in drive A.
❷  Click 🖫, the **Save button** on the Power Bar, to save the document to drive A using the default filename S3FILE1.DFT.

Melissa keeps the filename extension .DFT to signify that this is still a draft of the memo.

❸ Make sure your printer is turned on and ready to print, then print the document.

After she prints the document, Melissa gives it to Susan, who notes errors and suggests other changes. Susan returns the edited document to Melissa and asks her to make the changes before printing a copy for the file (Figure 3-10). Because Susan did, in fact, review the memo on 9/26/94, that date can remain.

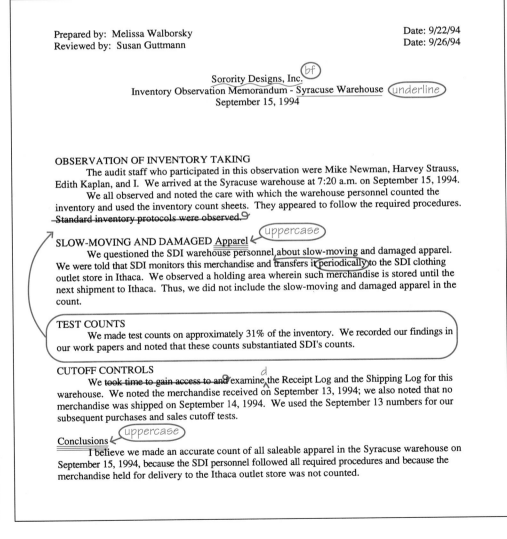

**Figure 3-10**
Memo with Susan's suggested corrections

*If you want to take a break* and resume the tutorial at a later time, you can exit WordPerfect. When you resume, launch WordPerfect and open S3FILE1.DFT into a document window.

## Block Operations

One of the most powerful editing features in WordPerfect is the Select command, which allows you to execute block operations. A **block operation** is a set of commands that allows you to modify or otherwise act on an existing block (or unit) of text. The block of text may be any portion of your document—a single character, a phrase, a sentence, a paragraph, a page, or a group of pages—that you select. Block operations are so important in editing documents that we will show you how to execute them using the mouse as well as the keyboard. Before you can execute a block operation, you have to select the text on which you want to execute it. The selected text becomes highlighted.

### Selecting Text

- Drag I over the desired block of text.

*or*

- Move the insertion point (using the mouse or the keyboard) to the beginning of the block, press and hold down [Shift], then move the insertion point to the end of the block and release [Shift].

*or*

- Move the insertion point to the beginning of the block, press [F8] (Select), and use the keyboard to move the insertion point to the end of the block.

Block operations are powerful and efficient because they allow you to move, copy, or modify a block of text *as a unit* instead of changing each character, word, or paragraph individually. For example, you could change all the text in a paragraph from regular type to boldface, from left-justified to centered, or from uppercase and lowercase to all uppercase. You can also use block operations to delete a block of text, save a block of text to a disk, or move a block of text from one location to another within your document.

Figure 3-11 shows the many Block operations that are available in WordPerfect. Some of these operations (such as Bold, Delete, and Flush Right) are familiar to you, but many of them may be unfamiliar—Append, Comment, and Convert Case. You'll learn many of these operations as you complete this and future tutorials.

## Block Operations

| Operation | Description |
|---|---|
| Append | Add block to the end of an existing file |
| Bold | Make blocked text boldface |
| Center | Center block horizontally |
| Comment | Convert selected text to a document comment |
| Convert Case | Switch all characters in block to uppercase, lowercase, or first letter uppercase (where appropriate) and others lowercase |
| Copy | Make a copy of block at another location in the document or copy to another document |
| Cut/Paste | Remove block and paste it into another location in the document |
| Delete | Erase block |
| Find | Find text or codes within block |
| Flush Right | Align block against the right margin |
| Font | Change the type style, size, or appearance of blocked text |
| Grammatik | Check grammar within block |
| Macro | Macro acts upon block |
| Mark Text | Mark block for lists, index, table of contents |
| Print | Send block of text to the printer |
| Protect | Keep block of text together on same page (protect against page break) |
| Replace | Find and replace text or codes within block |
| Save | Save block of text to the disk |
| Sort | Sort lines or records within block |
| Speller | Check the spelling within block |
| Style | Insert style formatting codes within block |
| Table | Convert block of text to a table |
| Underline | Underline block |

**Figure 3-11**
List of common
Block operations

### Modifying a Block of Existing Text

- Select (highlight) the block of text.

- Execute a WordPerfect block operation (see Figure 3-11), such as Bold, Underline, or Center, to modify the highlighted text without changing any other text in the document.

Block operations involve first selecting, or highlighting, the block of text that you want to modify and then executing the appropriate WordPerfect command to act on that block of text. Let's illustrate this procedure by changing an existing phrase in Melissa's inventory observation memo from regular type to boldface.

## Changing Existing Text to Boldface

Look at Figure 3-10 and notice that Susan's first suggested change is to make the client's name boldface in the document title. This is a common practice at McDermott & Eston.

Melissa already knows how to use the Bold button to create new boldface text, but to change *existing* text to boldface, she has to select the existing text first. Let's select and then change the client's name to boldface.

To change a block of existing text to boldface:

❶ Move I immediately to the left of the "S" in "Sorority" in the document title, press and hold down the left mouse button, drag I to the end of the phrase "Sorority Designs, Inc.," and release the mouse button.

WordPerfect activates—that is, changes from gray to black—the word "Select" on the status bar. See Figure 3-12.

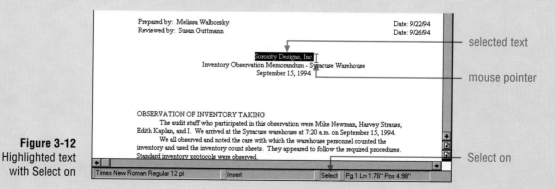

**Figure 3-12**
Highlighted text
with Select on

❷ Click B, the **Bold button** on the Power Bar, to make the highlighted text boldface.

The name of the company changes to boldface.

❸ Click I somewhere in the document window outside the selected text.

Clicking $\mathrm{I}$ outside the selected text turns off Select. For example, click $\mathrm{I}$ to the right of the selected text. The word Select on the status bar is deactivated (becomes gray). See Figure 3-13.

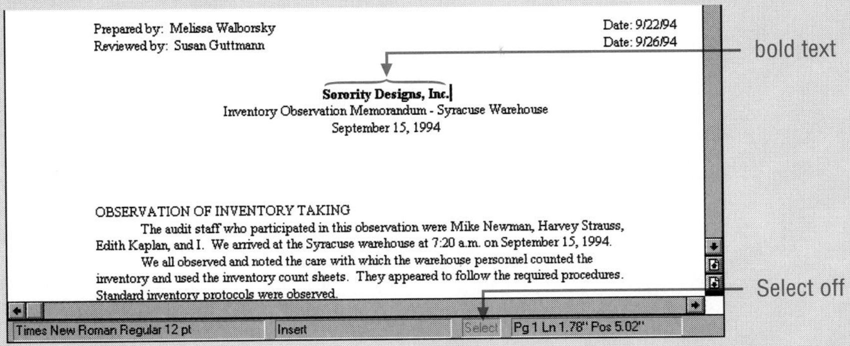

**Figure 3-13**
Document window
after you apply
boldface to a block
of text

**TROUBLE?**    If you accidentally apply boldface to a block of text that you want in regular type, select the text and click ⬛.

## Underlining a Block of Text

Look again at Figure 3-10. Susan's next suggestion is to underline "Syracuse Warehouse" in the second line of the memo title. Let's use a block operation to underline this text.

To underline a block of existing text:
❶   Click $\mathrm{I}$ to the left of the "S" in "Syracuse," which is the beginning of the block of text you want to highlight, press and hold **[Shift]**, click $\mathrm{I}$ to the right of the word "Warehouse," then release **[Shift]**.

WordPerfect activates the message "Select" on the status bar and highlights the selected block of text.
❷   Click 🄤, the **Underline button** on the Power Bar, to underline the block of text.
❸   Click the mouse pointer somewhere in the document window outside the highlighted text to turn Select off.

## Deleting a Block of Text

Another time-saving block operation is deleting a block of text. If you want to delete more than two or three words, you can save time by using Select. For example, in Figure 3-10, in the paragraph headed "CUTOFF CONTROLS," Susan suggests that Melissa delete the unnecessary and wordy phrase "took time to gain access to and." Let's use a block operation, this time using only the keyboard, to delete the phrase.

To delete a block of text using the keyboard:
❶   Move the insertion point to the beginning of the phrase "took time to gain access to and" just below the heading "CUTOFF CONTROLS."

❷ Press **[F8]** (Select). The "Select" message on the status bar becomes active.

❸ Using the keyboard (not the mouse), move the insertion point to the right of the space just after "and" (to the left of the "e" in "examine"). See Figure 3-14.

selected text ——

**Figure 3-14**
Selected text to
delete

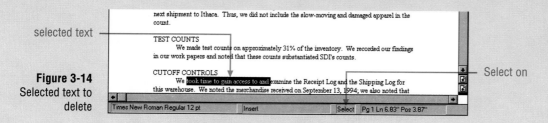

Select on

TROUBLE?   If, after pressing [F8] (Select), you try to move the insertion point with the mouse, Select turns off. You must move the insertion point with the keyboard after pressing [F8] (Select).

❹ Press **[Del]** or **[Backspace]**.

WordPerfect deletes the text without prompting you for confirmation. The more text you have to delete, the more keystrokes you will save by using the Select feature.

TROUBLE?   If you accidentally delete the wrong block of text, you can restore it by clicking the Undo button on the Power Bar or by clicking Undelete from the Edit menu and then clicking Restore.

❺ Change "examine" to "examined."

Now the phrase reads "We examined . . ." as Susan suggested.

## Converting a Block of Text to All Uppercase

Turn once again to Figure 3-10. In the second heading, Susan has marked the word "Apparel" to be all uppercase. When Melissa used find and replace to change "merchandise" to "apparel," she forgot to change "Apparel" to all uppercase in the heading. Susan also noted that the last heading, "Conclusions," should be in all uppercase letters as well. Melissa knows that she can use the Select operation to convert the case.

To convert the case of a block of text:

❶ Using any method you desire, select the word "Apparel" in the third heading as the block of text to be converted.

The text is highlighted.

❷ Click **Edit**, click **Convert Case**, then click **Uppercase**.

WordPerfect converts the word "Apparel" to "APPAREL."

❸ Turn off Select by clicking the mouse pointer anywhere in the document window or by pressing **[F8]** (Select).

Notice that the [F8] (Select) key is a toggle switch for the Select command.

❹ Select the word "Conclusions," which is the last heading in the memo.

❺ Click **Edit**, click **Convert Case**, then click **Uppercase**.

❻ Turn off Select either by clicking I anywhere in the document window or by pressing **[F8]** (Select).

The word "Conclusions" becomes "CONCLUSIONS." Your document window should now look similar to Figure 3-15.

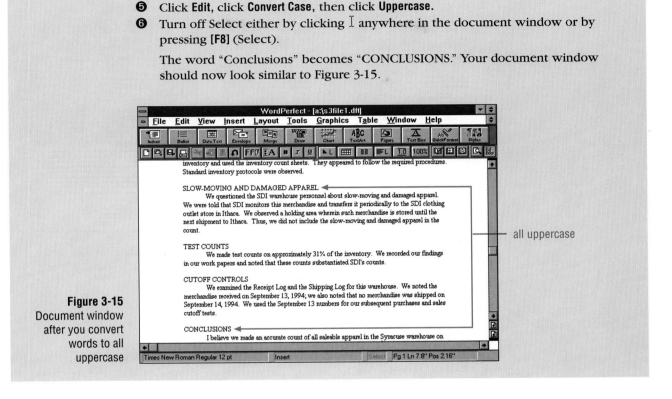

all uppercase

**Figure 3-15**
Document window
after you convert
words to all
uppercase

You can also use the Convert Case command to convert a block of text to all lowercase characters or, using Initial Capitals, make the first letter of each word (except prepositions and articles) uppercase and the other letters lowercase.

## Cutting and Pasting a Block of Text

One of the most important uses of the Select command is that of moving text. Suppose, for example, you have typed a paragraph into a document but then realize the paragraph is in the wrong place. You could solve the problem by deleting the paragraph and then retyping it at the new location. But a much more efficient approach is to use a block operation to move the paragraph. This is sometimes called "cut and paste," because after highlighting the block of text you want to move, you cut (delete) it from the document and then paste (restore) it back again in the appropriate place (Figure 3-16).

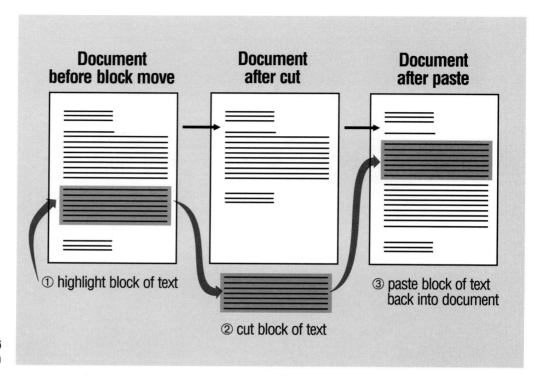

**Figure 3-16**
Cut and paste operation

Cut and paste is an important operation in virtually all Windows applications. For this reason, Windows allows you to cut and paste with the mouse or with the keyboard. In the following steps, you use either the mouse or the keyboard.

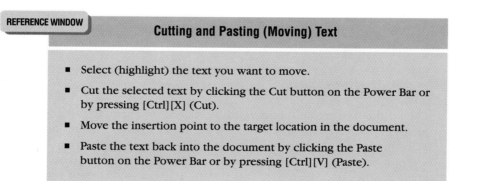

REFERENCE WINDOW

**Cutting and Pasting (Moving) Text**

- Select (highlight) the text you want to move.
- Cut the selected text by clicking the Cut button on the Power Bar or by pressing [Ctrl][X] (Cut).
- Move the insertion point to the target location in the document.
- Paste the text back into the document by clicking the Paste button on the Power Bar or by pressing [Ctrl][V] (Paste).

In Figure 3-10, Susan suggests that Melissa move the "TEST COUNTS" section so that it is the second section in the memo instead of the third. Melissa knows that instead of deleting and retyping the paragraph, she can use Select with the Move command to move it to a new position. Let's do this now.

To move a block of text:

❶ Click I immediately to the left of the first "T" in "TEST COUNTS," press and hold down **[Shift]**, then click I just before the "C" in "CUTOFF" at the beginning of the next section of text.

The entire block you want to move is highlighted. See Figure 3-17. Because you want to move the entire paragraph, you should select from the beginning of one heading to the beginning of the next to include the blank line between them.

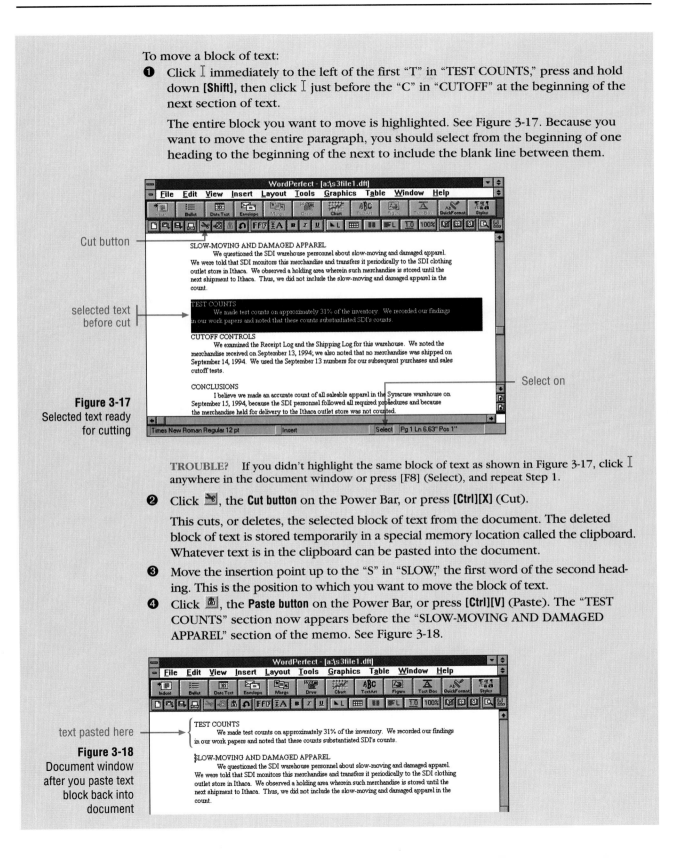

Cut button

selected text
before cut

Select on

**Figure 3-17**
Selected text ready
for cutting

**TROUBLE?**   If you didn't highlight the same block of text as shown in Figure 3-17, click I anywhere in the document window or press [F8] (Select), and repeat Step 1.

❷ Click ✂, the **Cut button** on the Power Bar, or press **[Ctrl][X]** (Cut).

This cuts, or deletes, the selected block of text from the document. The deleted block of text is stored temporarily in a special memory location called the clipboard. Whatever text is in the clipboard can be pasted into the document.

❸ Move the insertion point up to the "S" in "SLOW," the first word of the second heading. This is the position to which you want to move the block of text.

❹ Click 📋, the **Paste button** on the Power Bar, or press **[Ctrl][V]** (Paste). The "TEST COUNTS" section now appears before the "SLOW-MOVING AND DAMAGED APPAREL" section of the memo. See Figure 3-18.

text pasted here

**Figure 3-18**
Document window
after you paste text
block back into
document

## Selecting Whole Units of Text

WordPerfect provides another, more efficient method for selecting whole words, sentences, and paragraphs.

To use this method, you double-click the mouse pointer on the desired word to select it and the space to its right; you triple-click the mouse pointer within the desired sentence to select that sentence; and you quadruple-click within the desired paragraph to select that paragraph. Alternatively, you can move the mouse pointer to the left margin, where it becomes ↗, then click once to select a sentence or twice to select a paragraph.

---

**REFERENCE WINDOW**

### Selecting Whole Units of Text

- Double-click a word to select it.

- Triple-click any word within a sentence to select the sentence.

    *or*

    Click ↗ in the margin to the left of a sentence to select that sentence.

- Quadruple-click any word within a paragraph to select the paragraph.

    *or*

    Double-click ↗ in the margin to the left of a paragraph to select that paragraph.

---

## Deleting a Whole Sentence

Melissa wants to delete the unnecessary sentence at the end of the first section of her memo, as Susan suggests. (Refer to Figure 3-10.)

To delete a whole sentence:

❶ Triple-click I anywhere in the sentence or click the mouse pointer in the left margin. See Figure 3-19.

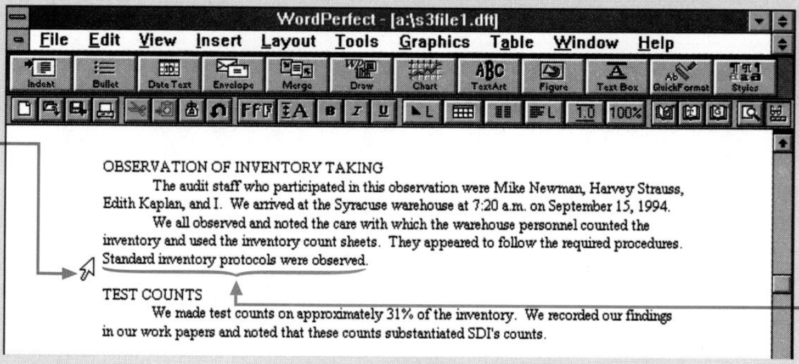

position mouse
pointer here

**Figure 3-19**
Mouse pointer in left
margin for selecting
sentences and
paragraphs

sentence to be selected

WordPerfect highlights the entire sentence. See Figure 3-20.

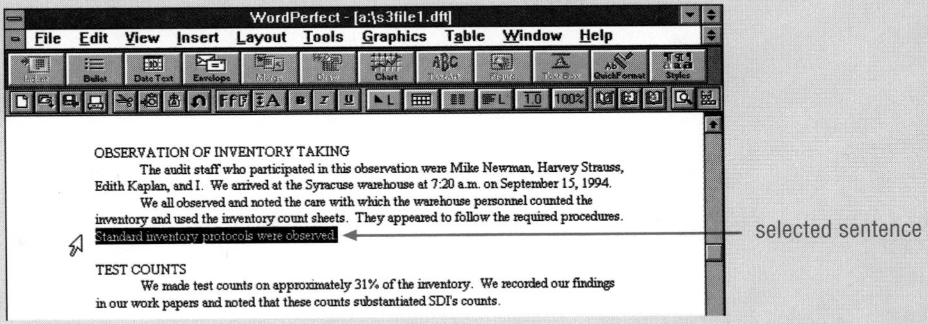

**Figure 3-20**
Document window
with selected
sentence

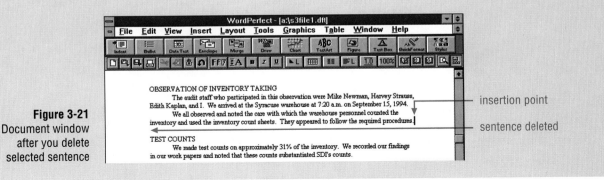

❷ Press **[Del]** or **[Backspace]** to delete the sentence.

Note that this *deletes* the text, which is different from *cutting* it. Cutting allows you to paste the text back into the document. Deleting doesn't save the text to the clipboard, so you can't paste it back into the document. (You can, however, restore the deleted block of text using Undelete.)

❸ Press **[Backspace]** twice to delete the extra spaces. Your screen should now look like Figure 3-21.

**Figure 3-21**
Document window
after you delete
selected sentence

## Copying a Whole Paragraph

You can also use the methods we've discussed in this tutorial to copy a sentence, a paragraph, or a page.

REFERENCE WINDOW

## Copying Text

- Select (highlight) the text you want to copy.
- Copy the text to the clipboard by clicking the Copy button on the Power Bar or by pressing [Ctrl][C] (Copy).
- Move the insertion point to the location in the document where you want the copy to appear.
- Paste the text back into the document by clicking the Paste button on the Power Bar or by pressing [Ctrl][V] (Paste).

Although Melissa has no reason to copy text in her memo, let's copy the second paragraph under the heading "Observation of Inventory Taking" to the end of the memo, for illustration purposes only, and then use Select to delete it.

To copy a paragraph using the Select command:

❶ Double-click 📐 in the margin to the left of the second paragraph under "OBSERVATION OF INVENTORY TAKING." The entire paragraph is highlighted. See Figure 3-22.

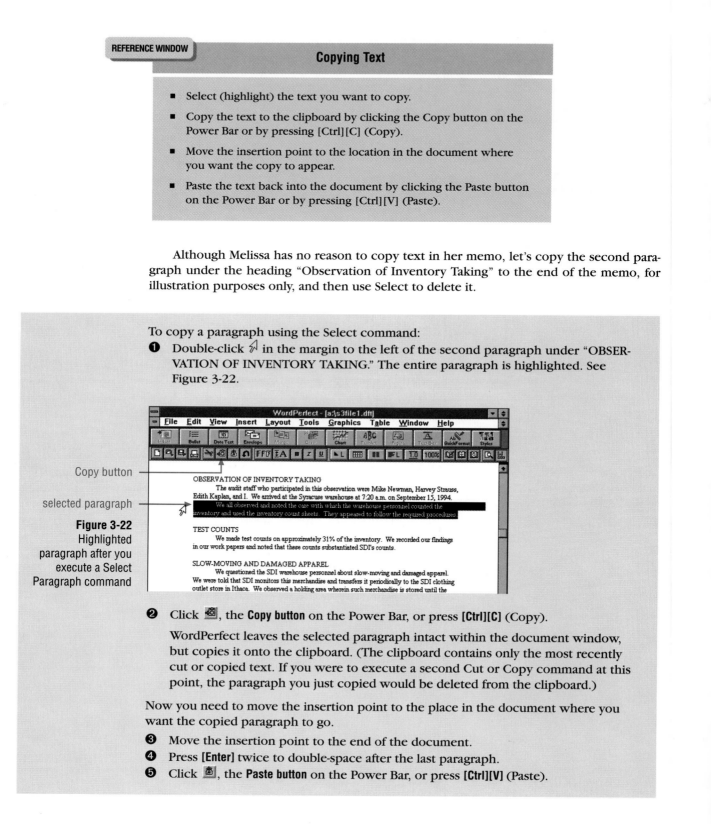

Copy button ⟶

selected paragraph ⟶

**Figure 3-22**
Highlighted paragraph after you execute a Select Paragraph command

❷ Click 📋, the **Copy button** on the Power Bar, or press **[Ctrl][C]** (Copy).

WordPerfect leaves the selected paragraph intact within the document window, but copies it onto the clipboard. (The clipboard contains only the most recently cut or copied text. If you were to execute a second Cut or Copy command at this point, the paragraph you just copied would be deleted from the clipboard.)

Now you need to move the insertion point to the place in the document where you want the copied paragraph to go.

❸ Move the insertion point to the end of the document.

❹ Press **[Enter]** twice to double-space after the last paragraph.

❺ Click 📋, the **Paste button** on the Power Bar, or press **[Ctrl][V]** (Paste).

A copy of the selected paragraph appears at this new location in the document. See Figure 3-23.

copied paragraph

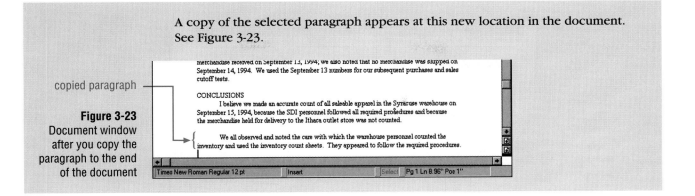

**Figure 3-23**
Document window
after you copy the
paragraph to the end
of the document

## Deleting a Whole Paragraph

Just as you can delete a sentence using Select, you can also delete a paragraph you just copied. To demonstrate this feature, let's delete the paragraph we just copied.

To delete a paragraph using Select:
❶ Double-click ⁄ in the margin to the left of the paragraph you just copied. WordPerfect highlights the entire paragraph.
❷ Press **[Del]** or **[Backspace]** to delete the paragraph.
❸ Press **[Backspace]** twice to delete the two blank lines after the last paragraph.

# Using Drag and Drop to Move Text

In addition to cut and paste, you can use the drag and drop method to move text. Let's use drag and drop to move the word "periodically" as Susan suggested in Figure 3-10.

To move text using drag and drop:
❶ Move the mouse pointer to the word "periodically," located in the paragraph under "SLOW-MOVING AND DAMAGED APPAREL."
❷ Select "periodically" and the space after it by double-clicking the word.
❸ Move the mouse pointer anywhere within the selected block, press and hold down the left mouse button, and (while still holding down the button) move the insertion point to the left of the letter "t" in "transfers," and release the mouse button.

As you move the mouse pointer, it displays a little box (called a move box) representing the text it's dragging. See Figure 3-24. Make sure, as you move the mouse pointer to the location where you want to drop the text, that you focus on the location of the *insertion point* rather than on the location of the mouse pointer or the move box. The insertion point marks the precise location of the drop.

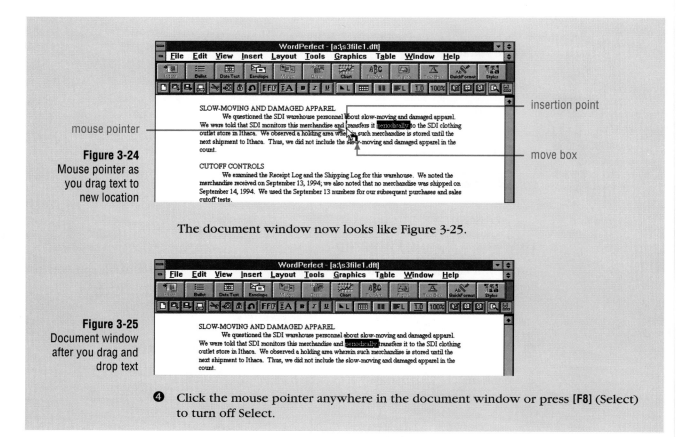

**Figure 3-24**
Mouse pointer as
you drag text to
new location

The document window now looks like Figure 3-25.

**Figure 3-25**
Document window
after you drag and
drop text

❹    Click the mouse pointer anywhere in the document window or press **[F8]** (Select)
to turn off Select.

With a little practice, you will see that using the drag and drop method to move
words, sentences, paragraphs, or any unit of text smaller than the screen itself is the most
efficient method.

You can also use drag and drop to copy text. Before dragging the highlighted text,
you press [Ctrl] and hold it down during the drag and drop. The selected text stays in its
original location, and the copy is inserted into the new location.

The final version of your document should now look similar to Figure 3-26.

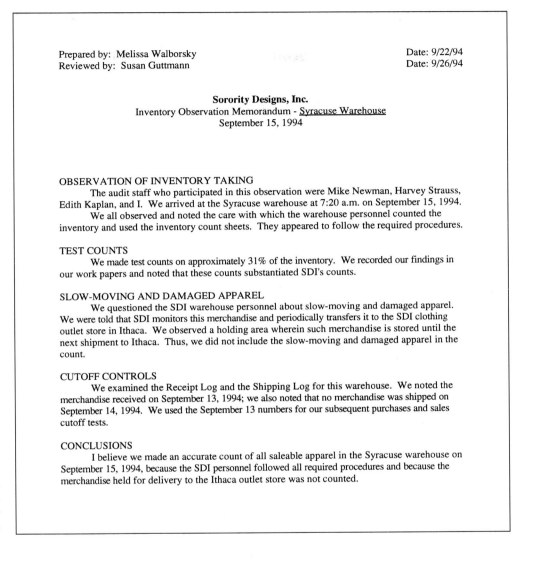

Prepared by: Melissa Walborsky                    Date: 9/22/94
Reviewed by: Susan Guttmann                       Date: 9/26/94

**Sorority Designs, Inc.**
Inventory Observation Memorandum - <u>Syracuse Warehouse</u>
September 15, 1994

OBSERVATION OF INVENTORY TAKING
    The audit staff who participated in this observation were Mike Newman, Harvey Strauss, Edith Kaplan, and I.  We arrived at the Syracuse warehouse at 7:20 a.m. on September 15, 1994.
    We all observed and noted the care with which the warehouse personnel counted the inventory and used the inventory count sheets.  They appeared to follow the required procedures.

TEST COUNTS
    We made test counts on approximately 31% of the inventory.  We recorded our findings in our work papers and noted that these counts substantiated SDI's counts.

SLOW-MOVING AND DAMAGED APPAREL
    We questioned the SDI warehouse personnel about slow-moving and damaged apparel. We were told that SDI monitors this merchandise and periodically transfers it to the SDI clothing outlet store in Ithaca.  We observed a holding area wherein such merchandise is stored until the next shipment to Ithaca.  Thus, we did not include the slow-moving and damaged apparel in the count.

CUTOFF CONTROLS
    We examined the Receipt Log and the Shipping Log for this warehouse.  We noted the merchandise received on September 13, 1994; we also noted that no merchandise was shipped on September 14, 1994.  We used the September 13 numbers for our subsequent purchases and sales cutoff tests.

CONCLUSIONS
    I believe we made an accurate count of all saleable apparel in the Syracuse warehouse on September 15, 1994, because the SDI personnel followed all required procedures and because the merchandise held for delivery to the Ithaca outlet store was not counted.

**Figure 3-26**
Final version of the
inventory
observation memo

# Saving and Printing the Memo

Melissa has completed all the corrections that Susan suggested and can now save and print the finished memo. Before she prints it, Melissa should run the speller and possibly Grammatik to check the final version for errors. She might also want to use the Page Zoom Full command to see how the memo fits on the page. We'll assume that she's already done these things and is ready to print the memo.

To save and print the memo:
❶  Make sure your Student Disk is still in drive A.
❷  Click **File**, then click **Save As**.

TROUBLE?    If a Save dialog box appears telling you that S3FILE1.DFT has text selected, you forgot to turn off Select before you clicked File and Save As. Click the button next to Entire File, then click the OK button.

❸ Save the document to your Student Disk as S3FILE2.MEM.

In this example, the .MEM filename extension signifies that this is the final version of the memo. WordPerfect saves the final version of the memo to the disk.

❹ Make sure your printer is on and ready to print, then print the document.

Melissa gives the completed memo to Susan for copying, filing, and distributing.

# Questions

1. List the button or pull-down menu commands that would perform the following operations:
   a. Center a line of text between the left and right margins
   b. Move a phrase flush against the right margin
   c. Find the first occurrence of the word "payment" in a document
   d. Replace all occurrences in a document of the word "Log" (as in "Shipping Log") with the word "Record."

2. How do you select a block of text
   a. using the mouse?
   b. using the keyboard?

3. What happens when you execute the following commands with a block of text selected?
   a. Click Edit, then click Cut.
   b. Click Edit, click Convert Case, then click Lowercase.
   c. Click ▨ on the Power Bar.
   d. Press [Del] or [Backspace].
   e. Click ▨ on the Power Bar.

**E**

4. What happens when you execute the following commands with a block of text selected? *Hint:* Look at Figure 3-11.
   a. Click File, then click Print.
   b. Click Layout, click Justification, then click Center.
   c. Click the Speller button on the Power Bar.
   d. Click the Font button on the Power Bar, then click a new font.
   e. Click File, then click Save As.
   f. Click ▨ on the Power Bar.

5. List five common commands you can execute with a block of text highlighted (Select on).

6. Describe how you would create boldface text as you type it, then describe how you would change existing text to boldface.

7. Describe the "drag and drop" operation.

8. How would you copy a sentence in your document
   a. using only the mouse?
   b. using only the keyboard?

9. What is the unit of text you can select by
   a. clicking the mouse pointer in the left margin?
   b. double-clicking the mouse pointer in the left margin?
10. What is the unit of text you select when you do the following on a word within the document window?
    a. double-click
    b. triple-click
    c. quadruple-click

# Tutorial Assignments

For the following Tutorial Assignments, make sure the document window is blank before you open a document.

Open the file T3FILE1.DFT and do the following:

1. Without retyping the title (the first line of the document), change it to all upper-case letters.
2. Center the first three lines of text.
3. Italicize the title using a Select command from the Edit menu.
4. Perform a find and replace operation to change all occurrences of "SDI" to "Sorority Designs, Inc."
5. Save the document as S3FILE3.DOC.
6. Print the document.

Open the file T3FILE2.DFT and do the following:

7. Use Flush Right to right-justify the date in the top line of the memo.
8. Center the title lines (the two lines under Melissa Walborsky's name).
9. Make the title, "Solving the Problem of Employee Turnover," uppercase and underlined.
10. Move numbered paragraph 2 above numbered paragraph 1, then renumber the paragraphs.
**E** 11. Without retyping them, italicize the first sentence in each of the three numbered paragraphs.
**E** 12. Without retyping it, italicize the phrase "ad hoc" in the last paragraph.
13. Copy the second (unnumbered) paragraph, which begins with "The major cause of turnover . . . ," to the end of the document.
14. Delete the last sentence of the (new) last paragraph.
15. Edit the beginning and end of the last sentence of the document from "The major cause of turnover . . . at Ithaca College" to "If the major cause of turnover . . . at Ithaca College, should we hire fewer students?"
16. Save the document as S3FILE4.MEM.
17. Print the document.

Open the file T3FILE3.DFT and do the following:

18. Use find and replace to change the occurrences of "ICOS" to "Ithaca Clothing Outlet Store" in the body of the letter, but not in the "Re:" statement.
**E** 19. Use the Replace command to replace all occurrences of the invisible Hd Left Ind format code (which indents every line of the paragraphs) with the Left Tab code (which indents only the first line of the paragraphs). *Hint:* In the Find and Replace Text dialog box, click Match, then click Codes to display the Codes dialog box. Then choose Hd Left Ind *(not* ...Hd Left Ind, which is preceded by three dots) from the Find Codes list and insert it as the Find string, and choose Left Tab *(not* ...Left Tab, which is preceded by three dots) as the Replace With string. You might want to turn on Reveal Codes here, but you can execute the command with Reveal Codes off.
20. Move numbered paragraph 3 above numbered paragraph 1, and then renumber the paragraphs.

21. Without retyping it, italicize the phrase "esprit de corps" in numbered paragraph 4.
22. Use a block command to delete the second sentence of the last (unnumbered) paragraph, which begins "Your suggestion will . . . ."
23. Save the document as S3FILE5.LET.
24. Print the document.

# Case Problems

## 1. Supplies Expenditures Memo

Flora Martínez, the office manager for the public accounting firm of Black, Doman & Zapata (BDZ), sends a report each month to the senior partners summarizing expenditures for office supplies. The report on expenditures, which provides comparisons with previous periods and with industry averages, includes a spreadsheet file printout summarizing expenditure data. The main purpose of this month's report is to summarize and explain a higher-than-normal expenditure rate for office supplies.

Do the following:

1. Open the file P3EXPEND.DFT.
2. In the first line, make the date (including the word "Date") flush right.
3. Center the two title lines of the memo.

**E** 4. Selecting the desired text only once, convert the first title line "Increase in Expenditures for Office Supplies" to all uppercase letters and then boldface type. After making both changes, turn Select off.

**E** 5. Change the three headings (which start "EXPENDITURES DURING," "REASONS FOR," and "ITEMS TO") to mixed uppercase and lowercase letters, according to the standard rules of capitalization for headings and titles. *Hint:* Use the Initial Capitals option of the Convert Case command.

6. Move the numbered paragraph 3 above numbered paragraph 2. Revise the paragraph numbers so they are consecutive.
7. Move the last sentence of the last paragraph to become the second sentence in that same paragraph.
8. Use a block operation to delete the second sentence, which begins "With the increased cost of wood," in the newly numbered paragraph 3.
9. Where such changes wouldn't cause an error in the meaning of the text, carry out a find and replace operation to change most occurrences of "the company" to "BDZ."

**E** 10. Carry out a find and replace to selectively change the tabs (Left Tab codes) that occur after the numbers in the numbered paragraphs to indents (Hd Left Ind codes). Don't change the other tabs. *Hint:* In the Find and Replace Text dialog box, click Match, then click Codes to display the Codes dialog box. Then choose Left Tab *(not* ...Left Tab, which is preceded by three dots) from the Find Codes list and insert it in the Find string, and choose Hd Left Ind *(not* ...Hd Left Ind, which is preceded by three dots) as the Replace With string. You may want to turn on Reveal Codes here, but you can execute the command with Reveal Codes off.

11. Save the memo as S3EXPEND.MEM.
12. Print the memo.

## 2. Review of a Fast-Growing, Small, Public Company

Grant Seymour is a freelance writer for *Investor's Review,* a financial magazine that reviews stocks and other investments. His editor has asked him to write an article on Innovo Group, a fast-growing business that manufactures and markets aprons. Figure 3-27 shows the first paragraphs of Grant's rough draft of the article.

Grant Seymour
811 West Heather Road
White Plains, NY 10602
(914) 384-4400

Word Count (approx): 1200
First World Serial Rights
November 10, 1994

**LETTING GO OF THE APRON STRINGS**
**The Innovo Group Success Story**

by Grant Seymour

Don't be fooled by its name or its product. Innovo Group--which sounds like a company that ought to make cellular phones or computer software--actually manufactures and markets aprons.

You heard me right: <u>aprons</u>. You know, those cloth things that you wear when you cook a meal in the kitchen or serve hamburgers in the back yard.  Sounds like an unlikely product for a new, thriving company.

But the Innovo Group has elevated aprons to new heights. They don't just make aprons--they make **APRONS**! Colorful, artistic, bizarre, humorous, personal, philosophical, and political aprons.

Want to make a political statement, create a mood, or just look wild? Innovo has an apron to fill the bill.

Want to make a wild investment? Innovo can probably help you out there, too.

**Figure 3-27**

Do the following:

1. Open a new document and type the header lines, as shown in Figure 3-27, at the beginning of the document. This header is a standard format used by freelance writers.
   a. On the left, type the author's name, address, and phone number.
   b. Flush right on the first line, type the word count for the article.
   c. Flush right on the second line, type the rights the author is offering: "First World Serial Rights."
   d. Flush right on the third line, insert today's date (not the date in Figure 3-27).
2. Type the two lines of the title in boldface type and center it between the left and right margins.
3. Make the first line of the title all uppercase.
4. Type the author's byline centered between the left and right margins.
5. Type the remainder of the article, as shown in Figure 3-27.
6. Save the article as S3INNOVO.DOC.
7. Print the document.

### 3. Collins Consulting, Inc.

Allison Sanders is director of Collins Consulting, Inc., a small financial consulting business. The company presents seminars on developing and managing small startup businesses. Allison is planning the program for a seminar to be held August 27, 1994, in Atlanta, Georgia. A copy of her tentative schedule is shown in Figure 3-28.

**MANAGING YOUR STARTUP BUSINESS**
Collins Consulting, Inc.
Peachtree Center Auditorium, Atlanta, Georgia
August 27, 1994

Welcome . . . . . . . . . . . . . . . . . . . . . . . . . . . . . . . . . . . . . . Allison Sanders
Director, Collins Consulting, Inc.

Comments . . . . . . . . . . . . . . . . . . . . . . . . . . . . . . . . . . . . . Paul Johnson
Atlanta Area Chamber of Commerce

Speaker . . . . . . . . . . . . . . . . . . . . . . . . . . . . . . . . . . Gabriella Trujillo
Professor of Marketing, Emory University
"The Entrepreneurial Climate in the Southeast"

Video . . . . . . . . . . . . . . . . . . . . . . . . . . . . . . Introduced by Allison Sanders
"Managing Your Startup Business"

Video . . . . . . . . . . . . . . . . . . . . . . . . . . . . . Introduced by Allison Sanders
"Profits vs. Cash Flow in Small Businesses"

**Figure 3-28**

Do the following:

1. Open a new document window and type the four title lines of the program.
2. Center all four title lines. Make the first title line boldface.
3. Type the first four items in the program. Make the text on the right side flush right with dot leaders. *Hint:* Press [Alt][F7] *twice* to move the text flush right with dot leaders. Center the titles of the speeches and the videos.
4. To create the fifth item in the program (the second video), use a copy and paste operation to copy the fourth item (the first video), and then edit the video title rather than retyping the entire text.
5. Save the document as S3FINANC.DOC.
6. Print the document.

# Formatting Multiple-Page Documents

## Writing a Sales Report

**CASE** **Camino Office Equipment Corporation** Steven Tanaka is a sales representative for the Camino Office Equipment Corporation (COEC), which sells photocopy machines, fax machines, dictaphones, telephone-answering equipment, and other high-technology office equipment. Steven's sales territory is Arizona and New Mexico. He is the only COEC representative covering that area.

At the end of every year, Steven writes a report that summarizes his sales results, compares these results with his previous years' sales, and presents strategies for future sales. Steven is currently working on his 1994 annual sales report.

## Planning the Document

Steven wrote his first annual sales report in 1989. At that time, he was trained by company personnel on how to write reports, and he studied several reports by successful COEC sales representatives. He now prepares for his annual report throughout the year by filing notes and data on his sales activities and results. At the end of the year, he organizes and analyzes this information and follows company guidelines for the content, organization, style, and format of his report.

### Content

The main contents of Steven's annual report, besides his own notes and observations, are his quarterly sales figures for the current year and the previous two years. He obtains prior-year sales figures from his previous annual reports and current-year sales figures from COEC's main office.

Just as important as the sales data are his interpretations of it. Steven knows that a good sales report includes analysis and recommendations.

### Organization

Steven organizes his report according to company policy, with a title page, an introduction, a presentation and interpretation of the gross sales for the current and the previous two years, an analysis and summary of the year's sales effort, and recommendations for improved sales in the future.

### Style

The report follows established standards of business-writing style, emphasizing clarity, simplicity, and directness.

### Format

In accordance with COEC policy, Steven's report will include a title page, with each line of text centered between the left and right margins and the entire text centered between the top and bottom margins. The text in the body of the report will be double-spaced. Every page except the title page will include a header and a page number. Tabs at the beginning of each paragraph will be 0.3 inch. The sales data will be presented in a table.

## Changing the Line Spacing

Steven has already written and edited the body of his report, but he has yet to type the title page and format the report as COEC requires. Let's open Steven's document.

To open the document:

1. Open the document c4file1.dft from your Student Disk into a new document window.
2. To avoid the potential problem of overwriting the original file, click **File**, click **Save As**, then save the document as s4file1.dft.

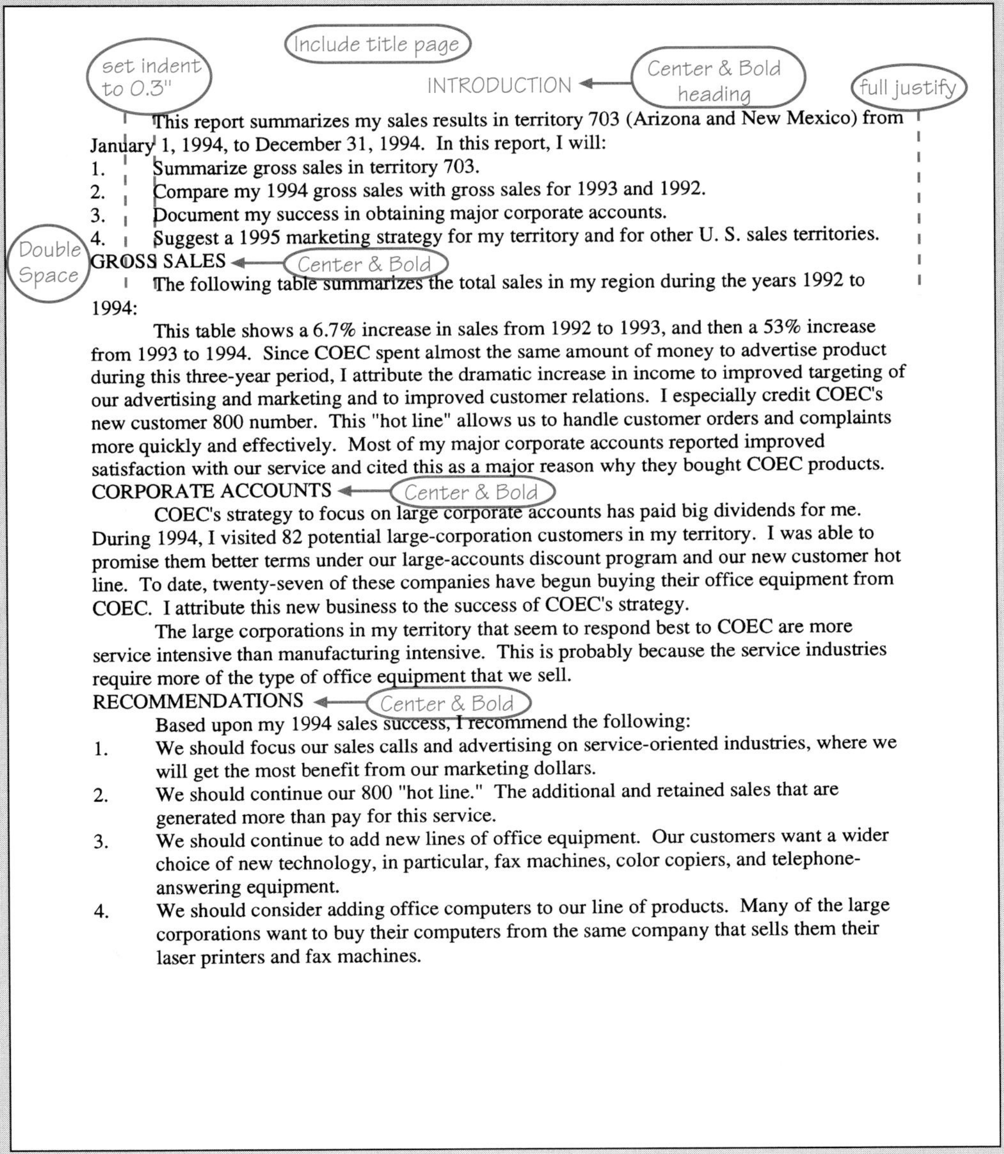


INTRODUCTION

This report summarizes my sales results in territory 703 (Arizona and New Mexico) from January 1, 1994, to December 31, 1994. In this report, I will:

1. Summarize gross sales in territory 703.
2. Compare my 1994 gross sales with gross sales for 1993 and 1992.
3. Document my success in obtaining major corporate accounts.
4. Suggest a 1995 marketing strategy for my territory and for other U. S. sales territories.

GROSS SALES

The following table summarizes the total sales in my region during the years 1992 to 1994:

This table shows a 6.7% increase in sales from 1992 to 1993, and then a 53% increase from 1993 to 1994. Since COEC spent almost the same amount of money to advertise product during this three-year period, I attribute the dramatic increase in income to improved targeting of our advertising and marketing and to improved customer relations. I especially credit COEC's new customer 800 number. This "hot line" allows us to handle customer orders and complaints more quickly and effectively. Most of my major corporate accounts reported improved satisfaction with our service and cited this as a major reason why they bought COEC products.

CORPORATE ACCOUNTS

COEC's strategy to focus on large corporate accounts has paid big dividends for me. During 1994, I visited 82 potential large-corporation customers in my territory. I was able to promise them better terms under our large-accounts discount program and our new customer hot line. To date, twenty-seven of these companies have begun buying their office equipment from COEC. I attribute this new business to the success of COEC's strategy.

The large corporations in my territory that seem to respond best to COEC are more service intensive than manufacturing intensive. This is probably because the service industries require more of the type of office equipment that we sell.

RECOMMENDATIONS

Based upon my 1994 sales success, I recommend the following:

1. We should focus our sales calls and advertising on service-oriented industries, where we will get the most benefit from our marketing dollars.
2. We should continue our 800 "hot line." The additional and retained sales that are generated more than pay for this service.
3. We should continue to add new lines of office equipment. Our customers want a wider choice of new technology, in particular, fax machines, color copiers, and telephone-answering equipment.
4. We should consider adding office computers to our line of products. Many of the large corporations want to buy their computers from the same company that sells them their laser printers and fax machines.

**Figure 4-1** Rough draft of Steven's report with his editing marks

Steven marks a copy of this report with the changes he needs to make (Figure 4-1). As he looks over his copy, Steven decides that first he should double-space the text. Let's change the line spacing in Steven's report.

To change the line spacing in a document:

❶ Make sure the insertion point is at the beginning of the document.

Remember that WordPerfect's formatting features take effect from the position of the insertion point to the end of the document. If you want to set new line spacing for the entire document, you must move the insertion point to the beginning of the document before you make the change.

❷ Click [1.0], the **Line Spacing button** on the Power Bar, and drag the mouse pointer down to **2.0**, then release the mouse button.

The text of the report is double-spaced. See Figure 4-2.

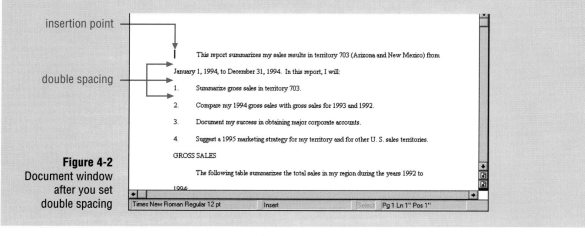

insertion point

double spacing

**Figure 4-2**
Document window
after you set
double spacing

You can set the line spacing to any value you want. The most common line spacings, however, are 1.0 for single spacing, 1.5 for one and one-half spacing, 2.0 for double spacing, and 3.0 for triple spacing.

## Centering a Page Top to Bottom

Steven next decides to create the title page. To do this, he must insert a hard page break at the beginning of the document, instruct WordPerfect to center the lines between the left and right margins, and then type the title page.

To create the title page:

❶ Make sure the insertion point is at the beginning of the document.

❷ Click **Insert,** then click **Page Break** to force a hard page break.

The page-break mark appears as lines across the document window, and the status bar indicates that the insertion point is now on page 2. See Figure 4-3. You can see the bottom margin of page 1 and the top margin of page 2. Having now created a separate page (page 1), you'll type the title of the report.

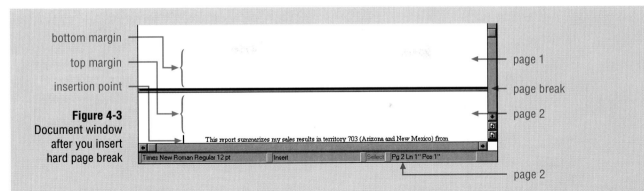

bottom margin
top margin
insertion point

**Figure 4-3**
Document window
after you insert
hard page break

page 1
page break
page 2

This report summarizes my sales results in territory 703 (Arizona and New Mexico) from

Times New Roman Regular 12 pt     Insert     Select     Pg 2 Ln 1" Pos 1"

page 2

❸ Click ▣, the **Justification button** on the Power Bar, and choose **Full** to set the body of the document—that is, everything except the title page—to full justification.

Setting full justification here accomplishes two things. First, it sets the body of the report to full justification, which Steven wants. Second, it avoids the problem of having WordPerfect center-justify the entire report when you move to the beginning of the document and center-justify the title page.

❹ Move the insertion point to the first page.

❺ Click ▣, and choose **Center** to set the first page of the document to center justification. This will cause all the text on the title page to be center-justified. The insertion point is now centered between the left and right margins of the document window.

❻ Type the text of the title page, as shown in Figure 4-4. After you type the title ("1994 ANNUAL SALES REPORT") in boldface characters, turn off Bold and press **[Enter]** four times to insert four double-spaced blank lines. Then type the next block of text (name, title, territory) and press **[Enter]** four times to insert four more double-spaced blank lines. Finally, insert today's date by clicking ▣, the **Date Text button.** Your screen should look similar to Figure 4-4.

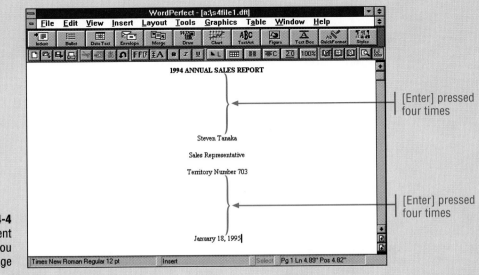

[Enter] pressed
four times

[Enter] pressed
four times

**Figure 4-4**
Document
window after you
type title page

❼ Click ▣, the **Page Zoom Full button**, to see a full-page view of the title page.

COEC requires that the text of the title page be centered between the top and bottom margins. As you can see from the full-page view, however, the text of the title page is too high up on the page. You could insert hard returns at the beginning of the page until the text is centered, but WordPerfect provides an easier, more accurate method to center text on a page—a feature called Center Page. Once Steven sets this feature at the beginning of a page, the text will stay centered between the top and bottom margins, regardless of how much or how little text there is. You can specify that this format command affect only the current page or the current and all subsequent pages.

REFERENCE WINDOW

### Centering a Page Top to Bottom

- Move the insertion point to the beginning of the page that you want to center top to bottom.
- Click Layout, click Page, then click Center to display the Center Page(s) dialog box.
- Click the Current Page button if you want to center only the current page, then click the OK button.

Let's center the title page, which is the current page.

To center the current page top to bottom:
1. With the document window still in full-page view, move the insertion point to the beginning of the document, before any text.
2. Click **Layout,** click **Page,** then click **Center** to display the Center Page(s) dialog box.
3. Click the button next to Current Page because you want to center only the title page, not the subsequent pages in the document, then click the **OK button.**

The document window now shows the text of the title page centered between the top and bottom margins. See Figure 4-5.

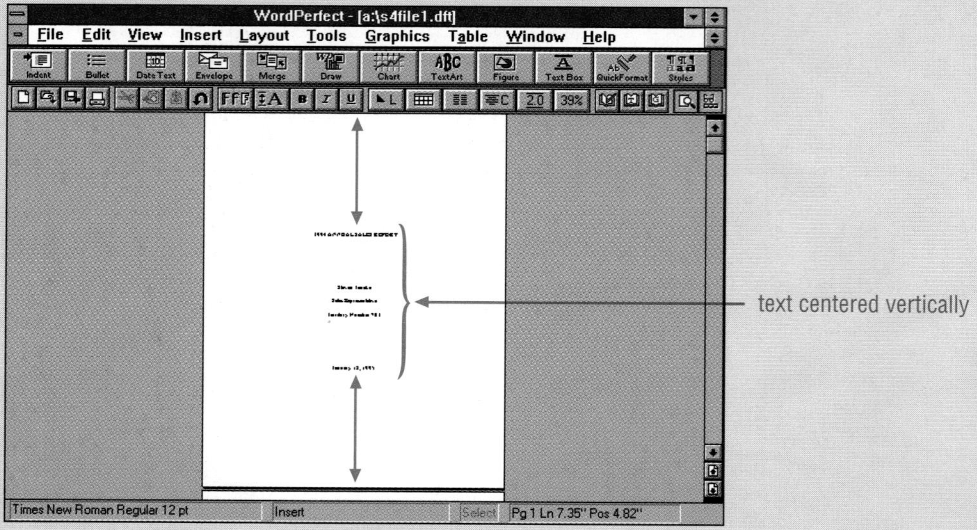

**Figure 4-5**
Full-page view
after you center page
top to bottom

text centered vertically

❹ Click [image], the **Page Zoom Full button**, to return the document window to normal (100%) page view.

## Changing the Tab Stops

Steven looks over his edited report (Figure 4-1) and decides to change the amount of indented space at the beginning of each paragraph from 0.5 inch to 0.3 inch, according to COEC requirements.

When Steven wrote the draft of his report, he pressed [Tab] at the beginning of each paragraph. This created a 0.5-inch space at the beginning of each paragraph, because the first tab stop was at 0.5 inch. A **tab stop** is a location (usually specified in inches) along each text line to which the insertion point moves when you press [Tab] or click the Indent button on the Button Bar. You can see the tab stops in your document by displaying the Ruler Bar.

To display the Ruler Bar:
❶ Click **View**, then click **Ruler Bar.** WordPerfect displays the Ruler Bar, as shown in Figure 4-6. The wedge-shaped markers indicate the locations of the tab stops.

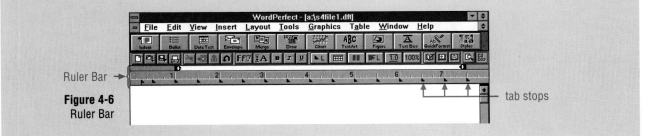

**Figure 4-6**
Ruler Bar

In WordPerfect, the default setting for tab stops is every 0.5 inch from the left margin. With a 1-inch left margin and the insertion point located at the left margin (Pos 1", as indicated on the status bar), pressing [Tab] moves the insertion point and all text to the right of the insertion point to the tab stop at Pos 1.5".

To create the numbered paragraphs in his report, Steven typed a number and a period, which positioned the insertion point at about Pos 1.13", and then he pressed [F7] (Indent). This caused the text of each numbered paragraph to be indented to the next tab stop at Pos 1.5", which is 0.5" from the left margin (Figure 4-7). The insertion point returns to the left margin (Pos 1") after you press [Enter] at the end of the paragraph.

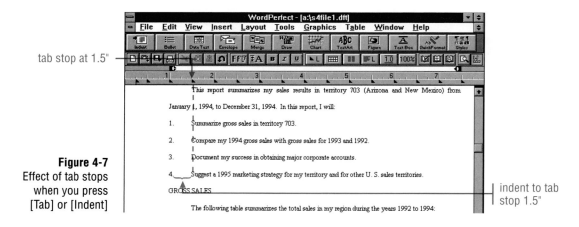

**Figure 4-7**
Effect of tab stops
when you press
[Tab] or [Indent]

Because the COEC format calls for the first line of each paragraph to be indented 0.3 inch, Steven will change one of the tab stops on the Ruler Bar.

To change a tab stop on the Ruler Bar:

❶ Move the insertion point to the beginning of page 2. (The status bar should say *Pg 2 Ln 1" Pos 1".*)

❷ Drag the tab stop marker located at 1.5 inches to about 1.3 inches. See Figure 4-8. As you drag the tab-stop marker, the location of the mouse pointer and tab stop is displayed on the right side of the status bar.

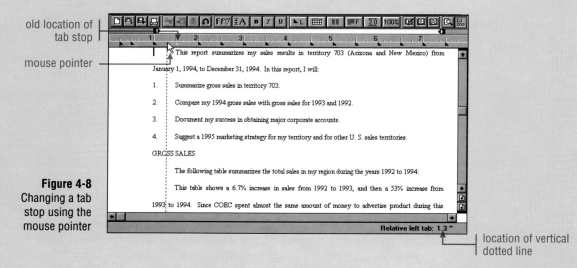

**Figure 4-8**
Changing a tab
stop using the
mouse pointer

**TROUBLE?**    As you drag the mouse pointer, the tab-stop marker might not stop exactly at 1.3 inches. Instead, it might stop at 1.31 or 1.28 inches, depending on your font. That's okay. The location of the tab stop does not have to be exactly 1.3".

Now scroll down through the body of the document. Notice that the first line of each paragraph is indented about 0.3 inch from the left margin (or 1.3 inches from the left edge of the paper), rather than 0.5 inch from the left margin (or 1.5 inches from the left edge of the paper).

❸ Click **View**, then click **Ruler Bar** to turn off the Ruler Bar.

# Numbering Pages

Because the report is now longer than one page, Steven wants to number the pages. He can do this automatically with the Page Numbering command. The COEC standard format requires that reports have page numbers centered at the bottom of each page.

### Numbering Pages

- Move the insertion point to the beginning of the document or to the location where you want page numbering to begin.
- Click Layout, click Page, then click Numbering to display the Page Numbering dialog box.
- Click the box to the right of Position and drag the highlight bar to the desired position for page numbering, then release the mouse button.
- Click the OK button.

Let's number the pages of Steven's report.

To set page numbering:
1. Move the insertion point to the beginning of the document, before any text.
2. Click **Layout**, click **Page**, then click **Numbering**. WordPerfect displays the Page Numbering dialog box.
3. Click the box to the right of Position and drag the highlight bar to **Bottom Center**, then release the mouse button. The dialog box displays the location of the page numbers on the sample pages.

   This Page Numbering command instructs WordPerfect to print a page number at the bottom center of every page, below the last line of text and just above the bottom margin.
4. Click the **OK button.**
5. Scroll down until you can see the page number at the bottom margin of page 1. See Figure 4-9.

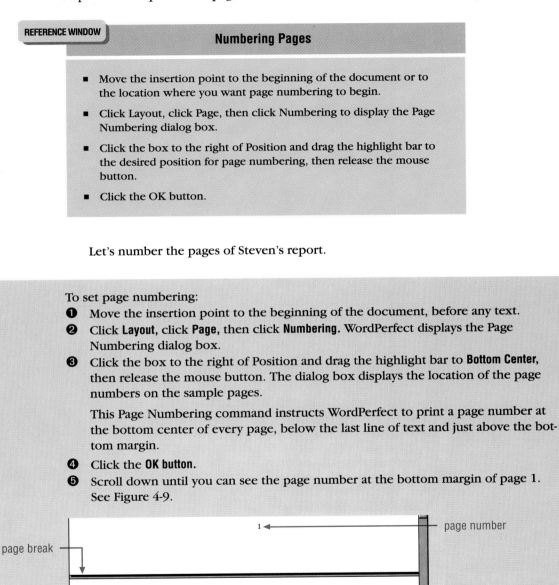

page number

page break

page 2

**Figure 4-9**
Page number at the
bottom of page 1

This report summarizes my sales results in territory 703 (Arizona and New Mexico) from January 1, 1994, to December 31, 1994. In this report, I will:

Times New Roman Regular 12 pt    Insert    Select    Pg 2 Ln 1.39" Pos 1"

## Creating Headers and Footers

Next, Steven wants to instruct WordPerfect to print the title of his report and his name at the top of every page. Text printed at the top of each page as a means of guiding the reader is called a **header.** Most books have headers that contain, for example, the page number and the name of the book or the chapter name or number. Similarly, a **footer** is one or more lines of text, intended to guide the reader, printed at the bottom of each page.

When you create a header, WordPerfect prints it just below the top margin and then inserts a blank line between the header and the first line of text on the page. Similarly, WordPerfect prints a footer just above the bottom margin and inserts a blank line between the footer and the last line of text on the page.

REFERENCE WINDOW

### Creating a Header or Footer

- Move the insertion point to the beginning of the document or to the beginning of the page where you want a header or footer to begin.

- Click Layout, then click Header/Footer. The Headers/Footers dialog box appears.

- Click the button next to the desired Header (A or B) or Footer (A or B) that you want to create.

- Click the Create button. The Header/Footer Bar appears on the screen below the Power Bar

- Type the text of the header or footer, then click the Close button on the Header/Footer Bar.

Let's create a header that includes the name of the report and Steven's full name.

To create a header:

❶ Again move the insertion point to the beginning of the document, before any text.

❷ Click **Layout,** then click **Header/Footer.** The Headers/Footers dialog box appears on the screen. See Figure 4-10.

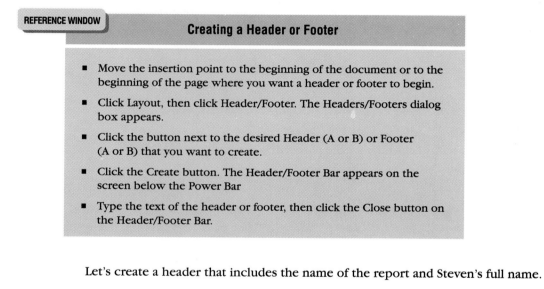

**Figure 4-10**
Header/Footers
dialog box

WordPerfect lets you define up to two different headers at a time, Header A and Header B. In this report you'll use only one header. In other documents you might want two headings—one heading, such as the title, on odd-numbered pages, and another heading, such as the author's name, on even-numbered pages.

❸ Make sure the button to the left of Header A is marked, then click the **Create button.** The Header/Footer Bar appears on the screen below the Power Bar, and the insertion point appears at the top of page 1, just below the top margin. This is where the header will appear in your printed document. See Figure 4-11.

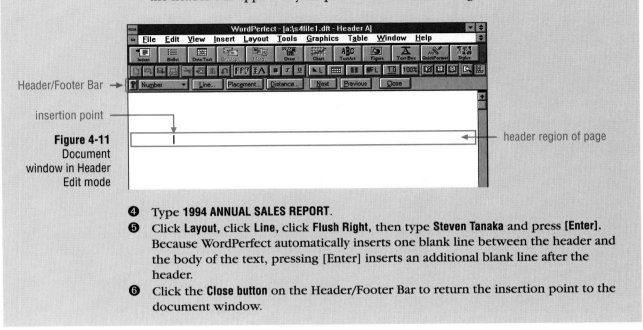

Header/Footer Bar →

insertion point —

**Figure 4-11**
Document
window in Header
Edit mode

header region of page

❹ Type **1994 ANNUAL SALES REPORT.**
❺ Click **Layout,** click **Line,** click **Flush Right,** then type **Steven Tanaka** and press **[Enter].** Because WordPerfect automatically inserts one blank line between the header and the body of the text, pressing [Enter] inserts an additional blank line after the header.
❻ Click the **Close button** on the Header/Footer Bar to return the insertion point to the document window.

If you want page numbers to be part of the header or footer, do not set Page Numbering. Instead, include the page number in the definition of the header or footer by clicking the Number button on the Header/Footer Bar, and then clicking Page Number. Then when you print the document, the page numbers will appear where the code appears in the definition of the header or footer. In his report, Steven put page numbers at the bottom of each page, so they won't interfere with the headers.

## Suppressing Page Numbering, Headers, and Footers

Steven has inserted the codes for page numbering and a header, but he doesn't want these elements to appear on the title page. To eliminate page numbering, headers, and footers on any particular page, you can use the Page Suppress feature.

REFERENCE WINDOW

## Suppressing Page Numbering, Headers, and Footers

- Move the insertion point to the beginning of the page where you want to suppress page numbering, headers, or footers.

- Click Layout, click Page, then click Suppress. WordPerfect displays the Suppress dialog box.

- Click the boxes of the items that you want to suppress on the current page, then click the OK button.

Let's suppress the page numbering and header on the title page of Steven's report.

To suppress the page numbering and the header on a specific page:

❶  Make sure the insertion point is at the beginning of the title page.

❷  Click **Layout,** click **Page,** then click **Suppress.** WordPerfect displays the Suppress dialog box.

❸  Click the **All checkbox** so that all options become checked. With these options checked, no header, footer, page numbers, or watermarks (background graphic images) will be printed on the current page.

❹  Click the **OK button** to return to the document window. The header and page number on the title page disappear from the screen.

Now when Steven prints his annual report, no page number or header will appear on the title page. The Suppress feature only suppresses the page number, header, footer, or watermark for one page—the page on which you execute the Suppress command.

## Setting a New Page Number

Even though a page number won't appear on the title page when Steven prints the report, the title page is still page 1 of the document, and the body of the report begins on page 2. But Steven wants the first page of the body of the report to be page 1. This requires that he change the page numbering for the document, beginning on the page after the title page.

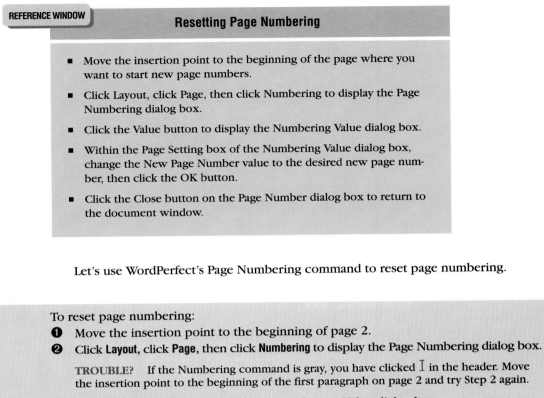

**REFERENCE WINDOW**

**Resetting Page Numbering**

- Move the insertion point to the beginning of the page where you want to start new page numbers.
- Click Layout, click Page, then click Numbering to display the Page Numbering dialog box.
- Click the Value button to display the Numbering Value dialog box.
- Within the Page Setting box of the Numbering Value dialog box, change the New Page Number value to the desired new page number, then click the OK button.
- Click the Close button on the Page Number dialog box to return to the document window.

Let's use WordPerfect's Page Numbering command to reset page numbering.

To reset page numbering:

❶ Move the insertion point to the beginning of page 2.

❷ Click **Layout**, click **Page**, then click **Numbering** to display the Page Numbering dialog box.

**TROUBLE?**   If the Numbering command is gray, you have clicked I in the header. Move the insertion point to the beginning of the first paragraph on page 2 and try Step 2 again.

❸ Click the **Value button** to display the Numbering Value dialog box.

❹ Within the Page Settings box of the Numbering Value dialog box, change the New Page Number value from 2 to 1, then click the **OK button.**

❺ Click the **Close button** on the Page Number dialog box to return to the document window.

Now when Steven prints the document, the body of the report will begin on page 1, with pages numbered consecutively after that.

## Viewing and Saving the Document

Let's see how Steven's document looks now in full-page view.

To view the document in full-page view:

❶ Make sure the insertion point is still on the first page of the body of the report.

❷ Click ▣, the **Page Zoom Full button.** The document appears in full-page view.

Even though the words are too small to read, you can see the position of the header at the top of the page and the page number at the bottom of the page.

Note that if you move the insertion point to the title page, the page number on the status bar is "Pg 1," because the title page is the first page of the document. But if you move the insertion point to the next page, which is the first page of the body of the report, the status bar still says "Pg 1" because you have changed the page number. Therefore, the document has two pages numbered as page 1. Don't worry about this. Just remember that when you print the document, the page numbers will appear only in the body of the report, not on the title page.

❸  Click 🔲, the **Page Down button** at the bottom of the vertical scroll bar. The next page of the document appears on the screen. This is the last page of the document.

❹  Click 🔲, the **Page Up button** near the bottom of the vertical scroll bar. Page 1 of the body of the report again appears on the screen.

❺  Click 🔲 to restore the document window to 100% view.

Having worked on this version of his report for about 15 minutes, Steven decides to save the document with the changes he's made so far.

To save the document:

❶  Click 🔲, the **Save button.** WordPerfect saves the document using the default file-name S4FILE1.DFT.

***If you want to take a break*** and resume the tutorial at a later time, you can exit WordPerfect. When you resume, launch WordPerfect and open S4FILE1.DFT into a document window.

## Using WordPerfect Styles

One of the most powerful features of WordPerfect is the ability to apply styles. A WordPerfect **style** is a set of format codes that you can apply to words, phrases, paragraphs, or even entire documents to change their appearance or format. Once you define the format codes of a particular style, WordPerfect saves the style as part of the document, allowing you to use the style over and over again in that document without having to go through the formatting keystrokes each time. For example, Steven wants to specify the format for section headings within his report. He can create a style (or edit an existing one) that tells WordPerfect to insert an extra blank line just before each heading, to change the font type and appearance, and to center the heading each time.

The advantages of using styles to format titles, headings, and other elements of your document include the following:

- **Efficiency.** Once you specify the format codes within a style, you can apply that style to every like element in the document. When Steven creates the style for the headings in his annual report, he has to change the font and set Center and Bold only once; he can then use that style for all the headings in his document.
- **Flexibility.** If you later decide to change the style, you have to change it only once, and the format of all the affected parts of the document will automatically change. If Steven decided that he wanted all headings to be underlined instead of boldface,

he could go through the entire document and change each heading individually. Using a style, however, he could make the change only once, in the style itself.

- **Consistency.** Without styles you can sometimes forget exactly how you formatted a particular element in your document. With styles, the same format codes apply to every instance of the element. Steven can be confident that his report will follow the required COEC style and that all headings will have the same format.

Once you understand how to create and use styles, you'll want to create styles for document titles, headings, numbered lists, and other features you encounter frequently as you create your own documents.

## Creating a Style

The headings in Steven's report don't follow the required COEC format. He decides to create a style to format all the headings efficiently and consistently.

**REFERENCE WINDOW**

### Creating a WordPerfect Style

- Click the Styles button on the Button Bar.
- Click Create. The Styles Editor dialog box appears on the screen.
- Give the style a name and a description
- Assign the style one of the following Types: Paragraph, Character, or Document.
- In the Contents box, insert the format codes for your style.
- Click the Down Arrow below the phrase "Enter Key will Chain to" and select one of the listed options, or click the checkbox to turn off the "Enter Key will Chain to" feature.
- Click the OK button to exit the Styles Editor dialog box.

Let's create the heading style now.

To create a style:
1. With the insertion point anywhere in the document window, click [Styles], the **Styles button** on the Button Bar. (Creating a style doesn't insert a code into the document, so the insertion point can be anywhere in the document when you define the style.) WordPerfect displays the Style List dialog box. See Figure 4-12. The styles listed are WordPerfect's built-in styles. The built-in styles are designed for headings within a document, but none of these fits the COEC specifications.

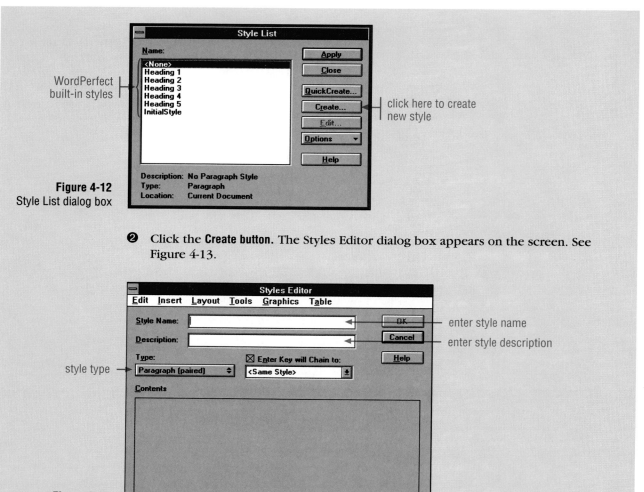

click here to create
new style

**Figure 4-12**
Style List dialog box

❷ Click the **Create button.** The Styles Editor dialog box appears on the screen. See Figure 4-13.

enter style name

enter style description

style type

**Figure 4-13**
Styles Editor
dialog box

Next, you want to name the style you're going to create and give it a description. Let's call the style "Heading."

❸ Type **Heading** into the Style Name text box. Then click I in the Description text box, or press **[Tab]** to move the insertion point there.

❹ Type **Heading of a section of text**.

Notice the option called Type. WordPerfect allows three types of styles: Paragraph, Character, and Document. "Paragraph" means that when you turn the style on, the new formatting features apply to the current paragraph (the one in which the insertion point is located). That is, the style turns on at the beginning of the paragraph and turns off at the end of the paragraph. "Character" means that when you apply the style, WordPerfect automatically inserts the codes to turn the style on and off. Character styles can apply to one character or to any string of characters of any length. "Document" means that when you turn the style on, the new formatting features begin and affect all of the text until the end of the document or until the formatting features are changed.

Steven wants his heading style to be Paragraph, so you don't need to change the default setting. In general, Paragraph is a good style type for headings and titles. This is because in WordPerfect, a paragraph is text of any length—a word, a phrase, a sentence, or several sentences—that end with a hard return. Now you're ready to specify the format codes (contents) for this style.

❺   Click I in the Contents box.

The insertion point is now a blinking rectangle in the Contents box.

Now you're ready to add format codes to the Contents box within the Styles Editor dialog box. You'll begin by entering a hard return, but you can't do it by pressing [Enter], because that would execute the OK button of the dialog box.

To add format codes to the Contents box:

❶   Click **Insert** on the Styles Editor menu bar (not on the WordPerfect document menu bar), then click **Hard Return**. This tells WordPerfect that you want a hard return above the paragraph to which you apply the Heading style.

❷   Click **Layout** on the Styles Editor menu bar, then click **Font** to display the Font dialog box. See Figure 4-14.

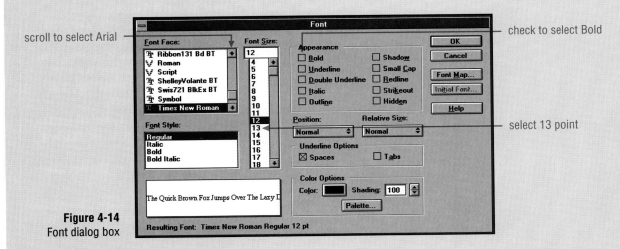

**Figure 4-14**
Font dialog box

❸   Scroll the Font Face list until Arial or some other sans serif font appears in the list, then click **Arial** (or the other font name).

❹   Click **13** in the Font Size list to choose a larger font size for the heading style.

❺   Click the **Bold checkbox** in the Appearance box. You have now selected a 13-point, bold, sans serif font for the heading style. Notice that the newly selected font appears in the sample text box in the lower-left corner of the dialog box.

❻   Click the **OK button** to return to the Contents box of the Styles Editor dialog box.

❼   Click **Layout** on the Styles Editor menu bar, click **Line**, then click **Center** to center the heading.

❽   Click the **Down Arrow** below the phrase "Enter Key will Chain to" and select **<None>**.

The Styles Editor dialog box should now look like Figure 4-15. You have completed the definition of your Heading style.

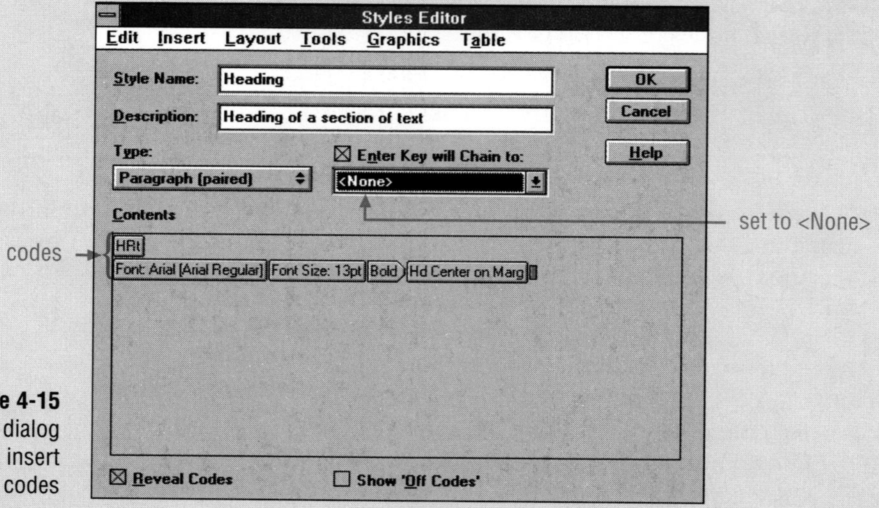

**Figure 4-15**
Styles Editor dialog box after you insert format codes

It is important in this case to make sure that "Enter Key will Chain to" is set to "<None>" for the following reason: When you apply a Paragraph style and then press [Enter] to end the paragraph, the style automatically turns off. If, however, the "Enter Key will Chain to" feature is set to another style, pressing [Enter] will also automatically apply that style to the next paragraph. Because you want to apply this style to headings and not to the paragraphs below the headings, you don't want the style to automatically turn on when you press [Enter].

❾  Click the **OK button** to exit the Styles Editor dialog box and return to the Styles List dialog box. The new style named "Heading" appears with the list of pre-defined headings in the Style List dialog box.

❿  Click the **Close button** to close the Style List dialog box and return to the document window.

**TROUBLE?**   If you accidentally press [Enter] with the focus on the Create button, WordPerfect will return you to the Styles Editor. If this happens, click the Cancel button and then click the Close button to return to the document window.

You have finished creating the style named "Heading," which contains the codes that Steven wants for the headings in his report. In the next section, you'll use this style to format the headings in the report.

### Applying a Style to New Text

Steven is now ready to apply the Heading style to a section heading in his report.

> **REFERENCE WINDOW**
>
> ### Applying a Style
>
> - Move the insertion point to the location where you want to apply the style.
> - Click the Styles button on the Button Bar.
> - Highlight the name of the desired style.
> - Click the Apply button.

Let's apply the Heading style Steven created.

To apply the Heading style:

❶ Move the insertion point to the top of the second page 1 of the report, the first page after the title page, to the left of the tab that indents the first paragraph.

❷ Click ▨, the **Styles button** on the Button Bar, to display the Style List dialog box. The Style List dialog box shows the name of the Heading style you just created (along with the names of the built-in styles).

❸ Highlight "Heading" and then click the **Apply button**. This turns on the style and returns you to the document window. Any text you type will be centered and bold-face until WordPerfect turns off the style when it encounters a hard return. Notice that the first paragraph of the body of the report moves to the right and becomes boldface. This is only temporary; when you type the heading and press [Enter] to turn off the style, the first paragraph will return to regular text.

❹ Type **INTRODUCTION** and press **[Enter]** to end the paragraph and turn off the style.

As you can see, the heading "INTRODUCTION" is centered and in boldface sans serif type. It is also preceded by a blank line as specified in the style, but this is hard to see at the top of the page. You can now use this style to format the other headings in the report.

### Applying a Style to Existing Text

Steven has already typed the other headings of the report: "GROSS SALES," "CORPO-RATE ACCOUNTS," and "RECOMMENDATIONS." He can apply his Heading style to these headings without retyping them, just as you can apply WordPerfect's Bold command to a phrase without retyping it.

To apply a style to existing text:

❶ Move the insertion point anywhere within the next heading, "GROSS SALES." You can scroll the document window to find this heading or use the Find feature, discussed in Tutorial 3.

With a Paragraph style, you don't have to block the text, nor does the insertion point have to be at the beginning of the paragraph.

❷ Click [Styles], the **Styles button** on the Button Bar, to display the Style List dialog box.

❸ Highlight "Heading" and then click the **Apply button.** Your screen now looks like Figure 4-16. This time the blank line is easy to see.

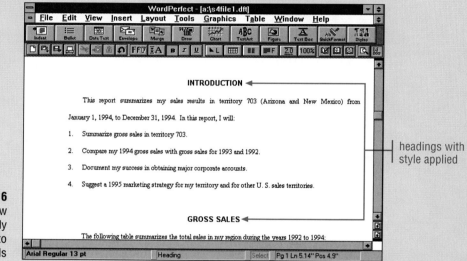

**Figure 4-16**
Document window
after you apply
Heading style to
two heads

❹ Repeat these steps for the other two headings, "CORPORATE ACCOUNTS" and "RECOMMENDATIONS."

All the headings in the report now have the same format.

## Viewing a Document in Draft Mode

Steven has determined that the page numbering and headers look good in his document, and now he wants to focus on other formatting features, such as page breaks, and to read through his draft. He decides to view the document in draft mode to maximize the amount of text within the document window. Draft mode allows you to view only the document—without top and bottom margins, headers and footers, or page numbering. Only the main text on each page of the document appears within the document window. Another advantage of draft mode is that you can distinguish the difference between *soft* page breaks (page breaks WordPerfect automatically inserts into your document when a page is filled with text) and *hard* page breaks (page breaks you force by choosing Page Break from the Insert menu). Let's switch to draft mode now.

To view a document in draft mode:

❶ Click **View**, then click **Draft.**

The document is now in draft mode.

❷ Move the insertion point to the beginning of the document and then scroll down until the first heading ("INTRODUCTION") is in view. See Figure 4-17.

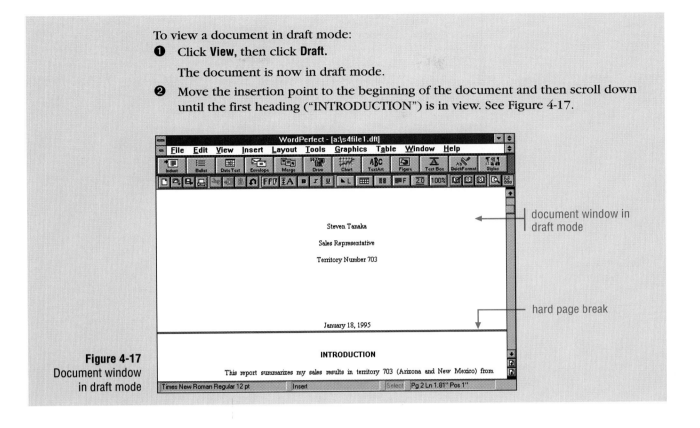

**Figure 4-17**
Document window
in draft mode

As you can see, WordPerfect displays a hard page break with a horizontal double line across the document window. You should leave the document in draft mode as you proceed through the exercises that follow.

## Setting a Conditional End of Page

As Steven continues to scroll down through his report, he notices a serious formatting problem: The heading "CORPORATE ACCOUNTS" is isolated at the bottom of page 1 (Figure 4-18). (Because of differences in type size among printers, your document might not have the heading isolated at the bottom of the page. Do the steps in this section anyway.)

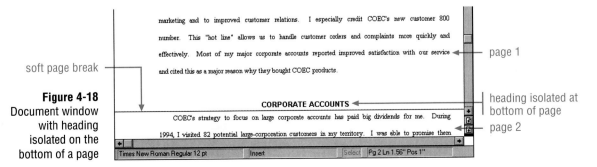

**Figure 4-18**
Document window
with heading
isolated on the
bottom of a page

One solution to the problem would be to insert a hard page break just before the heading. But if Steven later adds or removes text anywhere before the hard page break, the location of the page break would probably be unacceptable. For example, if Steven inserts a hard page break just before the heading and then adds three or four lines on page 1, one or two of the lines would spill over to page 2, the rest of page 2 would be blank, and "CORPORATE ACCOUNTS" would start on page 3, as shown in Figure 4-19.

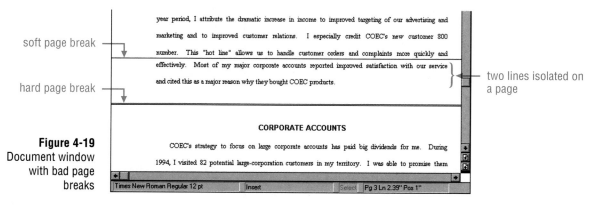

soft page break

hard page break

two lines isolated on a page

**Figure 4-19**
Document window with bad page breaks

A better solution is to use WordPerfect's Conditional End of Page command. The Conditional End of Page command allows you to prevent WordPerfect from inserting a soft page break that would separate a particular unit of text—such as a heading and the two lines that follow it—at an awkward point. For example, if you specify that six lines of text should be kept together, WordPerfect inserts a soft page break above the six lines if they would otherwise be split between two pages (Figure 4-20).

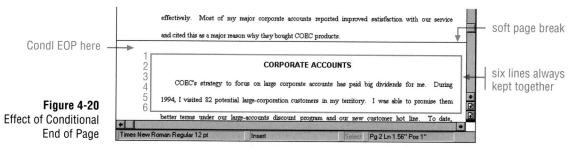

Condl EOP here

soft page break

six lines always kept together

**Figure 4-20**
Effect of Conditional End of Page

REFERENCE WINDOW

## Setting Conditional End of Page

- Move the insertion point to the line above the lines of text you want kept together.
- Click Layout, click Page, then click Keep Text Together. WordPerfect displays the Keep Text Together dialog box.
- Click the checkbox below Conditional End of Page and to the left of Number of lines to keep together.
- Type the number of lines you want kept together.
- Click the OK button to exit the Keep Text Together dialog box.

Steven decides to use the Conditional End of Page code above the "CORPORATE ACCOUNTS" heading. That way, regardless of any changes he makes to the document, the heading will never be isolated at the bottom of a page.

To set Conditional End of Page:

❶ Turn on Reveal Codes and move the insertion point immediately to the left of the Para Style: Heading code at the bottom of page 1, to the left of the heading "CORPORATE ACCOUNTS."

The insertion point in the document appears in the blank line above the heading. Whenever you specify Conditional End of Page, you should move the insertion point to the line above the block of text that you want kept together.

❷ Turn off Reveal Codes.

❸ Click **Layout**, click **Page**, then click **Keep Text Together**. WordPerfect displays the Keep Text Together dialog box.

❹ Click the checkbox below Conditional End of Page.

❺ Type **6** into the text box opposite Number of lines to keep together.

The number of lines that you want to keep together includes the blank lines in double-spaced text. So if you want the heading and the first two lines of text under the heading to be kept together, you should specify six (three lines of double-spaced text) as the number of lines to keep together.

❻ Click the **OK button** to exit the Keep Text Together dialog box.

WordPerfect inserts a soft page break above the heading, so that the heading is now on page 2. As you can see, a soft page break is a single line across the document window.

Steven realizes that every heading in his report should have the Conditional End of Page command applied to it, so that no heading (or a heading and only one line of text) is ever isolated at the bottom of a page. It occurs to Steven that the best way to handle this problem would be to put the Conditional End of Page code in the Heading style. The code would then take effect automatically at every heading. Let's insert the Conditional End of Page code into the Heading style.

To set Conditional End of Page in the style:

❶ Click [icon], the **Styles button**, highlight "Heading," then click the **Edit button**. The Styles Editor dialog box appears on the screen.

❷ Click I on the insertion point block in the Contents box. The colored insertion point begins to blink. Make sure the insertion point is to the left of the HRt code.

❸ Click **Layout** (in the Styles Editor dialog box, not in the document window), click **Page**, then click **Keep Text Together**. WordPerfect displays the Keep Text Together dialog box.

❹ Click the checkbox below Conditional End of Page, type **6** in the text box opposite Number of lines to keep together, then click the **OK button**.

The Condl EOP code appears in the style.

❺ Press the **OK button** to return to the Style List dialog box, then click the **Close button** (*not* the Apply button).

TROUBLE?    If you accidentally click the Apply button instead of the Close button, turn on Reveal Codes and delete the Para Style code that you just inserted into the document window.

With Conditional End of Page in the heading style, you don't need the code you inserted above the "CORPORATE ACCOUNTS" heading, although it won't hurt anything. (If you like, you can turn on Reveal Codes and delete the Condl EOP code above "CORPORATE ACCOUNTS.") Because the code is in the Heading style, the six lines that include each heading and the two lines of text after it will move as one unit in the event of a soft page break.

## Setting Widow/Orphan Protection

Steven realizes that long documents often have another potential formatting problem: widows and orphans. An **orphan** is the first line of a paragraph appearing alone at the bottom of a page. A **widow** is the last line of a paragraph appearing alone at the top of a page. See Figure 4-21. Widows and orphans detract from the appearance and readability of a document. Fortunately, you can solve the problem of widows and orphans by using WordPerfect's Widow/Orphan Protection.

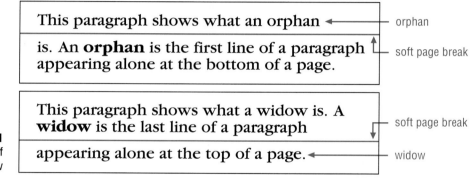

**Figure 4-21**
Illustration of
orphan and widow

---

**REFERENCE WINDOW**

### Setting Widow/Orphan Protection

- Move the insertion point to the beginning of the document.
- Click Layout, click Page, then click Keep Text Together. The Keep Text Together dialog box appears on the screen.
- Click the checkbox below Widow/Orphan, then click the OK button.

---

Let's set Widow/Orphan Protection in Steven's report.

---

To set Widow/Orphan Protection:

❶ Move the insertion point to the beginning of the document.

❷ Click **Layout**, click **Page**, then click **Keep Text Together**. The Keep Text Together dialog box again appears on the screen.

❸ Click the checkbox below Widow/Orphan, then click the **OK button**.

WordPerfect inserts the code Wid/Orph into the document. Now, no matter how you edit the document, no paragraph of two lines or more, when split between two pages, will ever leave only one line of the paragraph on a page.

## Saving an Intermediate Version of the Report

Having worked on the report for another fifteen minutes or so, Steven decides to save the file again.

To save the file using a different filename:
1 Click **File,** then click **Save As.**
2 Type the new filename **s4file2.dft** and click the **OK button**.
   WordPerfect saves the file using the filename S4FILE2.DFT.

*If you want to take a break* and resume the tutorial at a later time, you can exit WordPerfect. When you resume, launch WordPerfect and open S4FILE2.DFT into a document window.

## Using Tables

As Steven reads through his report, he realizes he forgot to include the table that summarizes his gross sales for the previous three years. WordPerfect's Tables feature allows you to specify the number of columns and rows, insert or delete columns and rows, change the width of columns, draw or remove lines between columns and rows, change the format of text and numbers within the table, and perform other tasks to make the table attractive and readable without having to retype any data.

### Creating a Table

Steven will use the Tables feature to create a table of his annual sales. His final table is shown in Figure 4-22. Let's create this table now.

**Figure 4-22**
Data table for
Steven's report

| TERRITORY 703 GROSS SALES (in dollars) | | | | | |
|---|---|---|---|---|---|
| Year | Qtr. 1 | Qtr. 2 | Qtr. 3 | Qtr. 4 | Total |
| 1992 | 542,197 | 591,287 | 588,841 | 498,276 | 2,220,601 |
| 1993 | 562,422 | 681,647 | 584,892 | 540,699 | 2,369,660 |
| 1994 | 891,322 | 904,498 | 896,217 | 934,228 | 3,626,265 |

To create a table:

❶ Move the insertion point to the end of the first sentence in the section "GROSS SALES," just after the colon at the end of the phrase "during the years 1992 to 1994:" This is the location in the document where you want the table to appear.

❷ Press [Enter] to insert blank lines between the text and the table. See Figure 4-23.

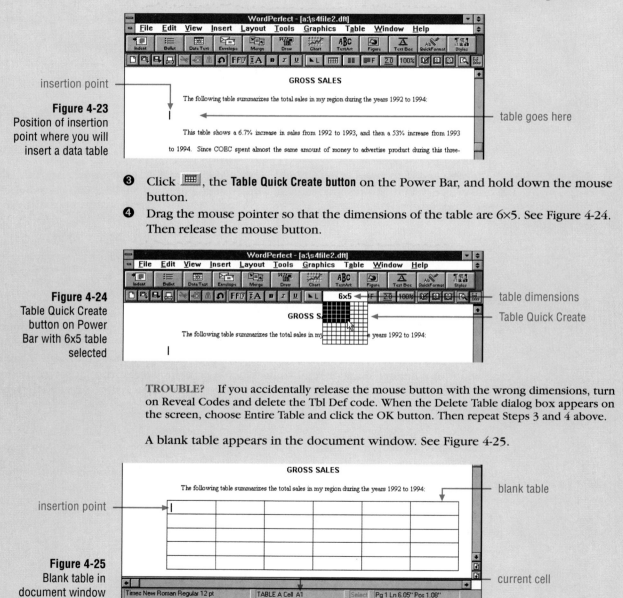

**Figure 4-23**
Position of insertion point where you will insert a data table

insertion point

table goes here

❸ Click the Table Quick Create button on the Power Bar, and hold down the mouse button.

❹ Drag the mouse pointer so that the dimensions of the table are 6×5. See Figure 4-24. Then release the mouse button.

**Figure 4-24**
Table Quick Create button on Power Bar with 6x5 table selected

table dimensions

Table Quick Create

**TROUBLE?** If you accidentally release the mouse button with the wrong dimensions, turn on Reveal Codes and delete the Tbl Def code. When the Delete Table dialog box appears on the screen, choose Entire Table and click the OK button. Then repeat Steps 3 and 4 above.

A blank table appears in the document window. See Figure 4-25.

insertion point

blank table

current cell

**Figure 4-25**
Blank table in document window

**TROUBLE?** Your Button Bar may change from the default WordPerfect Button Bar to the Tables Button Bar, depending on how your copy of WordPerfect was configured and how it has been used in the past. If a different Button Bar appears on your screen, don't worry about it. We will explain the Tables Button Bar shortly.

You have created a blank table with six columns and five rows, so that each row has six cells. In a WordPerfect table, a cell is a single box into which you can type a number or text. In order to identify each specific cell within a table, WordPerfect assigns letters to the columns and numbers to the rows. The first column on the left is column "A," the next column is "B," and so on, in alphabetical order. The rows are numbered from top to bottom, starting with row 1. Each cell, therefore, is designated by a letter and a number. The cell in the upper-left corner is A1, the cell to its right is B1, the cell below A1 is A2, and so forth, as shown in Figure 4-26.

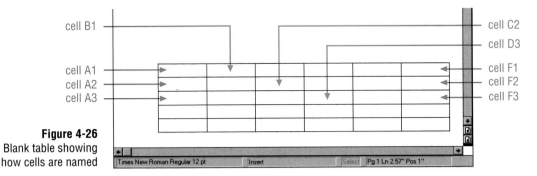

**Figure 4-26**
Blank table showing how cells are named

## Formatting a Table

Steven realizes that he'll have to modify the format of his table to make it attractive and readable. First he'll join the cells in the top row into one large cell, so it can contain the title of the table, as shown in Figure 4-22.

To join cells in a table:

❶ Make sure the insertion point is in cell A1, the first cell in the group of cells you want to join. The location of the insertion point is given in the center of the status bar at the bottom of the document window.

❷ Move the mouse pointer to the left edge of cell A1 until the pointer becomes ⇦. See Figure 4-27.

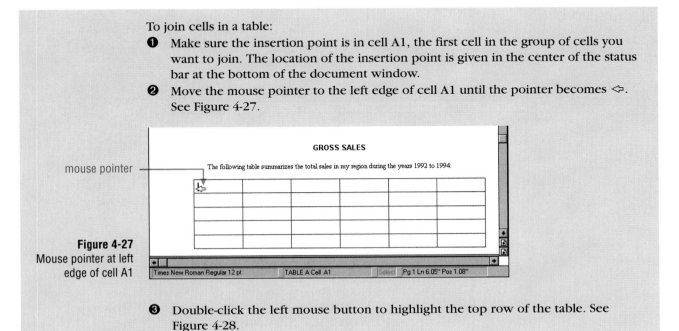

**Figure 4-27**
Mouse pointer at left edge of cell A1

❸ Double-click the left mouse button to highlight the top row of the table. See Figure 4-28.

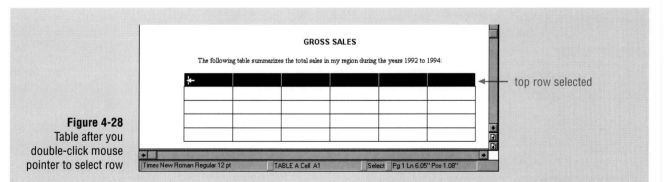

**Figure 4-28**
Table after you double-click mouse pointer to select row

TROUBLE? If you have difficulty double-clicking with the proper mouse pointer, just keep practicing. If you highlight the wrong cells, just click the mouse pointer in the middle of cell A1 to deselect the cells, then try Step 3 again.

❹ With the top row highlighted, click **Table**, click **Join**, then click **Cell** to join the cells. The top row is now a single cell in which you can type the title of the table.

## Using the Tables Button Bar

Steven realizes that he wants to make several other changes to the table. To help edit the table, he decides use the Tables Button Bar.

Let's select the Tables Button Bar now. (If the Tables Button Bar has automatically appeared on your screen, complete the following steps anyway so you'll learn how to select a desired Button Bar.)

To select the Tables Button Bar:
❶ Move the mouse pointer to the Button Bar and click the *right* (not the left) mouse button. WordPerfect displays a menu of Button Bars. See Figure 4-29.

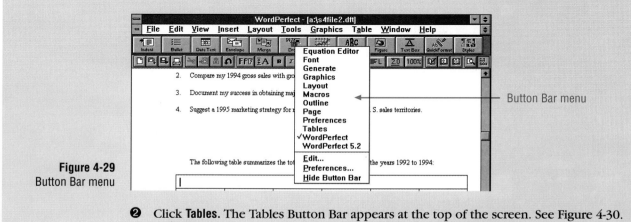

**Figure 4-29**
Button Bar menu

❷ Click **Tables**. The Tables Button Bar appears at the top of the screen. See Figure 4-30.

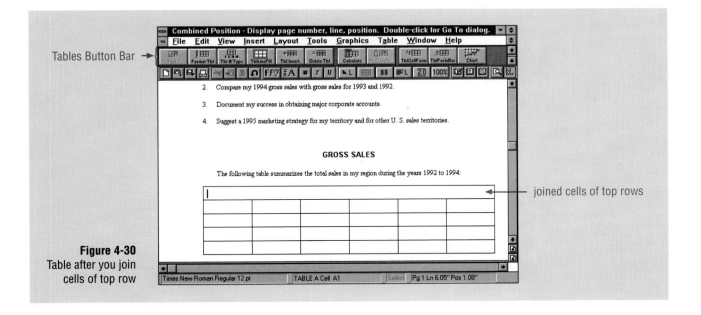

Tables Button Bar →

joined cells of top rows

**Figure 4-30**
Table after you join
cells of top row

With the Tables Button Bar on the screen, Steven decides that a double line under the top row would help separate the title from the rest of the table.

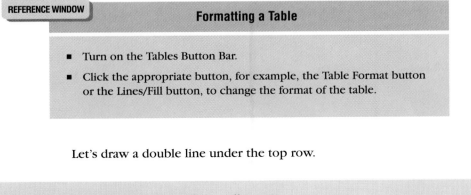

REFERENCE WINDOW

**Formatting a Table**

- Turn on the Tables Button Bar.
- Click the appropriate button, for example, the Table Format button or the Lines/Fill button, to change the format of the table.

Let's draw a double line under the top row.

To draw a double line under a cell:
❶ Make sure the insertion point is still in cell A1 (which now spans the entire top row).
❷ Click ▦, the **Lines/Fill button** on the Tables Button Bar. WordPerfect displays the Table Lines/Fill dialog box.
❸ Click the button to the right of Bottom to display the various line patterns. See Figure 4-31.

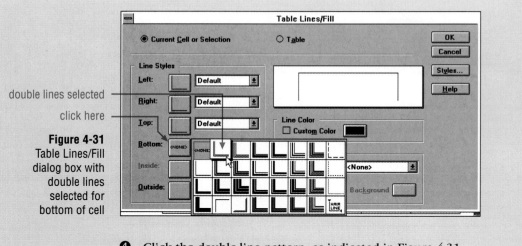

double lines selected ⎯

click here ⎯

**Figure 4-31**
Table Lines/Fill
dialog box with
double lines
selected for
bottom of cell

❹ Click the double-line pattern, as indicated in Figure 4-31.

The diagram in the dialog box shows a sample cell, with single lines on the top, left, and right sides, but double lines on the bottom.

❺ Click the **OK button** to return to the document window.

Steven also wants to draw a double line below the cells of row 2. As shown in Figure 4-22, this double line will separate the column labels from the data in the columns.

To draw a double line under a row of cells:

❶ Double-click ⇦ on the left edge of cell A2. See Figure 4-32.

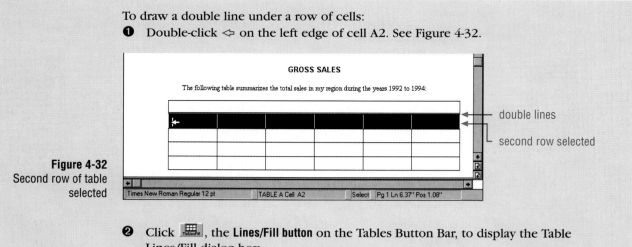

double lines

second row selected

**Figure 4-32**
Second row of table
selected

❷ Click [▦], the **Lines/Fill button** on the Tables Button Bar, to display the Table Lines/Fill dialog box.

❸ Again, click the **Bottom button** and select the double lines.

❹ Click the **OK button** to return to the document window.

Next Steven decides that the column labels and the numbers in the columns should be right-justified, that is, aligned along the right side of the cells. Let's change the format of the columns to be right-justified.

To right-justify text in columns:

❶ Make sure the second row is still selected.

❷ Click 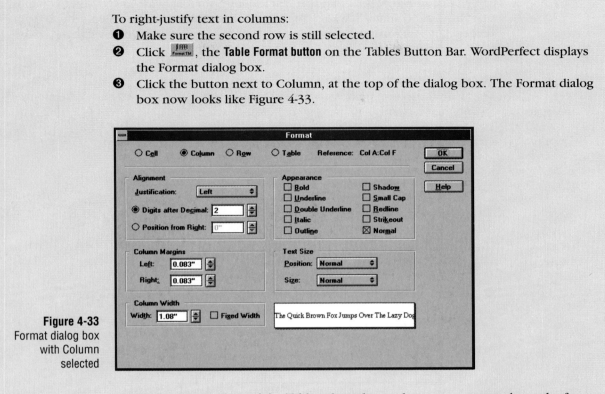, the **Table Format button** on the Tables Button Bar. WordPerfect displays the Format dialog box.

❸ Click the button next to Column, at the top of the dialog box. The Format dialog box now looks like Figure 4-33.

**Figure 4-33**
Format dialog box with Column selected

With an entire row of the Table selected, any change you now make to the format of the columns will affect all the columns in the table.

❹ In the Alignment box, to the right of Justification, click the button and choose Right.

❺ Click the **OK button.**

This sets right justification for all the columns of the table. Any text you type into the table will now be flush right in the cells.

Having set all the columns to right justification, Steven realizes that he wants the title, in cell A1, to be centered between the left and right edges of the table, as shown in Figure 4-22. Let's center-justify the text in cell A1.

To center-justify text (or numbers) in a cell:

❶ Move the insertion point to cell A1. The insertion point appears on the far right side of the cell.

❷ Click 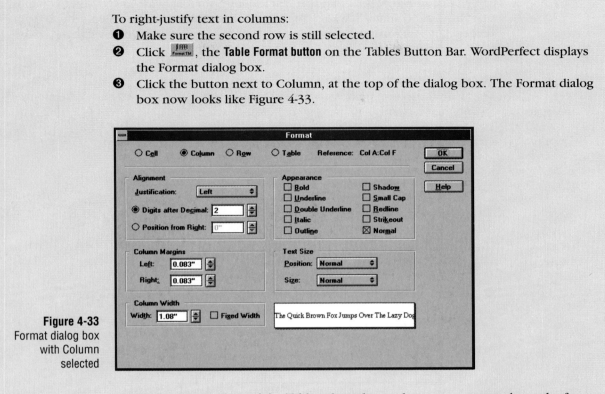, the **Format Table button** on the Tables Button Bar, to display the Format dialog box.

❸ Change the Justification to Center, then click the **OK button.**

The insertion point now appears in the middle of cell A1. Because you didn't highlight multiple cells (remember that cell A1 is now a single cell), this operation changes only cell A1 to center-justification. The other cells remain right-justified.

Notice in Figure 4-22 that the Year column is not as wide as the other columns, and that the Total column is wider. You can change the width of a column by dragging the vertical line that separates two columns. Let's change the width of the columns now.

**To change the width of the columns:**

❶ Move the mouse pointer to the vertical line to the right of cell A2, so the mouse pointer appears as ✛. See Figure 4-34.

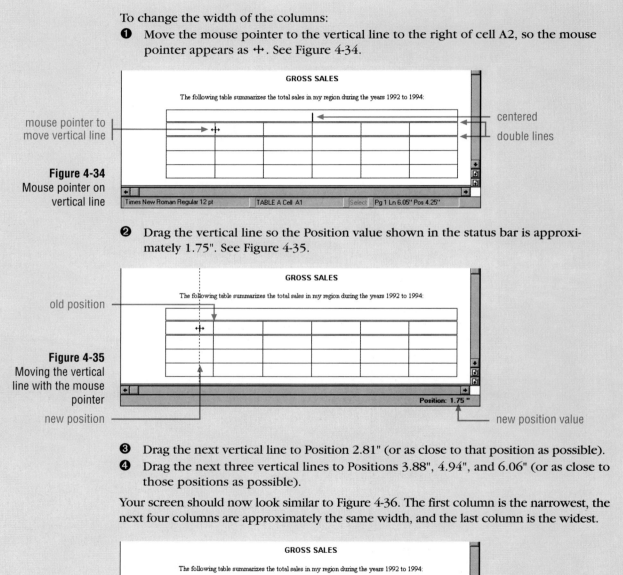

**Figure 4-34**
Mouse pointer on vertical line

❷ Drag the vertical line so the Position value shown in the status bar is approximately 1.75". See Figure 4-35.

**Figure 4-35**
Moving the vertical line with the mouse pointer

❸ Drag the next vertical line to Position 2.81" (or as close to that position as possible).

❹ Drag the next three vertical lines to Positions 3.88", 4.94", and 6.06" (or as close to those positions as possible).

Your screen should now look similar to Figure 4-36. The first column is the narrowest, the next four columns are approximately the same width, and the last column is the widest.

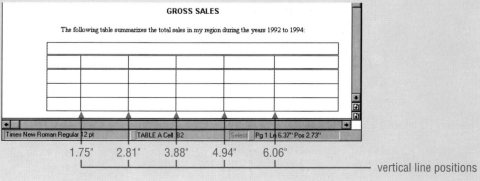

**Figure 4-36**
Blank table after you adjust the width of the columns

### Entering Labels and Data into the Table

Having created and formatted the table, Steven is now ready to enter data. To move the insertion point, you can click the mouse pointer in a cell or you can use the arrow keys. You can also use [Tab] to move the insertion point one cell to the right (without inserting a Tab code), or [Shift][Tab] to move the insertion point one cell to the left. Let's enter the labels and data into the table now.

To enter data into the table:
1. Move the insertion point to cell A1 and type **TERRITORY 703 GROSS SALES (in dollars)**, the title of the table, as shown in Figure 4-22.
2. Click I in cell A2.
3. Type **Year**.
4. Click I in cell B2, and type **Qtr. 1**.
5. Type the data into the other cells of the table, as shown in Figure 4-22.

Your screen should now look like Figure 4-22. You don't need to change back to the normal Button Bar, because WordPerfect automatically returns to it when the insertion point leaves the table. Because you chose the Tables Button Bar once while working with tables, WordPerfect automatically displays the Tables Button Bar again when you move the insertion point into a table.

## Using Bookmarks

Steven decides to take some time to look through his report to ensure that the narrative fits the data in the table. As he looks through the document, he wants to be able to return quickly to the heading "CORPORATE ACCOUNTS" (near the middle of the report), so he decides to create a bookmark. A WordPerfect **bookmark** is a tagged location within a document. Using WordPerfect's bookmark allows you to move quickly from any place in the document to the location you have tagged.

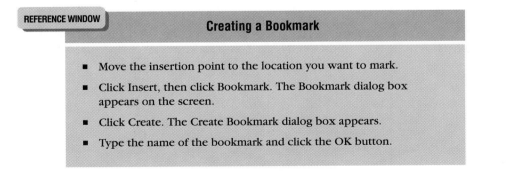

**REFERENCE WINDOW**

### Creating a Bookmark

- Move the insertion point to the location you want to mark.
- Click Insert, then click Bookmark. The Bookmark dialog box appears on the screen.
- Click Create. The Create Bookmark dialog box appears.
- Type the name of the bookmark and click the OK button.

Let's create a bookmark at the "CORPORATE ACCOUNTS" heading in Steven's report.

To create a bookmark:

❶ Move the insertion point to the right of the heading "CORPORATE ACCOUNTS" on page 2 of the report, the location where you want a bookmark.

❷ Click **Insert**, then click **Bookmark**. The Bookmark dialog box appears on the screen.

WordPerfect displays a built-in bookmark called QuickMark, which we'll describe later in this section. In this example, we want to set a user-defined bookmark.

❸ Click the **Create button**. The Create Bookmark dialog box appears on the screen.

❹ Type **Corporate Accounts** and click the **OK button**. Steven names the bookmark "Corporate Accounts" because the bookmark will be at that heading.

WordPerfect closes the Create Bookmark and the Bookmark dialog boxes and inserts a bookmark at the location of the insertion point.

You can turn on Reveal Codes to see that the Bookmark code appears in the document at the insertion point. Now let's use the bookmark to quickly move the insertion point to that location from anywhere else in the document.

**REFERENCE WINDOW**

### Moving to a Bookmark

■ Click Edit, then click Go To to display the Go To dialog box.

■ Click the Down Arrow to the right of the Bookmark text box and highlight the desired bookmark, then click the OK button.

To move the insertion point to a bookmark:

❶ Move the insertion point anywhere else in the document. For example, press **[Ctrl][End]** to move the insertion point to the end of the document. You're now ready to see how the bookmark works.

❷ Click **Edit**, then click **Go To**. WordPerfect displays the Go To dialog box.

❸ Click the button to the left of Bookmark, then, if necessary, click the **Down Arrow** to the right of the Bookmark text box, and then click **"Corporate Accounts."** See Figure 4-37.

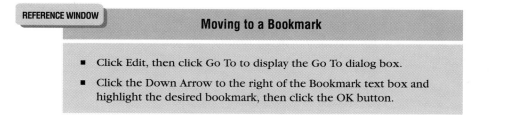

**Figure 4-37**
Go To dialog box

bookmark active

bookmark selected

click here to go to bookmark

❹  Click the **OK button.**

WordPerfect closes the dialog box and moves the insertion point to the Corporate Accounts bookmark.

WordPerfect's built-in bookmark, QuickMark, is a special bookmark because you set it or move the insertion point to it with simple keystrokes: Pressing [Ctrl][Shift][Q] sets the QuickMark at the current location of the insertion point, and pressing [Ctrl][Q] jumps the insertion point to the location of the QuickMark from anywhere in the document. You can also choose QuickMark from the Go To dialog box. A document can have only one QuickMark.

You can create as many user-defined bookmarks as you want in a document. For example, if you're writing a long report—say, 40 pages—you might want to insert a bookmark at each section heading and give the bookmark the name of that section. In this way, you could easily move the insertion point to any section of your report.

When you save a document, all the bookmarks are saved with it, including the QuickMark.

## Saving and Printing the Report

Steven now wants to look through the report one last time and then save and print it.

To view, save, and print the document:

❶  Click **View,** then click **Page** to return to page mode.

TROUBLE?    If you took a break while doing this tutorial and closed the document S4FILE2.DFT, WordPerfect automatically put the document in page mode when you opened it again.

Steven looks through the report and is pleased with the results.

❷  Preview the report in Full Page view, then save it as S4FILE3.REP.

❸  Print the report.

Your final copy of the report should look like Figure 4-38 on the following pages.

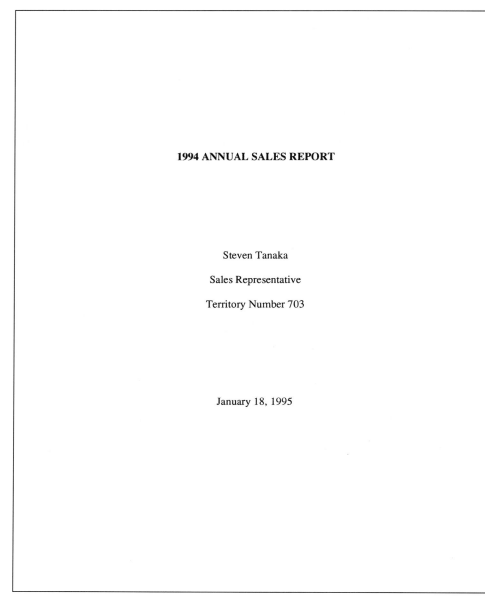

**1994 ANNUAL SALES REPORT**

Steven Tanaka

Sales Representative

Territory Number 703

January 18, 1995

**Figure 4-38**
Final version of
Steven's annual
sales report
(title page)

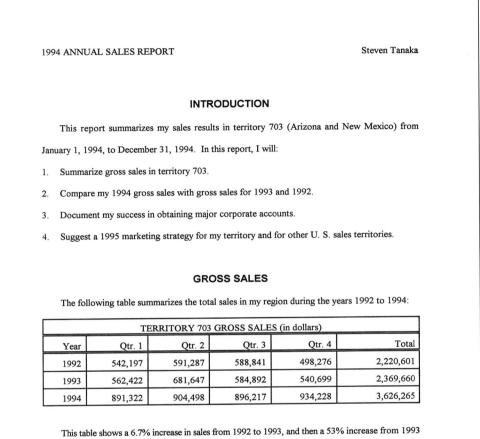

1994 ANNUAL SALES REPORT                                    Steven Tanaka

## INTRODUCTION

This report summarizes my sales results in territory 703 (Arizona and New Mexico) from January 1, 1994, to December 31, 1994.  In this report, I will:

1.  Summarize gross sales in territory 703.

2.  Compare my 1994 gross sales with gross sales for 1993 and 1992.

3.  Document my success in obtaining major corporate accounts.

4.  Suggest a 1995 marketing strategy for my territory and for other U. S. sales territories.

## GROSS SALES

The following table summarizes the total sales in my region during the years 1992 to 1994:

| TERRITORY 703 GROSS SALES (in dollars) | | | | | |
|---|---|---|---|---|---|
| Year | Qtr. 1 | Qtr. 2 | Qtr. 3 | Qtr. 4 | Total |
| 1992 | 542,197 | 591,287 | 588,841 | 498,276 | 2,220,601 |
| 1993 | 562,422 | 681,647 | 584,892 | 540,699 | 2,369,660 |
| 1994 | 891,322 | 904,498 | 896,217 | 934,228 | 3,626,265 |

This table shows a 6.7% increase in sales from 1992 to 1993, and then a 53% increase from 1993 to 1994.  Since COEC spent almost the same amount of money to advertise product during this three-year period, I attribute the dramatic increase in income to improved targeting of our advertising and marketing and to improved customer relations.  I especially credit COEC's new customer 800

1

**Figure 4-38**
Final version of
Steven's annual
sales report (page 1)

1994 ANNUAL SALES REPORT                                         Steven Tanaka

number.  This "hot line" allows us to handle customer orders and complaints more quickly and

effectively.  Most of my major corporate accounts reported improved satisfaction with our service

and cited this as a major reason why they bought COEC products.

### CORPORATE ACCOUNTS

COEC's strategy to focus on large corporate accounts has paid big dividends for me.  During

1994, I visited 82 potential large-corporation customers in my territory.  I was able to promise them

better terms under our large-accounts discount program and our new customer hot line.  To date,

twenty-seven of these companies have begun buying their office equipment from COEC.  I attribute

this new business to the success of COEC's strategy.

The large corporations in my territory that seem to respond best to COEC are more service

intensive than manufacturing intensive.  This is probably because the service industries require more

of the type of office equipment that we sell.

### RECOMMENDATIONS

Based upon my 1994 sales success, I recommend the following:

1.  We should focus our sales calls and advertising on service-oriented industries, where we will get
    the most benefit from our marketing dollars.

2.  We should continue our 800 "hot line."  The additional and retained sales that are generated
    more than pay for this service.

2

**Figure 4-38**
Final version of
Steven's annual sales
report (page 2)

1994 ANNUAL SALES REPORT                                                    Steven Tanaka

3.  We should continue to add new lines of office equipment.  Our customers want a wider choice
    of new technology, in particular, fax machines, color copiers, and telephone-answering
    equipment.

4.  We should consider adding office computers to our line of products.  Many of the large
    corporations want to buy their computers from the same company that sells them their laser
    printers and fax machines.

3

**Figure 4-38**
Final version of
Steven's annual
sales report (page 3)

## Questions

1. Define or describe the following terms:
   a. header
   b. footer
   c. page numbering
   d. Conditional End of Page
   e. widow
   f. orphan
   g. bookmark
2. How would you create a header that prints the title of your paper in the upper-right corner of every page?
3. How would you create a footer that prints your company name in the lower-left corner of every page?
4. Under what circumstances would you use each of the following features?
   a. Tables
   b. New Page Number
   c. Suppress
   d. Style
   e. Bookmark
5. What are the advantages of using a WordPerfect style to format the headings in your documents?
6. How would you change a tab stop from Position 1.5" to 1.25"?
7. How would you set tabs every one inch (instead of the default of every half-inch) from the left margin of a document? *Hint:* First display the Tab Set dialog box by clicking Layout, clicking Line, then clicking Tab Set.
8. When you use WordPerfect's Tables feature to create or edit a table, how would you do each of the following?
   a. Draw double lines at the bottom of a cell
   b. Create a single horizontal box that spans the entire width of the table
   c. Increase the width of a column in a table
9. How would you set a block of cells in a table to right justification?
10. As you edit a table, what is the advantage of using the Tables Button Bar? Is it necessary to use the Tables Button Bar, or does WordPerfect provide another method for editing a table?
11. Explain the difference between the built-in bookmark called QuickMark and a user-defined bookmark.

## Tutorial Assignments

Open the file T4FILE1.DFT from the Student Disk and do the following:
1. Change the format of the title to center justification.
2. Center the title page between the top and bottom margins.
3. Set the body of the report to full justification.
4. Change the line spacing to double spacing.
5. Number all the pages of the document in the upper-right corner.
6. Suppress page numbering on the title page.
7. Set the first page of the body of the report (after the title page) to page 1.
8. Change the first tab stop position from 1.5" to about 1.3".
9. At the beginning of the document, turn on Widow/Orphan Protection.

**E** 10. Apply the built-in style named "Heading 1" to the title of the document and the built-in style named "Heading 2" to each of the headings within the body of the report.

11. Save the file as S4FILE4.REP and print it.

Open the file T4FILE2.DFT from the Student Disk and do the following:

12. Create a style that formats the headings. Each heading should include a Conditional End of Page code (with six lines kept together) and a blank line. The text of the heading should be underlined, but remain flush left. Apply this style to the three headings in the document.

**E** 13. Create a footer that prints your name in the lower-left corner and the page number in the lower-right corner of each page. *Hint:* Within a footer, click Number and Page Number to insert the page number.

**E** 14. Create a Character style that centers a title page top to bottom, center-justifies the lines of the title, makes the text of the title boldface, and suppresses page numbering and your footer. Then use this style to create a title page with the title "Preparing for Sales Calls," your name, and the current date. *Hint:* When you want to apply a Character style, turn it on, type the desired text, and then turn it off. Turn off the "Enter Key will Chain to" checkbox or cause [Enter] to chain to "<None>."

15. Save the file as S4FILE5.DOC and print it.

Clear the document window and do the following:

16. Create an empty table that has three columns and seven rows.

17. Make the top row of cells into one cell, then change its justification to center. Type the heading "People to Contact in Territory 703" into the top row of the table.

18. In the second row of cells, type the following headings (one heading per cell): "Name," "Company," and "Phone Number." Adjust the widths of the cells so that each heading fits neatly on one line within the cell.

19. In the other five rows of the table, type the following data:
Mary Fox, Kaibab Construction Co., (602) 429-8652
Carl Gallegos, Sandia Electronics Corp., (505) 322-4858
Bruno Kline, Santa Fe Travel, Inc., (505) 841-2828
Sarah Dahlberg, Grand Canyon Tourist Assoc., (602) 335-8181
Candice Laake, Las Cruces Auto Parts, Inc., (505) 821-7474

20. If necessary, adjust the width of the columns so that all the information fits neatly in each cell.

**E** 21. Insert a blank row in the table beneath the name Carl Gallegos. *Hint:* Click the Table Insert button on the Tables Button Bar and use the dialog box to insert one row. Then type the following information into that row of cells: Arlene Hatch, Grizzly Gift Store, (406) 621-5951.

22. Save the file as S4FILE6.TAB and print it.

# Case Problems

## 1. Information on Most Popular Movies

Jennifer Wong is the entertainment editor of the newspaper *The Daily Review.* She is writing an article about the movie industry and its popularity. She decides to include in her article a table listing the five most popular movies in history.

Do the following:

1. Prepare a title page for the article on the popularity of movies.
   a. Title the report, "MAKE MY DAY," with the subtitle "Take Me to a Movie."
   b. Also include on the title page the author of the article, the name of the newspaper, and today's date.
   c. Center-justify the lines of the title page.
   d. Center the entire page between the top and bottom margins.

2. On a second page (separated by a page break), create a table with four columns and seven rows.
   a. Join the cells in the top row into one cell.
   b. Insert into that cell the title "ALL-TIME TOP FIVE AMERICAN MOVIES."
   c. In the second row of cells, type the headings "Rank," "Title," "Year," and "Income (millions)," with one heading per cell.
3. Adjust the width of the cells as follows:
   a. Make the "Rank" column very narrow, to fit the numbers 1 through 10.
   b. Make the "Title" column wide enough to fit the names of the movies. (Refer to #4, below.)
   c. Make the "Year" column narrower, to fit the dates.
   d. Make the "Income" column moderately wide.
4. Into the other five rows, insert the following data:

| | | | |
|---|---|---|---|
| 1 | Jurassic Park | 1993 | 330 |
| 2 | E.T, The Extra-Terrestrial | 1982 | 229 |
| 3 | Star Wars | 1977 | 194 |
| 4 | Return of the Jedi | 1983 | 168 |
| 5 | Batman | 1989 | 151 |

**E**
5. Use the Table Number Type button on the Tables Button Bar to change the number type for the Income values to Currency.
6. Save the file as S4MOVIES.TAB and print it.

## 2. Report on Computer Cost and Speed

David Sokol is a graduate student at the Carlton University School of Business. As part of a class project, he must prepare a short report comparing several popular types of computers used in business offices. In his paper, he includes a table to compare each computer's cost and speed.

Do the following:
1. Open the file P4COMP.DFT from the Student Disk into a document window.
2. Change the line spacing to double spacing.

**E**
3. Change the tab stops so that they begin at 0.4 inches from the left margin and are spaced every 0.4 inches thereafter.
4. Set the body of the report to full justification.
5. Turn on Widow/Orphan Protection for the entire report.
6. Create a header.
   a. Set the text of the header to flush right.
   b. Type the text of the header: "Comparison of Computers page" followed by a space. Make the title "Comparison of Computers" italics.
   c. After the text of the header, insert the code for page numbering.
7. Suppress the header so it won't appear on the title page when you print the report.
8. Create a title page for the report.
   a. Insert a hard page break to separate the title page from the body of the report.
   b. On the title page, type the title "A Comparison of the Speed of Common Business Computers." Press [Enter] three times after the title.
   c. Type the following information: "A Report for BusMng 617." Press [Enter] twice after this information.
   d. Type "by David Sokol," press [Enter] twice, and insert the current date using WordPerfect's Date Text command.
   e. Center the text of the title between the left and right margins.
   f. Center the text of the title between the top and bottom margins.
9. Make the first page of the body of the report page 1.

10. Create and apply a style for the four headings: "INTRODUCTION," "COMPUTER SYSTEMS," "METHODS," and "RESULTS."
    a. Within the style, insert a single-spaced line above the text of the heading.
    b. On the blank line above the heading, insert a Conditional End of Page code to keep six lines together.
    c. Insert the code to make the headings a sans serif font, such as Arial, Helvetica, or Univers.
11. As David writes his report, he often has to refer to the Methods section. Immediately after the METHODS heading, insert a bookmark named "Methods."
12. Look through the report. Make sure no heading is left alone at the bottom of a page. If necessary, insert a Conditional End of Page.
13. Move the insertion point to the end of the report, insert two blank lines, and create the following table. Make your table look as much like this one as possible.

| Comparison of Popular PC Models | | | | |
|---|---|---|---|---|
| Model | Test #1 | Test #2 | Test#3 | Cost |
| 286-12Mhz | 35 sec | 447 sec | 351 sec | $700 |
| 386SX-16 | 27 sec | 286 sec | 349 sec | $950 |
| 386-20Mhz | 26 sec | 285 sec | 240 sec | $1100 |
| 386-33Mhz | 9 sec | 105 sec | 237 sec | $1300 |
| 486SX-25 | 25 sec | 102 sec | 162 sec | $1500 |
| 486-33Mhz | 6 sec | 52 sec | 154 sec | $1800 |
| 486-50Mhz | 5 sec | 21 sec | 142 sec | $2100 |
| 486DX2-66 | 4 sec | 15 sec | 142 sec | $2700 |

**E**  14. Use the Table Lines/Fill command to change the top row (cell A1) to a Fill Style of 10% Fill. *Hint:* The Fill Style is an option in the Fill Options box of the Table Lines/Fill dialog box.
15. Save the report as S4COMP.REP and print it.

## 3. Investment Accounts Report

Karen Brueck is the president of Omaha Investors Group, an investment club of about 30 members. Karen asks her secretary, Christopher Manning, to prepare a quarterly report to send to each club member, telling them how each of the club's four investment accounts is doing. She tells Christopher to include in the report a table that compares each of the accounts over the last five years.

Do the following:
1. Open P4INVEST.DFT from the Student Disk into a document window.
2. Set the entire report to double spacing.
3. Make a header that prints the shortened title "Club Q2 Report page 1," but instead of typing the "1" in page 1, insert the Page Number code, so that the page number will print as part of the heading.
4. Insert a hard page break after the date (and above the heading "Introduction") to create a separate title page.
5. Set up the format of the title page so it is center-justified.
6. Center the text of the title page between the top and bottom margins.
7. Suppress the header for the title page.
8. Turn on Widow/Orphan Protection for the entire document.
9. Change the page number after the title page to page 1.
10. Set the body of the report to full justification.

11. Create a style for the headings within the report. Make the headings a boldface, sans serif font, centered between the left and right margins. Apply the style to all of the headings: "Introduction," "Fund Description," and "Fund Performance."

12. Move the insertion point to the phrase "(Insert first table here)." Delete the phrase, and then create the following table at that location:

| Total Annual Returns(%) | | | | | | | |
|---|---|---|---|---|---|---|---|
| FUND NAME | 1988 | 1989 | 1990 | 1991 | 1992 | 1993 | 1994 |
| Fixed Income | 9.8 | 9.0 | 9.0 | 9.0 | 9.9 | 9.7 | 9.6 |
| Common Stock | 5.3 | 16.6 | 31.2 | -3.3 | 30.1 | 20.7 | 18.7 |
| Windlow Stock | 1.2 | 24.7 | 15.0 | -5.7 | 25.2 | 17.6 | 37.7 |
| Growth Stock | 13.1 | 2.7 | 43.1 | -19.8 | 65.7 | 31.1 | 21.1 |

**E** 13. Use the Table Lines/Fill command to change the top two rows to a Fill Style of 10% Fill. *Hint:* The Fill Style is an option in the Fill Options box of the Table Lines/Fill dialog box.

**E** 14. Use the Table Format button to set the justification of the numeric cells in the table to Decimal Align.

**E** 15. Change the appearance of the text in the top two rows to Bold. *Hint:* With the insertion point still in the table, make sure the Tables Button Bar is active, then click the Format Tbl button and choose Cell, where you can change the fonts appearance to Bold.

**E** 16. Move the insertion point to the phrase "(Insert second table here)." Delete the phrase, and then create the following table at that location:

| The Current Value of Each Investment Fund (based on a 12/31/87 value of $1000) | | |
|---|---|---|
| FUND NAME | Current Value | Avg. Yearly Ret. |
| Fixed Income | 1755.44 | 9.42 |
| Common Stock | 2560.44 | 16.23 |
| Windlow Stock | 2204.87 | 13.49 |
| Growth Stock | 3048.58 | 19.52 |

*Hint:* Use the normal Bold command to make the first line boldface, then press [Enter] and type the second line. To set the second row to 10% Fill (gray shading), use the Fill Style in the Fill Options box of the Table Lines/Fill dialog box.

**E** 17. Use the Table Format button to set the justification of the numeric cells in the table to Decimal Align.

**E** 18. Use the Table Number Type button to change the number type for the Current Value numbers to Currency.

**E** 19. Use the Table Number Type button to change the number type for the Average Yearly Return values to Percent.

20. Save the report as S4INVEST.REP and print it.

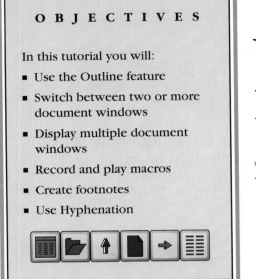

# Using Special Word-Processing Features

## Writing a Feasibility Report

**CASE**

**Connolly/Bayle Publishing Company**   Since graduating last year with a degree in business management, Jonathan Lew has worked in outside sales for Connolly/Bayle (C/B) Publishing Company, which publishes computer magazines. Recently Jonathan took an in-house job as an assistant to Ann McMullen, the business manager for C/B Publishing. The company's cofounders, Stephen Connolly and John Bayle, have asked Ann to head a task force to investigate the feasibility of starting a new magazine aimed at graphic designers who use personal computers. The task force consists of Ann, Jonathan, two marketing managers, and two editors who manage other magazines at C/B Publishing.

The task force met to map out strategies for the feasibility study. They decided to send out questionnaires, conduct interviews, and, with David Palermo, an accountant at C/B Publishing, make financial projections. After completing the study, the task force met again to analyze the information, draw conclusions, and make recommendations. Ann asked Jonathan to draft an outline for the group's final report and to distribute copies of the outline to the other task force members for their approval. Once the outline has been approved, Ann will write the main body of the report and Jonathan will prepare the report for final distribution by adding footnotes, section headings, and other features.

## Planning the Document

The responsibility for planning the document rests with Jonathan, although the other members of the task force will respond to his ideas and give their final approval.

## Content

The content of the feasibility report will come from the results of the feasibility study itself, from the financial analysis, and from the discussion notes Ann and Jonathan took during the task-force meetings.

## Organization

Jonathan will organize the feasibility report by creating an outline. He decides to have an introductory section, which will state the purposes of the report and explain how the data were gathered. He will then include sections on the target audience for the new magazine, operating expenses, and projected costs. The report will conclude with a summary and the recommendation of the task force.

## Style

Jonathan wants the feasibility report to conform to standard business-writing style, with straightforward logic and clear, concise sentences.

### Format

C/B Publishing has no policy on how to format in-house reports. Jonathan will use WordPerfect's default settings for margins, tabs, and justification and the standard format he learned in college for titles, headings, and page numbering.

## Creating an Outline

Jonathan's task is to organize the data collected in the feasibility study and outline the report. He decides to use WordPerfect's Outline feature. In an outline, each paragraph is preceded by a paragraph number. The paragraph numbers represent levels: Level-1 paragraphs (major ideas) are usually preceded by Roman numerals (I, II, III, etc.); level-2 paragraphs (supporting ideas) by uppercase letters (A, B, C, etc.); level-3 paragraphs by Arabic numerals (1, 2, 3, etc.); level-4 paragraphs by lowercase letters (a, b, c, etc.), and so forth (Figure 5-1). Paragraph numbering in a WordPerfect outline reflects this standard hierarchy. WordPerfect's Outline feature allows up to eight levels of paragraph numbers. Notice that the "numbers" in WordPerfect's Outline feature can be either numerals or letters.

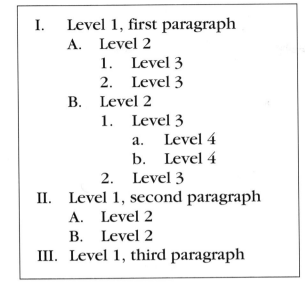

I.  Level 1, first paragraph
    A.  Level 2
        1.  Level 3
        2.  Level 3
    B.  Level 2
        1.  Level 3
            a.  Level 4
            b.  Level 4
        2.  Level 3
II.  Level 1, second paragraph
    A.  Level 2
    B.  Level 2
III.  Level 1, third paragraph

**Figure 5-1**
Standard outline paragraph levels and paragraph numbers

The advantage of WordPerfect's Outline feature is that paragraph numbering is automatic. When Outline is on and you press [Enter] to end one paragraph and start a new one, WordPerfect automatically inserts the appropriate number or letter for the next paragraph in the outline. With a simple keystroke, you can change a paragraph number from a higher level to a lower level or from a lower level to a higher level. When you move a paragraph or a group of paragraphs in the outline, WordPerfect automatically renumbers them.

The first draft of Jonathan's outline is shown in Figure 5-2. In the following steps, you'll use WordPerfect's Outline feature to create this outline.

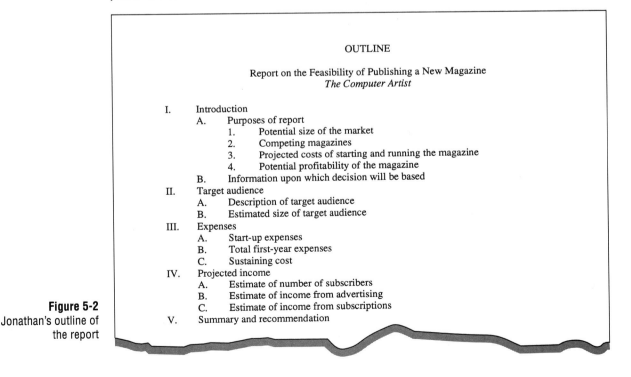

OUTLINE

Report on the Feasibility of Publishing a New Magazine
*The Computer Artist*

I.  Introduction
    A.  Purposes of report
        1.  Potential size of the market
        2.  Competing magazines
        3.  Projected costs of starting and running the magazine
        4.  Potential profitability of the magazine
    B.  Information upon which decision will be based
II.  Target audience
    A.  Description of target audience
    B.  Estimated size of target audience
III.  Expenses
    A.  Start-up expenses
    B.  Total first-year expenses
    C.  Sustaining cost
IV.  Projected income
    A.  Estimate of number of subscribers
    B.  Estimate of income from advertising
    C.  Estimate of income from subscriptions
V.  Summary and recommendation

**Figure 5-2**
Jonathan's outline of the report

First you need to create the title of the outline.

To create the outline title:

❶ Make sure a blank WordPerfect document window appears on the screen.

❷ Click **Layout**, click **Line**, then click **Center**.

Because you want to center only one line, you use the Line Center command on the Layout menu rather than the Center command on the Justification button of the Power Bar.

❸ Type **OUTLINE** and press **[Enter]** twice.

❹ Using the Line Center command, type the next two lines of the title, as shown in Figure 5-2. Make sure that you italicize the name of the magazine, *The Computer Artist*.

❺ Press **[Enter]** twice to double-space after the title. Your screen should look like Figure 5-3.

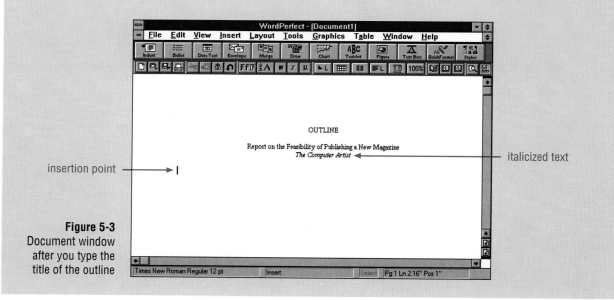

insertion point

italicized text

**Figure 5-3**
Document window
after you type the
title of the outline

Now you're ready to turn on WordPerfect's Outline feature and create the outline. With Outline on, whenever you press [Enter], WordPerfect automatically inserts the next number in the paragraph level you are currently in. If you want to change to a lower level (for example, from II to A), you can do so by clicking the Next Level button on the Outline Bar or pressing [Tab]. Similarly, if you want to change to a higher level (for example, from A to II), you can do so by clicking the Previous Level button on the Outline Bar or pressing [Shift][Tab]. If you want to delete the paragraph number entirely, simply press [Backspace]. As you work through the following steps, you'll see how these commands work to help you create an outline quickly and efficiently.

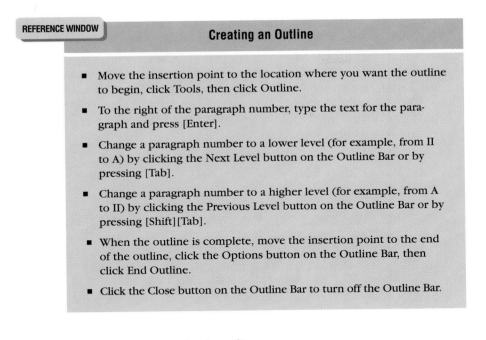

**REFERENCE WINDOW**

**Creating an Outline**

- Move the insertion point to the location where you want the outline to begin, click Tools, then click Outline.

- To the right of the paragraph number, type the text for the paragraph and press [Enter].

- Change a paragraph number to a lower level (for example, from II to A) by clicking the Next Level button on the Outline Bar or by pressing [Tab].

- Change a paragraph number to a higher level (for example, from A to II) by clicking the Previous Level button on the Outline Bar or by pressing [Shift][Tab].

- When the outline is complete, move the insertion point to the end of the outline, click the Options button on the Outline Bar, then click End Outline.

- Click the Close button on the Outline Bar to turn off the Outline Bar.

Let's create Jonathan's outline now.

To create an outline:

❶ With the insertion point at the left margin and two lines below the title, click **Tools**, then click **Outline**. WordPerfect displays the Outline Bar, inserts a paragraph number at the location of the insertion point, and displays symbols in the left margin to help you identify text and outline paragraphs. See Figure 5-4.

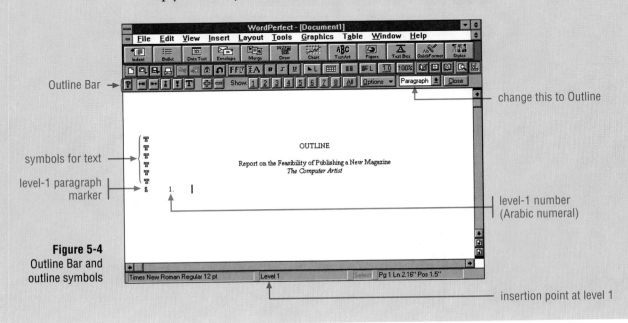

**Figure 5-4**
Outline Bar and outline symbols

❷   Click the **Down Arrow** to the right of the text box that currently contains the word "Paragraph."

When you first execute the Outline command, the default outline style is Paragraph, meaning that WordPerfect automatically numbers the paragraphs using Arabic numerals. Let's change the outline style to Outline, which uses the numbering system I., A., 1., a., (1), (a), i), and a).

❸   Click **Outline**.

WordPerfect sets the style to Outline and changes the level-1 paragraph number from an Arabic to a Roman numeral. See Figure 5-5. You are now ready to type the text of Jonathan's draft outline.

level-1 number
(Roman numeral)

Outline paragraph
numbering style

**Figure 5-5**
Document window
after WordPerfect
changes to Outline
paragraph
numbering style

❹   Type **Introduction** and press **[Enter]**. See Figure 5-6.

click here to raise
outline level

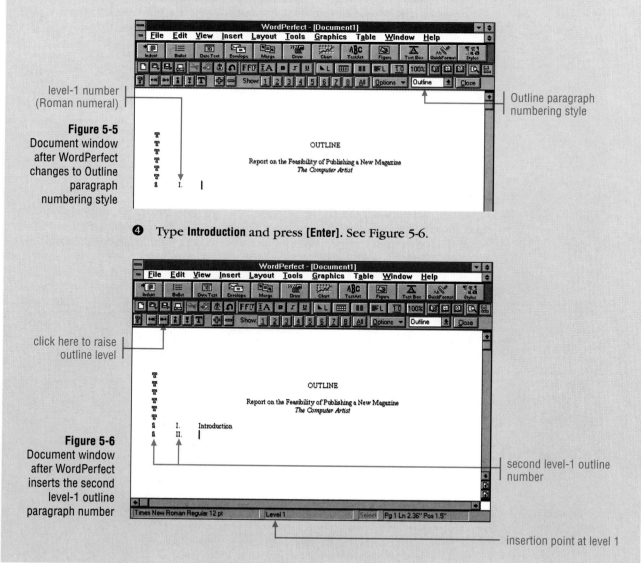

**Figure 5-6**
Document window
after WordPerfect
inserts the second
level-1 outline
paragraph number

second level-1 outline
number

insertion point at level 1

Because the Outline feature is on, pressing [Enter] moves the insertion point down one line and automatically inserts the next level-1 paragraph number, which is II. However, you want the level-2 paragraph number A, not II, on this line, as shown in Figure 5-2.

❺ Click 🔳, the **Next Level button** on the Outline Bar (see Figure 5-6), or press **[Tab]** to change from level 1 to level 2 and indent to the next tab stop. See Figure 5-7.

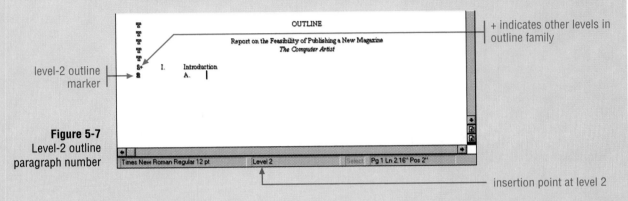

level-2 outline marker

+ indicates other levels in outline family

insertion point at level 2

**Figure 5-7**
Level-2 outline paragraph number

WordPerfect now displays the symbol "2" in the left margin to mark the level-2 paragraph. The plus sign (+) after the level-1 symbol means that this paragraph has subparagraphs below it. You're now ready to type the text of the level-2 paragraph.

❻ Type **Purposes of report** and press **[Enter]**. Notice that when you press [Enter], WordPerfect again inserts a paragraph number, but this time it is a level-2 number because that is the *current* level.

❼ With the insertion point to the right of the level-2 paragraph number B, click 🔳 on the Outline Bar or press **[Tab]** to change from level 2 to level 3 and to indent to the next tab stop. The "B" changes to "1."

❽ Type **Potential size of the market** and press **[Enter]**. When you press [Enter] here, the insertion point moves to the next line, and WordPerfect inserts the next paragraph number in the current level—in this case, the level-3 number 2.

❾ Type **Competing magazines**, press **[Enter]** to insert the next paragraph number (3), and type **Projected costs of starting and running the magazine**. Press **[Enter]** again and type **Potential profitability of the magazine**. See Figure 5-8.

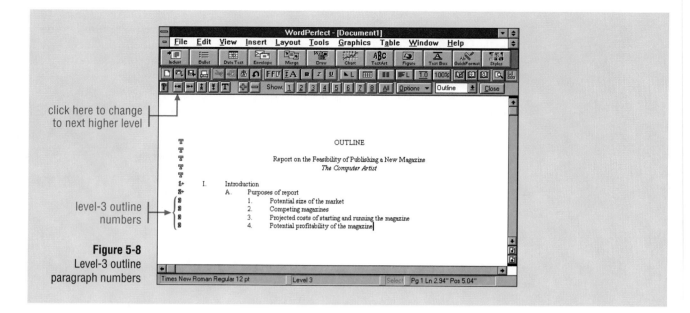

click here to change to next higher level

level-3 outline numbers

**Figure 5-8**
Level-3 outline paragraph numbers

You have now completed four items at level 3. In the next steps, you'll instruct WordPerfect to change a lower-level paragraph number to a higher-level paragraph number.

To change to a higher level:

❶ Press **[Enter]**. WordPerfect inserts the level-3 paragraph number 5, which you don't want.

❷ Click ▦, the **Previous Level button** on the Outline Bar (see Figure 5-8), or press **[Shift][Tab]** to return to the next higher level of paragraph numbering. The level-3 paragraph number 5 changes to the level-2 paragraph number B.

**TROUBLE?**  If you pressed [Backspace] instead of [Shift][Tab], WordPerfect deleted the paragraph number and displayed a "T" (for text) in the left margin, indicating that the line contains normal text, not an outline paragraph. To restore the deleted paragraph number, press the Body Text button on the Outline Bar, to toggle from text to paragraph number. Then repeat Step 2.

❸ Type **Information upon which decision will be based.** Your screen should now look like Figure 5-9.

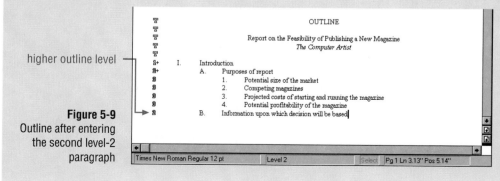

higher outline level

**Figure 5-9**
Outline after entering the second level-2 paragraph

❹ Complete the outline shown in Figure 5-2. Remember that when you want to change to a lower level in the outline, click ▣ on the Outline Bar or press **[Tab]**, and when you want to change to a higher level, click ▣ on the Outline Bar or press **[Shift][Tab]**. Do not press [Enter] after typing the last line.

❺ Click the **Close button** on the Outline Bar to close it.

❻ Save this intermediate version of the outline as S5OUTLIN.DFT on your Student Disk.

If you scroll your document window to see as much of the outline document as possible, your screen will look like Figure 5-10.

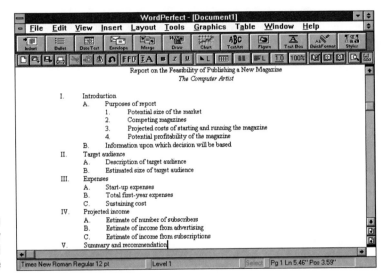

**Figure 5-10**
Document window
with the completed
outline

*If you want to take a break* and resume the tutorial at a later time, you can exit WordPerfect. When you resume, launch WordPerfect and open S5OUTLIN.DFT into the document window.

## Inserting New Paragraph Numbers into an Outline

Jonathan gives the task force members a copy of the outline at their next meeting. The task force decides to add a new section on competing magazines, as shown in Figure 5-11. They also suggest that item III ("Expenses") and item IV ("Projected income") be switched, so that projected income is presented before expenses. Finally, they suggest that items B and C under "Projected income" be switched, so that the estimate of income from subscriptions comes immediately after the estimate of the number of subscribers. Jonathan will use WordPerfect's outline editing features to make these changes.

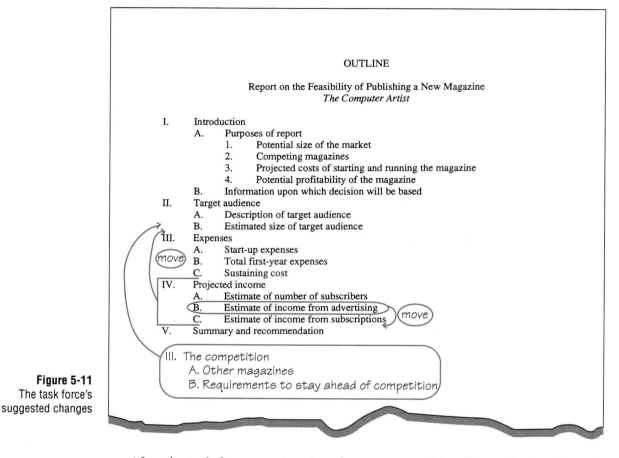

**Figure 5-11**
The task force's
suggested changes

After the task force meeting, Jonathan returns to his office and edits the outline according to the committee's suggestions. First let's insert the text on competing magazines, which begins with outline paragraph number III.

To insert new paragraph numbers into an outline:

❶ Turn on the Outline Bar by clicking **Tools**, then clicking **Outline**.

❷ Move the insertion point to the end of item II.B., which is the end of the line above the point at which you want to make the insertion.

❸ Press **[Enter]**. WordPerfect inserts a hard return, moves the insertion point down a line, and inserts the paragraph number "C" under the "B."

Because Jonathan wants a level-1 paragraph number (III) here, he must change the paragraph number "C" to a higher level.

❹ Click 🔲, the **Previous Level button** on the Outline Bar, or press **[Shift][Tab]** to change the paragraph number from a lower to a higher level.

The "C" disappears, the insertion point moves one tab stop to the left, and "III" appears on the screen. WordPerfect automatically increments the subsequent level-1 paragraph numbers in the outline.

❺ Type **The competition**.

Next you'll insert the two level-2 paragraphs under "The competition."

❻ Press **[Enter]** to insert a hard return and a new paragraph number, click ⏭, the **Next Level button** on the Bar, or press **[Tab]** to change from a level-1 to a level-2 paragraph number, and type **Other magazines**.

❼ Press **[Enter]** and type **Requirements to stay ahead of competition**.

Your screen should now look like Figure 5-12.

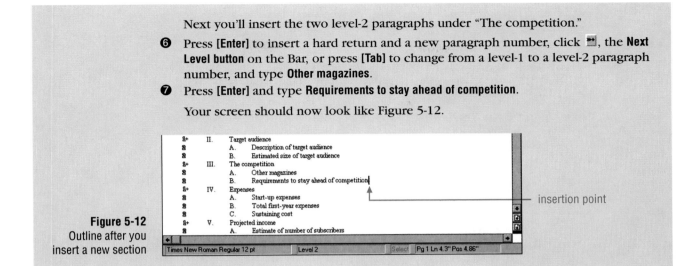

**Figure 5-12**
Outline after you insert a new section

## Moving an Outline Family

Jonathan's next task is to move the outline family that begins with paragraph number V ("Projected income"). An **outline family** is a group of paragraph numbers and accompanying text that includes the level where the insertion point is located and all levels subordinate to it, as shown in Figure 5-13. You can use a normal cut-and-paste operation to move outline paragraphs, but the WordPerfect Outline feature provides a simpler method.

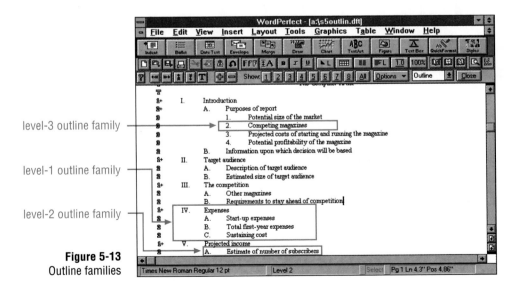

**Figure 5-13**
Outline families

## Moving an Outline Family

- Move the mouse pointer, which becomes ⇕, to the paragraph number symbol in the left margin adjacent to the outline family you want to move.
- Drag ⇕ so that the horizontal line marks the new location of the outline family.

Let's move the outline family that begins with number V.

To move an outline family:

❶ Move the mouse pointer to the "1+" symbol to the left of "V. Projected income," so the mouse pointer becomes ⇕.

❷ Press and hold down the left mouse button to highlight family V (paragraph V and the subordinate paragraphs A, B, and C below it), then drag the pointer so that the horizontal line that marks the new location of the outline family is above "IV. Expenses." See Figure 5-14. Then release the mouse button. (In other words, execute the normal "drag" operation with the mouse.)

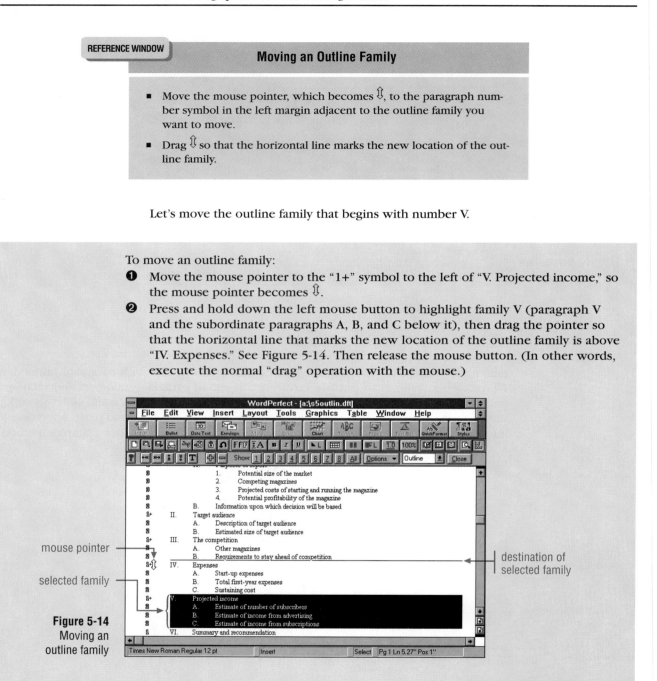

mouse pointer

destination of selected family

selected family

**Figure 5-14**
Moving an outline family

**TROUBLE?**   If you moved the wrong outline family or moved the correct outline family to the wrong location, click the Undo button on the Power Bar to undo your action. Then repeat the above steps correctly.

You have now moved the "Projected income" family above the "Expenses" family. Your next task is to move item "B. Estimate of income from advertising" below item "C. Estimate of income from subscriptions." This time let's use a method that allows you to move one paragraph at a time.

To move a single-paragraph outline family:

**①** Move the insertion point to the left of "E" in "Estimate" in paragraph IV. B. See Figure 5-15.

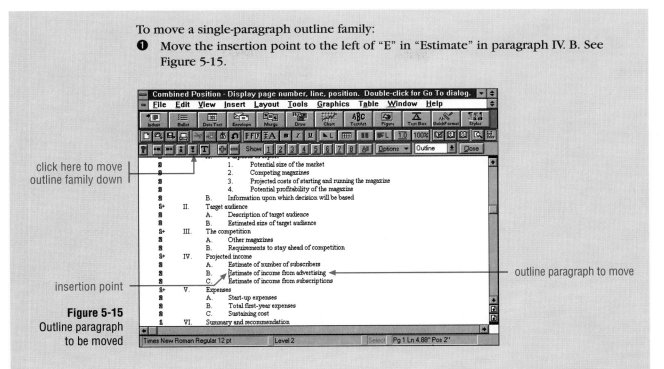

click here to move outline family down

insertion point

outline paragraph to move

**Figure 5-15**
Outline paragraph
to be moved

You will now use ⬇, the Move Down button on the Outline Bar, to move the outline paragraph.

**②** Click ⬇, the **Move Down button** on the Outline Bar. The paragraph moves down one position, so that it becomes paragraph C.

As usual, WordPerfect automatically renumbers the outline. This completes the outline.

You can now turn off the Outline feature just in case you wanted to add more text after the outline.

To turn off the Outline feature:

**①** Move the insertion point to the end of the outline, after the word "recommendation."

**②** Click the **Options button** on the Outline Bar, and click **End Outline.** The insertion point moves down to the line below the outline, and the symbol in the left margin is a "T," indicating that the insertion point is now on a text line, not in an outline paragraph.

**③** Click the **Close button** on the Outline Bar to turn off the Outline Bar.

This completes Jonathan's preparation of the outline.

**④** Save the outline as S5OUTLIN.DOC and print it.

The final version of your outline should now look like Figure 5-16.

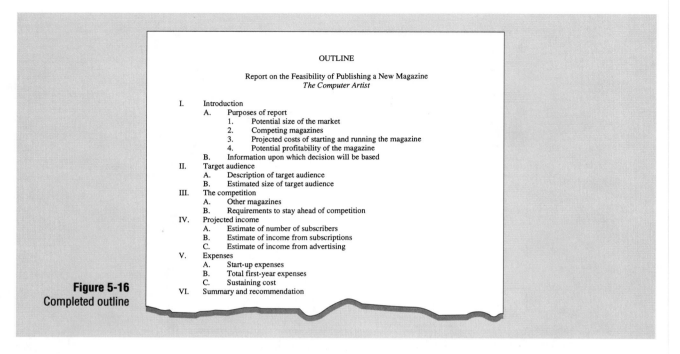

OUTLINE

Report on the Feasibility of Publishing a New Magazine
*The Computer Artist*

   I.    Introduction
        A.    Purposes of report
            1.    Potential size of the market
            2.    Competing magazines
            3.    Projected costs of starting and running the magazine
            4.    Potential profitability of the magazine
        B.    Information upon which decision will be based
  II.    Target audience
        A.    Description of target audience
        B.    Estimated size of target audience
 III.    The competition
        A.    Other magazines
        B.    Requirements to stay ahead of competition
 IV.    Projected income
        A.    Estimate of number of subscribers
        B.    Estimate of income from subscriptions
        C.    Estimate of income from advertising
  V.    Expenses
        A.    Start-up expenses
        B.    Total first-year expenses
        C.    Sustaining cost
 VI.    Summary and recommendation

**Figure 5-16**
Completed outline

*If you want to take a break* and resume the tutorial at a later time, you can exit WordPerfect. When you resume, launch WordPerfect and open S5OUTLIN.DOC into the document window.

## Using Multiple Document Windows

After approving Jonathan's revised outline, the task force agrees that Ann should begin writing the first draft of the report.

Ann wants to have the approved outline handy at all times without cluttering her desk; therefore, she decides to use the **multiple document window feature.** The multiple document window feature allows you to have up to nine document windows open at once. You can then easily switch back and forth among them. This is helpful if you want to read one document while creating another, copy text from one document to another, or edit two or more documents together. In this case, Ann will write her report in document window 2 (labeled "Document 2" on the title bar) while keeping the outline in document window 1. In that way, she will always have access to the approved outline in WordPerfect.

Let's use WordPerfect's multiple document feature to begin writing the report.

To use document window 2:

❶ Make sure the final version of the outline (S5OUTLIN.DOC) is in the document window. If it isn't, open S5OUTLIN.DOC now.

❷ Click 🗋, the **New Document button** on the Power Bar. WordPerfect opens a new, blank document window. The title bar of the WordPerfect window displays the message "Document 2 unmodified."

With blank document window 2 open, Ann is ready to start writing the report.

## Copying Text Between Document Windows

Ann can now use Document 2 to write her report and switch to Document 1 whenever she wants to see the outline. She will use the Window pull-down menu or a function-key command to switch between the two documents.

So that she doesn't have to retype the title of the report, Ann decides to copy it from the outline.

**REFERENCE WINDOW**

### Copying Text from One Document to Another

- Open each document into a document window.

- Make sure the source document window is active. If necessary, click Window and then click the name of the desired document window to display it.

- Select (highlight) the text you want to copy.

- Click the Copy button on the Power Bar.

  *or*

  Press [Ctrl][C].

- Make the target document active by clicking Window, then clicking the name of the desired document.

- Move the insertion point to the location in the target document where you want to insert the copied text.

- Click the Paste button on the Power Bar.

  *or*

  Press [Ctrl][V].

Let's copy the title from Document 1 to Document 2 using a copy-and-paste operation.

To copy text from Document 1 to Document 2:

❶ Click **Window**, then click **1 a:\s5outlin.doc - unmodified.**

❷ Select (highlight) the two lines of the title. See Figure 5-17. Make sure to select all of both lines, including the codes to center the lines. If you have selected the center codes, the highlighted region on your document window will appear as shown in Figure 5-17. If you haven't selected the center codes, the highlighted region will begin immediately with the words "Report on the . . . ." If this is the case, you might need to turn off the selection, then try again.

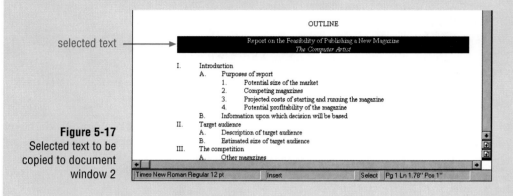

selected text →

**Figure 5-17**
Selected text to be copied to document window 2

❸  Click 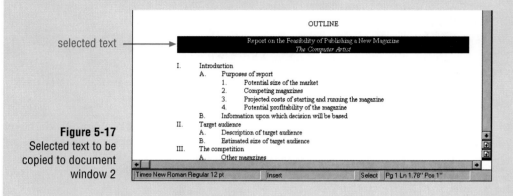, the **Copy button** on the Power Bar, or press **[Ctrl][C]**. WordPerfect copies the selected text to the Windows clipboard.

❹  Click the mouse pointer at the beginning of the document to turn off Select mode, or press **[F8]** (Select).

❺  Click **Window,** then click **2 Document2 - unmodified.**

❻  Click , the **Paste button** on the Power Bar, or press **[Ctrl][V]**. WordPerfect inserts a copy of the title of the report into Document 2. See Figure 5-18.

second document window →

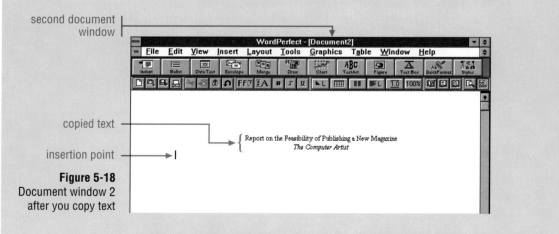

copied text →

insertion point →

**Figure 5-18**
Document window 2 after you copy text

**TROUBLE?**   If the first line of the title isn't centered, you did not select the code to center the line before you copied it. Move the insertion point immediately before the "R" in "Report," click Layout, click Line, then click Center.

These steps demonstrate that you can use the familiar copy and cut-and-paste operations, not only within a document, but also between documents.

## Using Tiled Windows

Ann decides that she would like to be able to see the outline while she is typing her report. Using the Switch command, she can easily switch between the two documents, but she can't see them both on the screen at once. To view the documents simultaneously, she will use the Tile Window feature.

To tile document windows 1 and 2:

❶ Click 📇 , the **View Button Bar button** on the Power Bar. This turns off the Button Bar and removes it from the screen, leaving more space to display the two document windows.

❷ Make sure that Document 2 still appears on your screen.

❸ Click **Window,** then click **Tile.** WordPerfect fits both document windows onto the screen, like tiles on a floor. See Figure 5-19. The active window—the one with the insertion point in it, where all editing takes place—has a highlighted title bar. In this case, Document 2 is active; a:\s5outlin.doc is inactive.

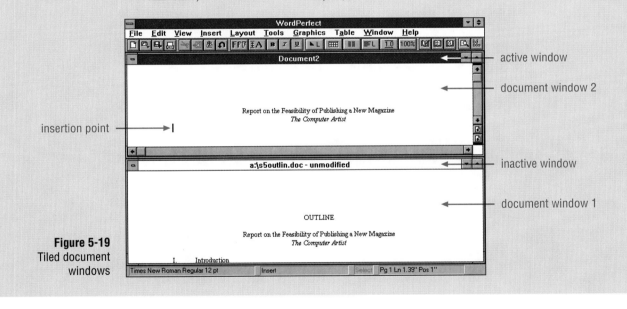

**Figure 5-19**
Tiled document
windows

Now Ann can see both documents simultaneously. She can edit only one document at a time, because the insertion point must be in one window or the other. She can, however, move the insertion point between the two windows by clicking in the window she wants to activate.

Ann decides that her report should be double-spaced, so her next task is to set double spacing for Document 2. Let's insert the format code for double spacing.

To double-space Document 2:

❶ Move the insertion point to the beginning of document window 2, before the title.

❷ Click 🔟 , the **Line Spacing button** on the Power Bar, and choose **2.0.**
The document is now double-spaced.

Next Ann wants to type a heading for the first section of her report.

To insert a heading:

❶ In Document 2, move the insertion point to the blank line below the title.

   TROUBLE?    If the insertion point won't move past the end of the second line of the title, you didn't copy the Hard Return code from the outline. With the insertion point in Document 2, turn on Reveal Codes, move the insertion point after the code for Italics at the end of the line, and press [Enter] to insert a blank line. Turn off Reveal Codes.

❷ Click ▣ , the **Bold button** on the Power Bar, to turn on boldfacing, then type **Introduction**, click ▣ again to turn off boldfacing, and press [Enter].

Ann continues to type her report in document window 2. The WordPerfect commands she carries out in the report don't affect the outline in document window 1.

In the next steps, you'll insert the remainder of Ann's draft of the report into Document 2 and maximize the document windows. To insert a file into an existing document, you do *not* use the Open command, which opens a document into a new document window. Rather, you use the Insert File command.

**REFERENCE WINDOW**

### Inserting a File into a Document Window

- Move the insertion point to the location in the document where you want to insert another document file.
- Click Insert, then click File.
- If necessary, change the disk or the directory to the location of the file that you want to insert.
- Highlight the desired file.
- Click the Insert button.
- Click the Yes button to verify that you want to insert the specified file into the current document window at the location of the insertion point.

Let's insert Ann's draft into Document 2.

To insert the remainder of the report:

❶ With the insertion point underneath the first heading ("Introduction") in Document 2 and the WordPerfect Student Disk in the disk drive, click **Insert**, then click **File.** The Insert File dialog box appears on the screen.

❷ Make sure the Drives option is set to the drive containing your Student Disk.

❸ Highlight **c5file1.dft** and click the **Insert button.**

   WordPerfect now asks you to verify that you want to insert the selected file into the current document.

❹ Click the **Yes button.** WordPerfect inserts the document file into document window 2.

Now that you're ready to work on the retrieved document, you don't need to see the outline in document window 1. So let's maximize the windows.

❺ Click ▲, the **Maximize button** in the upper-right corner of document window 2. Document window 2 now fills the entire WordPerfect screen.

❻ Click 🔲, the **View Button Bar button,** to restore the Button Bar to the screen. See Figure 5-20.

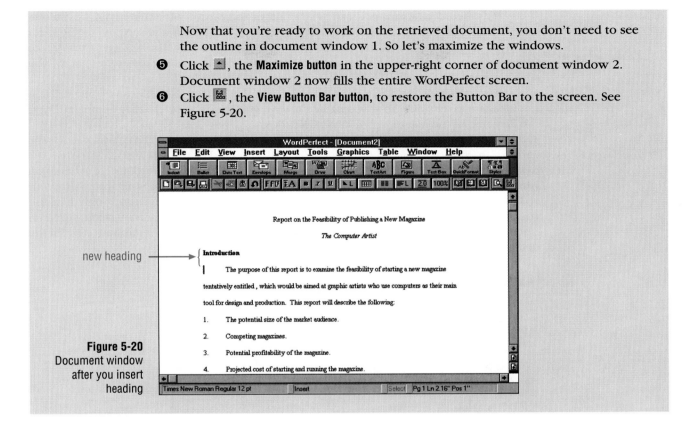

new heading

**Figure 5-20**
Document window
after you insert
heading

Take a few minutes to read the report, so you'll be familiar with its contents. (Remember, you can use draft mode to get more of the text on the screen at a time. Don't forget to switch back to page mode when you're finished.) Notice that the title of the magazine is missing from the first paragraph. You'll fix that problem later.

## Using Macros

Ann knows that while writing the feasibility study she will have to type the name of the proposed magazine, "The Computer Artist," many times. For any word-processing procedure that you use frequently—such as a series of WordPerfect commands, a word, a phrase, or a combination of commands and text—you can record a macro to perform the procedure for you. A **macro,** in its simplest sense, is a recording of keystrokes and mouse operations that you can play back at any time by pressing just a few keys.

Recording a macro to play back frequently written phrases or frequently executed commands has several advantages:

• Macros save time. By playing a macro, you can save many keystrokes and mouse operations, which means you can complete your work faster.

• Macros are accurate. When you play a macro, you don't have to worry about typos or other mistakes. If you record the macro correctly, every time you use it the keystrokes and mouse operations will play back without error.

• Macros are consistent. Macros that insert text and formatting codes create the same text and format each time.

When you record a macro, you can select one of three ways of naming it. A **keystroke macro** is a macro you name by pressing [Ctrl] or [Ctrl][Shift] and a letter or digit, for example, [Ctrl][M] or [Ctrl][Shift][8]. You can't use symbols like [Ctrl][/] or [Ctrl][Shift][=] or punctuation to name the macro. To play back a keystroke macro, you simply press [Ctrl] or [Ctrl][Shift] and the letter or digit you have chosen.

A **named macro** is a macro you name by typing a legal DOS filename (but without the filename extension). To play a named macro, you issue the Macro Play command, type the filename of the macro, and choose OK.

A **temporary macro** is a macro without a name. When WordPerfect asks you for the name of the macro to record or play, you just click Record or press [Enter].

Before you record any macros, however, you should instruct WordPerfect where you want the macros saved. Because you will want WordPerfect to save your macros to your Student Disk, let's specify drive A as the storage location. This is necessary only because you are recording macros as part of your classwork and want the macros saved to drive A. Under normal circumstances, you would want your macros saved to your hard disk, in the default directory specified by WordPerfect.

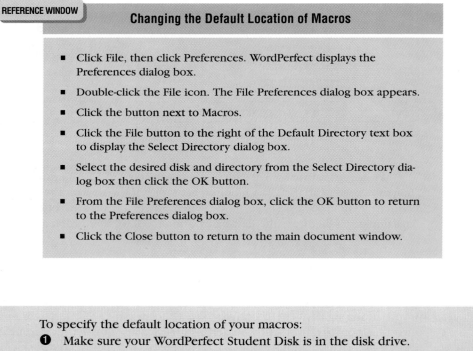

REFERENCE WINDOW

### Changing the Default Location of Macros

- Click File, then click Preferences. WordPerfect displays the Preferences dialog box.

- Double-click the File icon. The File Preferences dialog box appears.

- Click the button next to Macros.

- Click the File button to the right of the Default Directory text box to display the Select Directory dialog box.

- Select the desired disk and directory from the Select Directory dialog box then click the OK button.

- From the File Preferences dialog box, click the OK button to return to the Preferences dialog box.

- Click the Close button to return to the main document window.

To specify the default location of your macros:

❶ Make sure your WordPerfect Student Disk is in the disk drive.

❷ Click **File**, then click **Preferences**. WordPerfect displays the Preferences dialog box. See Figure 5-21.

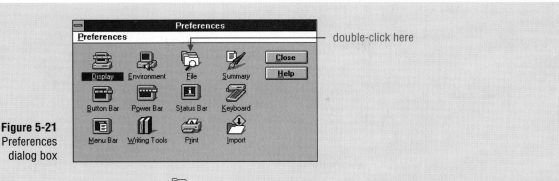

**Figure 5-21**
Preferences
dialog box

double-click here

❸ Double-click 🗁, the **File icon**. The File Preferences dialog box appears. See Figure 5-22.

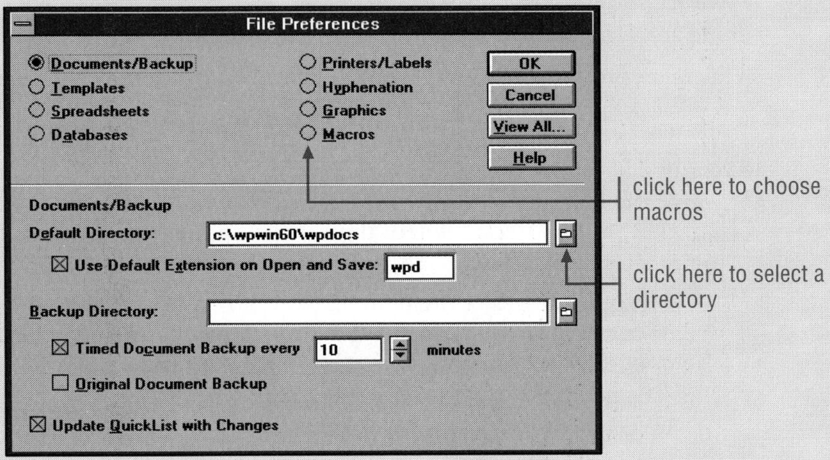

**Figure 5-22**
File preferences
dialog box

click here to choose macros

click here to select a directory

❹ Click the button next to Macros to tell WordPerfect that you want to change the directory where your macros are saved.

❺ Click 🗐, the **File button** to the right of the Default Directory text box, to display the Select Directory dialog box.

Before you go to Step 6, note the current Directory name in the upper-left corner of the dialog box. (It's probably c:\wpwin60\macros.) You will change the default directory back to this later in the tutorial.

❻ Click the **Down Arrow** to the right of the Drives text box, and click the letter of the disk drive containing your Student Disk, then click the **OK** button. WordPerfect returns you to the File Preferences dialog box.

❼ From the File Preferences dialog box, click the **OK button** again to return to the Preferences dialog box.

❽ Click the **Close button** to return to the main document window.

From now on, any macro you record will be saved to the disk in drive A.

## Recording a Keystroke Macro

In the following steps, you'll define a keystroke macro that inserts the name of the proposed magazine into Ann's report.

### Recording a Keystroke Macro

- Click Tools, click Macro, then click Record. The Record Macro dialog box appears on the screen.

- Type the name of the macro into the Name text box, then click the Record button or press [Enter].

- Record the desired mouse operations and/or keystrokes.

- Click Tools, click Macro, then click Record to turn off Macro Record.

Lets record the marco to insert the italicized name of the magazine.

To record a keystroke macro:

❶ Move the insertion point to the right of the space after the words "tentatively entitled" in the second line of the first paragraph of Ann's report. The insertion point should be immediately to the left of the comma.

As you create a macro, the commands you record are executed simultaneously in the document. If the macro inserts text, move the insertion point to the position in the document where you want that text *before* you create the macro.

❷ Click **Tools,** click **Macro,** then click **Record.** WordPerfect displays the Record Macro dialog box.

The text box labeled Name is where you type the name of the macro. Because you are going to record a keystroke macro to insert the name of the magazine, you'll use the name "ctrlm" where "ctrl" is the Control key and "m" stands for magazine.

Do not create a keystroke macro that uses the same keystrokes as a built-in WordPerfect command, for example [Ctrl][B] to turn on Bold, or [Ctrl][Shift][D] to insert the Date Code. The built-in shortcut key takes precedence over the macro, so you could create a macro which, when you try to play it, executes a built-in WordPerfect command instead. The only letters that you can use with [Ctrl] are A, M, and Y; all the other [Ctrl][*letter*] combinations are WordPerfect shortcut keys. The only letters that you cannot use with [Ctrl][Shift] are B, D, O, P, Q, S, and Z; all the other [Ctrl][Shift][*letter*] combinations are available for use in creating macros. All the [Ctrl][*digit*] and [Ctrl][Shift][*digit*] key combinations are available for use in creating macros.

❸ Press **[Ctrl][M]** to name the macro. This creates a keystroke macro, which WordPerfect saves using the filename CTRLM.WCM. (WCM stands for WordPerfect Control Macro.)

❹ Click the **Record button** or press **[Enter]**. The insertion point returns to the document window, the message "Macro Record" appears in the status bar at the bottom of the screen, and the mouse pointer becomes ⊘ when located in the document window. See Figure 5-23.

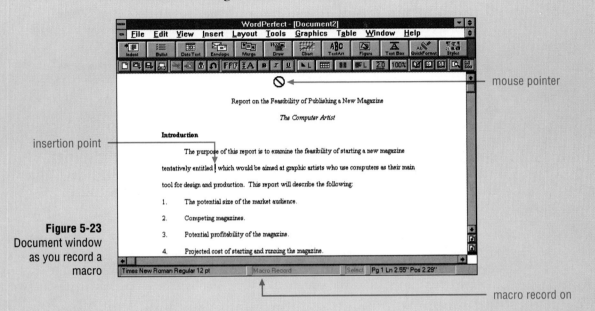

insertion point

mouse pointer

macro record on

**Figure 5-23**
Document window
as you record a
macro

The ⊘ symbol reminds you that you can't use the mouse pointer to move the insertion point while recording a macro. You can, however, use the mouse pointer to execute a command, because when you move the mouse pointer to the buttons or menu items, it becomes ⤢. Now you're ready to record the keystrokes and commands of the macro that inserts the name of the magazine.

❺ Click ⊡, the **Italics button** on the Power Bar, to turn on Italics.

❻ Type **The Computer Artist**.

❼ Click ⊡ to turn off Italics.

Now that you have recorded the keystrokes for your macro, you need to stop recording.

❽ Click **Tools**, click **Macro**, then click **Record**. The message "Macro Record" disappears from the status bar. WordPerfect now "compiles" the macro, which means that it translates the macro into a form that it can play back. WordPerfect also saves the completed macro as CTRLM.WCM on the Student Disk in drive A.

You can use this same procedure to record virtually any sequence of keystrokes or commands, such as your company or school name, your own name and address, or the commands for setting double spacing.

### Correcting an Error in a Macro

Take a moment to look at your document. Did you spell "The Computer Artist" correctly? Is it in italics? Did you remember to turn off Italics after you typed the magazine name? If you made a mistake, you can record the macro again. Let's assume you made a typing error and have to re-record the keystroke macro.

To correct an error in a macro:

❶ Delete "The Computer Artist" and the italics code that you inserted while creating the macro.

❷ Click **Tools,** click **Macro,** then click **Record** to display the Record Macro dialog box.

❸ Press **[Ctrl][M]** to name the macro, then click the **Record button** or press **[Enter].** WordPerfect displays a prompt telling you that the macro a:\ctrlm.wcm already exists and asks you if you want to replace it.

> **TROUBLE?**    If you pressed the wrong keys during this procedure, and WordPerfect doesn't prompt you that the macro already exists, click Tools, click Macro, then click Record to stop recording the macro, and then repeat Steps 2 and 3.

❹ Click the **Yes button** to instruct WordPerfect to replace the existing (erroneous) macro with a new one of the same name. WordPerfect erases the old macro file from the disk and displays "Recording Macro" on the status bar.

❺ Carefully type the correct keystrokes for your macro. In this case, click 🔲, the **Italics button** on the Power Bar, type **The Computer Artist**, and click 🔲 again.

❻ Click **Tools,** click **Macro,** then click **Record** to stop recording the macro.

If, while recording a macro, you make a simple typing error and correct it immediately by pressing [Backspace] and typing the correct characters, you don't need to stop recording the macro. WordPerfect records only the corrected keystrokes. If you make more serious errors, however, you should stop recording the macro and then start over.

### Executing a Keystroke Macro

Now that you've correctly recorded a keystroke macro, you're ready to use it to insert the magazine name into the document. To play a [Ctrl] keystroke macro, you press [Ctrl] and, while holding it down, press the letter or digit you used to name the macro.

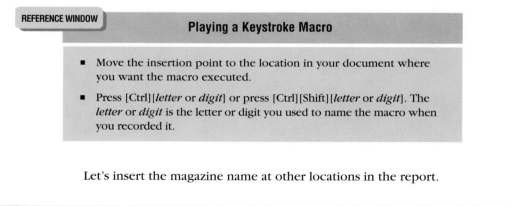

**REFERENCE WINDOW**

**Playing a Keystroke Macro**

- Move the insertion point to the location in your document where you want the macro executed.

- Press [Ctrl][*letter* or *digit*] or press [Ctrl][Shift][*letter* or *digit*]. The *letter* or *digit* is the letter or digit you used to name the macro when you recorded it.

Let's insert the magazine name at other locations in the report.

To play a keystroke macro:

❶ Move the insertion point to the location in your document where you want the macro executed. In this case, move the insertion point just to the right of the phrase "target audience" on the first line under the heading "The Target Audience." (Remember, you already inserted the magazine title in the introductory paragraph when you created the macro.)

❷ Press **[Spacebar]**, type **of**, and press **[Spacebar]**.

Now you're ready to insert the italicized name of the magazine. But instead of using the Italics command and typing the text, you'll simply execute the macro you just recorded.

❸ Press **[Ctrl][M]**. The italicized magazine title appears in the document at the insertion point.

   **TROUBLE?**   If you pressed the wrong key combination, such as [Ctrl][N], WordPerfect will not execute your macro but may execute a different command. For example, [Ctrl][N] opens a new document window. If you made that error, close the new document window and repeat Step 3.

❹ Now move the insertion point after "The potential audience" at the beginning of the second sentence of the next paragraph.

❺ Press **[Spacebar]**, type **for**, press **[Spacebar]**, then use the keystroke macro to insert *"The Computer Artist."*

❻ Click **View**, then click **Draft** to change your document window to draft mode so you can see more of the text near the page break. Then scroll your document window so the heading "The Target Audience" is near the top. Your screen should look similar to Figure 5-24.

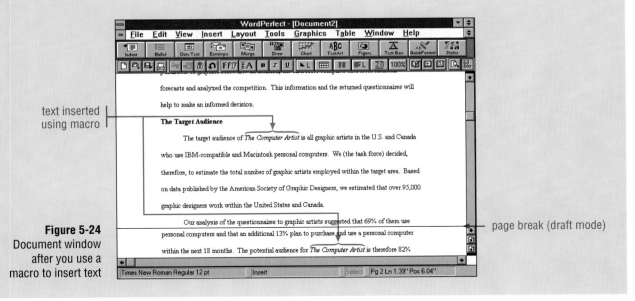

text inserted using macro

**Figure 5-24**
Document window after you use a macro to insert text

page break (draft mode)

Although Ann recorded and played the keystroke macro while writing her feasibility report, the macro is not associated exclusively with the report, but is saved to the disk as a separate file. She can use the macro in this report and in any future documents she writes using the disk on which the macro is stored.

## Creating and Executing a Named Macro

Ann knows that in this report and in other documents, she will frequently have to type the abbreviated name for Connolly/Bayle Publishing Company—C/B Publishing—so she decides to record a macro for it.

As you record this macro, you'll insert the name "C/B Publishing" into the document at the beginning of the title; later, you'll play the macro to insert the name elsewhere in the document. First let's insert a new line in the title.

To insert a new line in the title:

❶ Move the insertion point to the beginning of Ann's report.

❷ Press **[Enter]** to insert a blank line at the beginning of the document, then move the insertion point back to the beginning of the blank line.

    TROUBLE?   If the first line of the text becomes left-justified after you press [Enter], you clicked I before the "R" in "Report" instead of at the left margin (before the invisible Line Center code). With the insertion point in the first line of text, click Layout, click Line, then click Center. Then move the insertion point back to the beginning of the blank line and skip Step 3.

❸ Click **Layout**, click **Line**, then click **Center** to center the title line.

You're now ready to record the macro that will insert the abbreviated company name. Ann decides to create a named macro using the name "CB," which stands for "C/B Publishing." In a named macro you can use any legal DOS filename, but don't add an extension; WordPerfect automatically adds .WCM. Remember, if you make a mistake while recording keystrokes, turn off Record Macro and start again.

To record a named macro:

❶ Click **Tools,** click **Macro,** then click **Record** to display the Record Macro dialog box.

❷ Type **cb** and click the **Record button** or press **[Enter]** to name the macro. The message "Macro Record" appears on the status bar.

❸ Type **C/B Publishing** but do *not* press [Enter]. (If you do press [Enter], the macro will record a hard return, and every time you play the CB macro, a hard return will be inserted into the document.)

    TROUBLE?   If you made a mistake while typing the keystrokes of the macro, turn off Record Macro and start over, replacing the original CB macro with the correct version.

❹ Click **Tools,** click **Macro,** then click **Record** to stop recording the macro.

The message "Macro Record" disappears from the status bar, and WordPerfect automatically saves the macro as CB.WCM. Your screen should now look like Figure 5-25.

newly inserted text ——

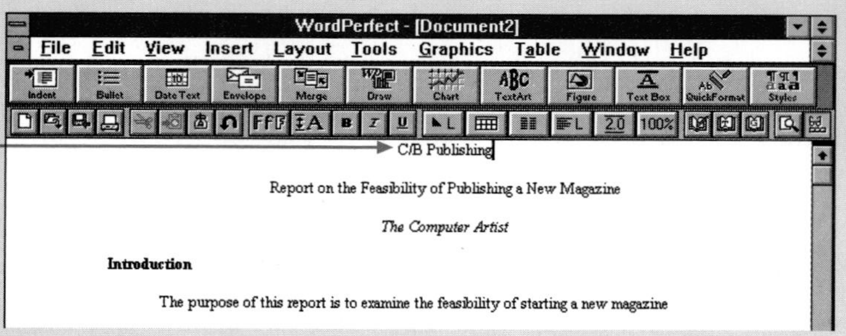

**Figure 5-25**
Document window
after you add a new
line to the title

Now that you've recorded the CB macro, you can use it to insert the name of the company at various other locations in the report.

### Playing a Named Macro

- Move the insertion point to the location in your document where you want the macro executed.
- Click Tools, click Macro, then click Play to display the Play Macro dialog box.
- Type the name of the macro and click the Play button or press [Enter].

Let's insert the company name at other locations in the report.

To play a named macro:

❶ Move the insertion point to the right of the words "will help," just above the heading "The Target Audience" and press **[Spacebar]**. This places the insertion point where you want the name "C/B Publishing" inserted.

❷ Click **Tools**, click **Macro**, then click **Play.** The Play Macro dialog box appears on the screen.

❸ Type **cb** and click the **Play button** or press **[Enter].** The macro inserts the name of the company into the document at the location of the insertion point.

Next let's use the CB macro to insert the company name elsewhere in the document.

❹ Move the insertion point to the "b" in "board of directors" in the middle of the paragraph titled "The Competition." You might want to use the Search command to find "board of directors" and then move the insertion point back to the "b."

❺ Click **Tools**, click **Macro**, then click **Play**, type **cb**, and click the **Play button** or press **[Enter].** Press **[Spacebar]** to leave a space after the company name.

Ann has now completed her work on this draft of the document and is ready to save the intermediate version to the disk.

❻ Save the document as S5FILE2.DFT.

So far you have defined two types of macros—keystroke macros and named macros. The advantage of a named macro over a keystroke macro is that you can use easy-to-remember names for it. The advantage of the keystroke macro is that it takes fewer keystrokes to play than a named macro. For example, to play the CB macro, you have to make three menu selections (Tools, Macro, Play), type "CB," and click the OK button or press [Enter]—a total of six keystrokes or mouse operations. To play the keystroke macro, you simply press [Ctrl][M]—two keystrokes.

The third type of macro—the temporary macro—is similar to the named macro, except that you don't type the name of the macro when you record it or play it.

Having completed the macros in this tutorial, you can now reset the default location of the macro files. Under normal circumstances, you would save your macros to the default path on your hard drive, and the following steps would be unnecessary. They are necessary here only because you created macros as part of your classwork and wanted them saved to drive A.

To reset the location of macro files:

❶ Click **File,** then click **Preferences.** WordPerfect displays the Preferences dialog box.

❷ Double-click 🗂, the **File icon.** The File Preferences dialog box appears on the screen.

❸ Click the button next to Macros.

❹ Click 🖫, the **File button,** to the right of the Default Directory text box. The Select Directory dialog box appears on the screen.

❺ Click the **Down Arrow** to the right of the Drives text box and click **c:,** then click the original macros directory in the Directories display box to highlight it. It is probably "c:\wpwin60\macros." The desired directory name should now appear in the Directory Name text box in the upper-left corner of the Select Directory dialog box.

TROUBLE?    If you're unsure what the default macros directory should be, consult your instructor or technical support person.

❻ Click the **OK button** to accept the selected directory name and return to the File Preferences dialog box, then click the **OK button** to return to the Preferences dialog box.

❼ Click the **Close button** to return to the main document window.

From now on, any macro you record will be saved to the original macros directory.

❽ Click **View,** then click **Page** to return your screen to page mode so that you can see both top and bottom margins.

*If you want to take a break* and resume the tutorial at a later time, you can exit WordPerfect. When you resume, launch WordPerfect and open S5FILE2.DFT into a document window.

## Using Footnotes

Jonathan prints and distributes a copy of the feasibility report to the members of the task force, who then suggest some minor revisions. They think the report should include three footnotes: the first giving the source of the data published by the American Society of Graphic Designers, the second explaining how the task force arrived at the proposed subscription rate of $55, and the third giving the source of the expenses required to start up the proposed magazine (Figure 5-26).

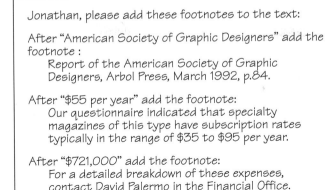

**Figure 5-26**
The task force's
footnotes for
the report

Jonathan, please add these footnotes to the text:

After "American Society of Graphic Designers" add the footnote :
    Report of the American Society of Graphic Designers, Arbol Press, March 1992, p.84.

After "$55 per year" add the footnote:
    Our questionnaire indicated that specialty magazines of this type have subscription rates typically in the range of $35 to $95 per year.

After "$721,000" add the footnote:
    For a detailed breakdown of these expenses, contact David Palermo in the Financial Office.

---

**REFERENCE WINDOW**

### Creating a Footnote

- Move the insertion point to the location in the text where you want the footnote number to appear.
- Click Insert, click Footnote, then click Create. The Footnote Bar appears at the top of the document window and the insertion point appears in a blank footnote at the bottom of the page.
- Type the text of the footnote.
- Click the Close button of the Footnote Bar to return the insertion point to the document window.

Let's create these footnotes now.

To create a footnote:
1. Move the insertion point to the location in the text where you want the footnote number to appear. In this case, move the insertion point to the right of the comma that follows the phrase "American Society of Graphic Designers" in the paragraph under "The Target Audience."
2. Click **Insert**, click **Footnote**, then click **Create**. The Footnote Bar appears at the top of the document window, the footnote number appears in the text, and the insertion point appears in a blank footnote at the bottom of the page. See Figure 5-27. The footnote is separated by a short horizontal line from the main body of the document, and the footnote number, both in the text and in the footnote, appears as a superscript.

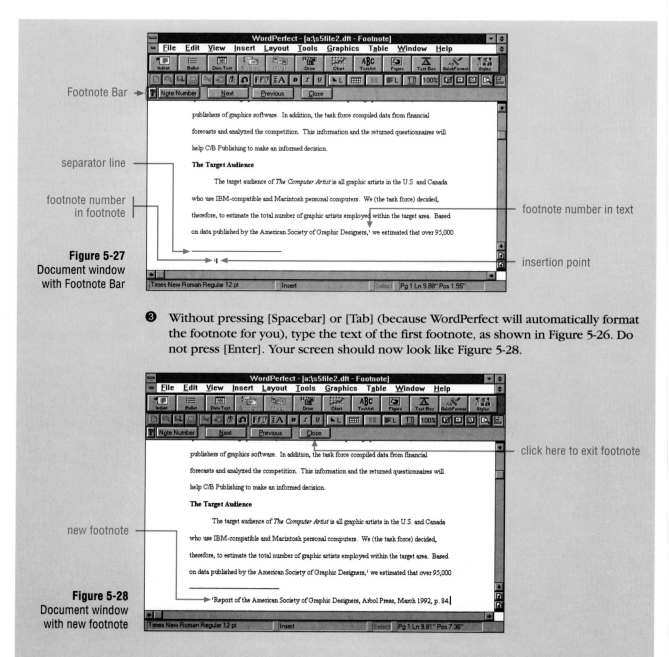

Footnote Bar →

separator line

footnote number in footnote

footnote number in text

insertion point

**Figure 5-27**
Document window with Footnote Bar

❸ Without pressing [Spacebar] or [Tab] (because WordPerfect will automatically format the footnote for you), type the text of the first footnote, as shown in Figure 5-26. Do not press [Enter]. Your screen should now look like Figure 5-28.

click here to exit footnote

new footnote

**Figure 5-28**
Document window with new footnote

TROUBLE?   If you made a mistake, you can use any of WordPerfect's editing features to modify the footnote. Your screen might not look exactly like Figure 5-28. Because of differences in font sizes and printers, the phrase "American Society of Graphic Designers," may appear elsewhere on page 1 or even near the top of page 2.

❹ Click the **Close button** of the Footnote Bar to return the insertion point to the document window.

WordPerfect has automatically inserted the correct footnote number into the body of the report and formatted the text of the footnote at the bottom of the page.

### Editing a Footnote

After typing the first footnote, Jonathan remembers that the report cited in the footnote was published in 1993, not in 1992. The footnote given to him by the task force is incorrect. Thus, he needs to edit the footnote to make this correction.

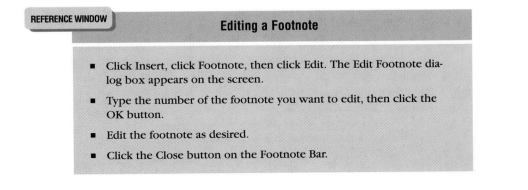

**REFERENCE WINDOW**

**Editing a Footnote**

- Click Insert, click Footnote, then click Edit. The Edit Footnote dialog box appears on the screen.

- Type the number of the footnote you want to edit, then click the OK button.

- Edit the footnote as desired.

- Click the Close button on the Footnote Bar.

Let's edit the first footnote in Jonathan's report.

To edit a footnote:

❶ Click **Insert**, click **Footnote**, then click **Edit.** The Edit Footnote dialog box appears on the screen. See Figure 5-29.

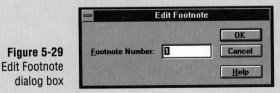

**Figure 5-29**
Edit Footnote
dialog box

❷ Make sure the Footnote Number text box contains the number 1, because you want to edit footnote number 1, then click the **OK button.**

The Footnote Bar again appears on the screen, and the insertion point appears within the footnote you created earlier.

❸ Using the WordPerfect insertion-point movement and edit keys, change "1992" to "1993."

❹ Click the **Close button** on the Footnote Bar to exit the footnote and return to the main body of the document.

The text of footnote 1 is now correct.

## Adding a New Footnote

Jonathan now wants to add the second and third footnotes.

To add a footnote:

❶ Move the insertion point to the space after the final "r" in the phrase "$55 per year" in the second paragraph under "Projected income."

❷ Click **Insert**, click **Footnote**, then click **Create**. The Footnote Bar again appears on the screen, and WordPerfect inserts a new, blank footnote at the bottom of page 3.

❸ Type the text of the second footnote, as shown in Figure 5-26. Your screen should now look like Figure 5-30.

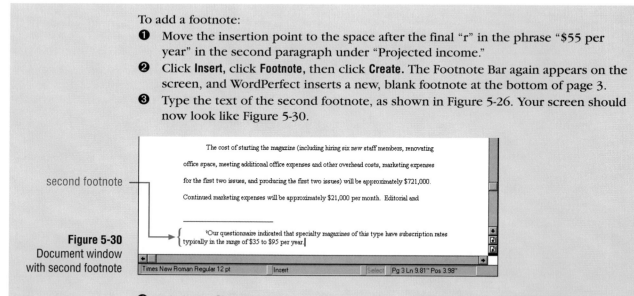

second footnote

**Figure 5-30**
Document window
with second footnote

❹ Click the **Close button** of the Footnote Bar to exit the footnote and return to the main body of the document.

❺ Repeat Steps 1 through 4 to create the third footnote, shown in Figure 5-26. Put this footnote after the period following the number "$721,000" in the paragraph headed "Expenses."

## Benefits of the Footnotes Feature

Using the Footnotes feature provides three benefits:
- WordPerfect automatically numbers the footnotes. If you add a footnote anywhere in the document, delete a footnote, or move a footnote, WordPerfect automatically renumbers all the footnotes consecutively.
- WordPerfect automatically formats the footnote text at the bottom of the page.
- WordPerfect allows you to edit the footnote.

What is true of footnotes is also true of **endnotes,** which are notes printed at the end of the document rather than at the bottom of each page. You can create and edit endnotes the same way you do footnotes, except that you would select Endnotes rather than Footnotes from the Insert menu.

To delete a footnote, you move the insertion point to the footnote number in the document and use the deletion keys to delete the footnote code. When you delete a footnote number, WordPerfect automatically deletes the text of the footnote and renumbers the remaining footnotes consecutively.

To move a footnote, you move the insertion point to the footnote, turn on Reveal Codes, highlight the footnote code, and use a regular cut-and-paste block operation to move the footnote to another point in your document. Again, WordPerfect automatically renumbers the footnotes.

# Using Hyphenation

When text is full-justified, WordPerfect inserts small spaces between words and characters to keep the lines of text aligned along the right margin. Sometimes this causes unsightly "rivers," or blank areas, in the text which distract the reader. Similarly, when text is left-justified, an extremely ragged right edge may occur (Figure 5-31). To solve these problems, you can use WordPerfect's automatic Hyphenation feature. With Hyphenation on, long words that would otherwise wrap to the next line are divided in two, so that part of the word stays on the original line. Thus, the occurrence of "rivers" or of extremely ragged right margins is decreased.

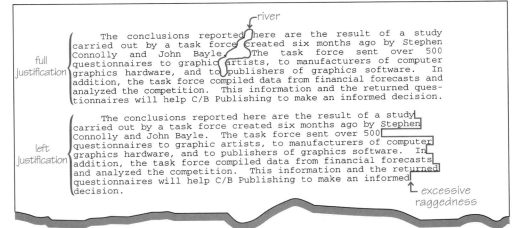

**Figure 5-31**
Text with a "river"
and excessively
ragged right margin

When you turn on Hyphenation and then move the insertion point through your document, WordPerfect analyzes each word that falls at or near the end of a line and checks to see if it should be wrapped to the next line, kept on the same line without hyphenation, or hyphenated. If WordPerfect needs help in deciding how to hyphenate a word, a Position Hyphen dialog box appears on the screen to ask you where or if you want the word hyphenated.

As the final step in formatting his document, Jonathan decides to turn on Hyphenation to minimize raggedness along the right margin of the report. You should turn on Hyphenation as the last step in preparing the final version of a document; otherwise, WordPerfect will constantly interrupt you with hyphenation prompts as you type and modify the text.

REFERENCE WINDOW

### Hyphenating a Document

- Move the insertion point to where you want hyphenation to begin, usually at the beginning of the document.

- Click Layout, click Line, then click Hyphenation. The Line Hyphenation dialog box appears on the screen.

- If desired, change the Hyphenation Zone.

- Click the checkbox to the left of Hyphenation On to turn on Hyphenation.

- Click the OK button to exit the Line Hyphenation dialog box.

Let's add hyphenation to Jonathan's report.

To turn on Hyphenation:

❶ Move the insertion point to the beginning of the document.

Hyphenation occurs only from the point in the document where you position the insertion point the end of the document. Because you want to hyphenate the entire document in this case, you should move the insertion point to the beginning of the document.

❷ Click **Layout**, click **Line**, then click **Hyphenation.** The Line Hyphenation dialog box appears on the screen. See Figure 5-32.

click here to turn on Hyphenation ⊢

**Figure 5-32**
Line Hyphenation
dialog box

Line Hyphenation

☐ Hyphenation **O**n

Hyphenation Zone
Percent **L**eft:    10%
Percent **R**ight:    4%

OK
Cancel
**H**elp

❸ Click the checkbox to the left the Hyphenation On to turn on Hyphenation.

The **hyphenation zone** specifies which words should wrap to the next line and which words should be hyphenated. Any word that extends past the right margin will wrap to the next line unless the word begins before the left hyphenation zone and extends past the right hyphenation zone. See Figure 5-33. The larger the hyphenation zone, the fewer words will be hyphenated; the smaller the hyphenation zone, the more words will be hyphenated. A hyphenation zone set to the default values of 10% on the left and 4% on the right is acceptable for most circumstances. For instructional purposes, let's decrease the hyphenation zone in order to increase the amount of hyphenation.

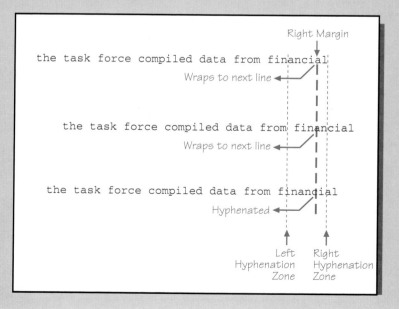

**Figure 5-33**
Hyphenation zone

❹ In the Line Hyphenation dialog box, change the Percent Left value to **8%** and the Percent Right value to **3%**.

❺ Click the **OK button** to return to the document window.

❻ Move the insertion point to the end of the document, forcing WordPerfect to hyphenate the entire document, as necessary.

As the insertion point moves through the document, WordPerfect automatically hyphenates some words. The words that WordPerfect selects for hyphenation depend on the type and size of the font you're using.

If WordPerfect's hyphenation dictionary doesn't recognize a particular word that needs hyphenation, WordPerfect stops and asks you for help in positioning the hyphen. You can then instruct WordPerfect where to hyphenate, or you can choose not to hyphenate the word at all. For example, WordPerfect might stop at a word like "Stanislowski" and display the Position Hyphen dialog box, shown in Figure 5-34.

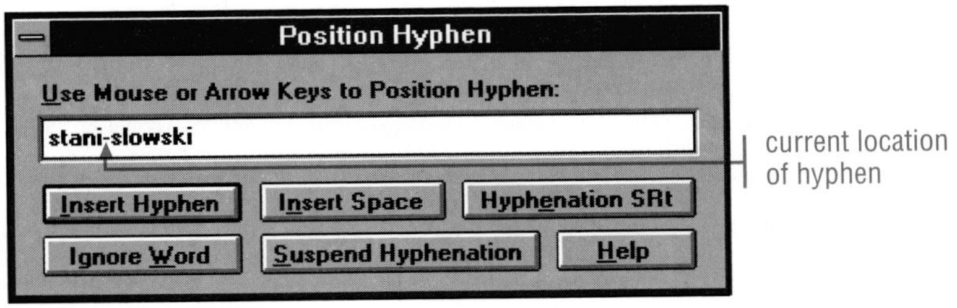

**Figure 5-34**
Position Hyphen
dialog box

If the Position Hyphen dialog box appears on your screen, you should position the hyphen where you want it using the mouse pointer or the arrow keys, then click the Insert Hyphen button. On the other hand, if you decide that you don't want to hyphenate the word, you can click the Ignore Word button. If you have inadvertently typed two words together, for example, "productionexpenses," instead of "production expenses," you can position the hyphen between the two words and then click the Insert Space button.

For example, if WordPerfect stopped at "Stanislowski" (a proper noun that doesn't appear in WordPerfect's hyphenation dictionary), you would press [→] to move the hyphen so the word in the dialog box is Stani-slowski. If you press [→] and the hyphen doesn't move to the right, WordPerfect is telling you that you have reached the maximum size for the partial word to fit on the current line.

If you make a mistake in hyphenating a word, move the insertion point to the word and delete the hyphen.

This completes the feasibility report, the final version of which is shown in Figure 5-35. Your document may look slightly different because of differences in font size and hyphenation. Ann and Jonathan are now ready to save and print the document and exit WordPerfect.

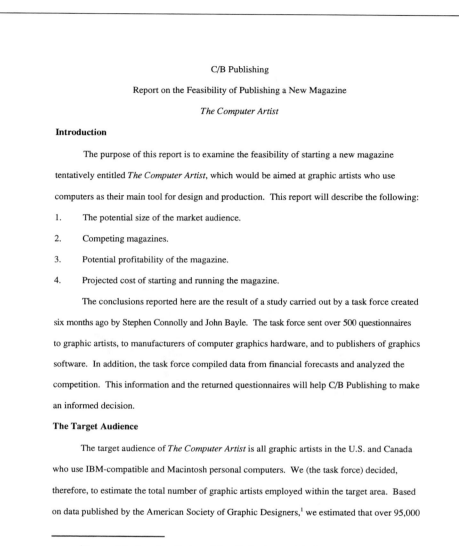

C/B Publishing

Report on the Feasibility of Publishing a New Magazine

*The Computer Artist*

**Introduction**

The purpose of this report is to examine the feasibility of starting a new magazine

tentatively entitled *The Computer Artist*, which would be aimed at graphic artists who use

computers as their main tool for design and production.  This report will describe the following:

1.    The potential size of the market audience.

2.    Competing magazines.

3.    Potential profitability of the magazine.

4.    Projected cost of starting and running the magazine.

The conclusions reported here are the result of a study carried out by a task force created

six months ago by Stephen Connolly and John Bayle.  The task force sent over 500 questionnaires

to graphic artists, to manufacturers of computer graphics hardware, and to publishers of graphics

software.  In addition, the task force compiled data from financial forecasts and analyzed the

competition.  This information and the returned questionnaires will help C/B Publishing to make

an informed decision.

**The Target Audience**

The target audience of *The Computer Artist* is all graphic artists in the U.S. and Canada

who use IBM-compatible and Macintosh personal computers.  We (the task force) decided,

therefore, to estimate the total number of graphic artists employed within the target area.  Based

on data published by the American Society of Graphic Designers,[1] we estimated that over 95,000

_____

[1]Report of the American Society of Graphic Designers, Arbol Press, March 1993, p. 84.

**Figure 5-35**
Final version of the
feasibility report
(page 1)

graphic designers work within the United States and Canada.

Our analysis of the questionnaires to graphic artists suggested that 69% of them use personal computers and that an additional 13% plan to purchase and use a personal computer within the next 18 months. The potential audience for *The Computer Artist* is therefore 82% (69% + 13%) of 95,000, or a total of 78,000 artists. We expect that this number will increase in the coming years because nearly 100% of the new graphic artists coming into the field will use computers on the job, while those retiring tend to be the artists who don't use computers. In the next five years, the target audience could number over 100,000.

**The Competition**

About eight trade magazines regularly cover the subjects of graphics software, desktop publishing, and graphic design, but no magazine published today focuses specifically on graphic design using personal computers. From experience with other professional magazines that C/B Publishing has published under similar circumstances, we expect that 12% of the potential audience will initially subscribe to the new magazine. We believe, however, that as the number of computer-based graphic designers increases, other publishers will certainly recognize this growing market and launch new magazines of their own. For this reason, the success of *The Computer Artist* will largely depend on our securing a commitment from the C/B Publishing board of directors to aggressive marketing and adherence to high publication standards. We must secure this commitment if we hope to increase or even maintain our subscription level two or three years into circulation. Being the first magazine to tap this market will help us, but we must be ever vigilant of the competition.

**Projected Income**

Our income from *The Computer Artist* has two sources, subscriptions and advertising.

**Figure 5-35**
Final version of the
feasibility report
(page 2)

From the estimated size of the potential audience (78,000 graphic designers in the U.S. and Canada) and the expected percentage of subscribers (12%), we project that we will have 9400 subscribers within the first year of publication. Assuming a subscription rate of $55 per year[2] and 9400 subscribers, the potential income from subscriptions will be $517,000.

Results of the questionnaires sent to manufacturers of computer graphics hardware and to publishers of graphics software were very encouraging. We have verbal commitments for full-page, half-page, and quarter-page advertisements from several large hardware and software companies who market graphics programs, laser printers, plotters, soft fonts, printer cartridges, and optical character recognition software. The marketing members of the task force are confident that with effort and focus, they can sell all of our advertisement space in *The Computer Artist*.

We have budgeted 16 of the 64-page issues for ad space. If we fill all 16 pages in 12 issues per year, and if we assume an average gross income per page of $4000, the total revenues from page advertisements will be approximately $768,000 per year.

The total projected income from publication of the magazine will, therefore, be approximately $1,285,000 per year.

**Expenses**

The cost of starting the magazine (including hiring six new staff members, renovating office space, meeting additional office expenses and other overhead costs, marketing expenses for the first two issues, and producing the first two issues) will be approximately $721,000.[3]

---

[2]Our questionnaire indicated that specialty magazines of this type have subscription rates typically in the range of $35 to $95 per year.

[3]For a detailed breakdown of these expenses, contact David Palermo in the Financial Office.

**Figure 5-35**
Final version of the
feasibility report
(page 3)

Continued marketing expenses will be approximately $21,000 per month. Editorial and production expenses (based on our experience with our other magazines of similar size and format) will be approximately $44,000 per month. The total expense the first year will, therefore, be about $1,371,000, and the repeating expense after the initial investment will be about $780,000 per year.

**Summary and Recommendation**

*The Computer Artist* is a magazine that fits within the mission of C/B Publishing. We have the knowledge and experience necessary to publish this magazine.

The financial analysis given above suggests that the first year's expenses will exceed income by about $86,000. But in subsequent years, the income will exceed expenditures by about $505,000.

Based on the above analysis, we recommend publication of the new magazine *The Computer Artist.*

**Figure 5-35**
Final version of the
feasibility report
(page 4)

To save and print the document and exit WordPerfect:

❶ Save the document as S5FILE3.REP and print it.

❷ Click **File**, then click **Exit.**

If you haven't saved either or both of the documents within the WordPerfect document windows, WordPerfect displays a prompt asking if you want to save the document.

❸ If WordPerfect displays a prompt, make sure that you save any valuable documents.

# Questions

1. Define or describe each of the following terms:
   a. paragraph number in an outline
   b. outline level
   c. outline family
2. Why would you want to prepare an outline?
3. How would you begin an outline?
4. What is the Outline Bar?
5. How would you turn on Hyphenation?
6. When is the best time, during preparation of a document, to turn on Hyphenation?
7. What is the hyphenation zone?
8. Is the number of hyphenated words in your document increased or decreased when you increase the width of the hyphenation zone?
9. What is a macro?
10. List the four major steps used in recording a macro.
11. Describe how to execute each of the following types of macros:
    a. Keystroke macro
    b. Named macro
    c. Temporary macro
**E** 12. Name one advantage and one disadvantage of each of the three types of macros.
13. What would you do to have two different documents open at the same time?
14. How would you view two different documents on the screen simultaneously?
15. Suppose you needed to copy several nonconsecutive sentences and paragraphs from one document to another. How would you perform that task?
16. What is
    a. a footnote?
    b. an endnote?
17. How would you create a footnote?
**E** 18. How would you create an endnote?
19. If WordPerfect needs help in positioning the hyphen when Hyphenation is on, the Position Hyphen dialog box appears on the screen with a suggested position for the hyphen. What would you do to change the position of the hyphen and instruct WordPerfect to continue checking through the document?

# Tutorial Assignments

Open the file T5FILE1.DFT from your WordPerfect Student Disk and do the following:
1. With T5FILE1.DFT in Document 1, write an outline of the report in Document 2, switching between your outline and the report as needed and using WordPerfect's Outline feature. Use the headings of the report to help you in preparing the outline.
2. Save the outline as S5FILE4.OTL.
3. Print the outline.
4. In Document 1, position the insertion point at the beginning of the report and turn on Hyphenation. Move the insertion point to the end of the document and respond to any Position Hyphen dialog boxes that WordPerfect displays.
5. Change the location of macro files to your Student Disk in drive A.
**E** 6. Record a macro named TITLE.WCM that makes a heading boldface and switches it to all uppercase letters (for example, "Introduction" to "**INTRODUCTION**"). *Hint:* To bold or capitalize existing text, you have to select the text first.

7. Use the macro you just created to bold and capitalize the other four major headings in the report in Document 1.

8. Record a keystroke macro ([Ctrl][Shift][A]) that inserts the magazine name *Aldus Magazine* (in italics). Use the macro to insert the magazine name at each occurrence of double question marks (??) in the report in Document 1. Then delete the double question marks.

9. Restore the default location of macro files to C:\WPWIN60\MACROS or to the path given by your instructor or technical support person.

10. Save the report as S5ALDUS.DFT.

11. Print the report.

12. Move the insertion point to the right of the comma after the phrase "Aldus Magazine" in the first paragraph of the report. Insert the following footnote: *Aldus Magazine* is published by Aldus Corporation, 411 First Avenue South, Seattle, WA 98104-2871.

13. Move the insertion point to the right of the article title "Pattern Recognition" (and just after the close quote) and insert the following footnote: Olav Martin Kvern, "Pattern Recognition," *Aldus Magazine,* Vol. 4, No. 2, 1993, p. 64.

14. Move the insertion point to the right of the article title "Beating Banding" (and just after the close quote) and insert the following footnote: Greg Stumph, "Beating Banding," *Aldus Magazine,* Vol. 4, No. 2, 1993, p. 41.

15. Save the document as S5ALDUS.REP.

16. Print the final version of the document.

17. Close all the documents so that only the blank Document 1 window is open.

Open the file T5FILE2.DFT from your WordPerfect Student Disk and do the following:

18. With T5FILE2.DFT in Document 1, write an outline of the report in Document 2, switching between your outline and the report as needed and using WordPerfect's Outline feature. Use the headings and subheadings of the report to help you in preparing the outline.

19. Save the outline as S5FILE5.OTL.

20. Print the outline.

21. In Document 1, position the insertion point at the beginning of the report and turn on Hyphenation. Move the insertion point to the end of the document and respond to any Position Hyphen dialog boxes that WordPerfect displays.

22. Change the location of macro files to your Student Disk in drive A.

23. Move the insertion point to the first occurrence of "??" in the document, delete the double question marks, and then record a macro named FH.WCM that inserts the phrase "Aldus FreeHand" into the document.

24. Use the macro to insert "Aldus FreeHand" at the other occurrences of "??" in the document.

25. Restore the default location of macro files to C:\WPWIN60\MACROS or to the path given by your instructor or technical support person.

26. Move the insertion point immediately to the right of the first occurrence of "Aldus FreeHand" in the first paragraph of the report and insert the following endnote: Aldus FreeHand is published by Aldus Corporation, 411 First Avenue South, Seattle, WA 98104-2871.

27. Move the insertion point immediately to the right of "EPS" in the first paragraph of the report and insert the following endnote: EPS stands for Encapsulated PostScript. PostScript is a printer language developed by Adobe Systems, Inc.

28. Move the insertion point immediately to the right of "TIFF" in the first paragraph of the report and insert the following endnote: TIFF stands for Tag Image File Format.

29. Save the report as S5FILE6.REP.

30. Print the report.

# Case Problem

## 1. Justification Report for New Office in San Jose

Charles Mataoa is an assistant business manager for the Custom Cables and Connectors Company. He wants to write a justification report, in memorandum format, to propose that the company open a new business office in San Jose, California.

Do the following:

1. Open the document P5SANJOS.DFT, the first few paragraphs of a draft of the justification report.
2. Write a short outline of the contents of the report to this point, using the headings of the report as your guide. Make sure to use WordPerfect's Outline feature in creating your outline.
3. Save the outline as S5SANJOS.OTL.
4. Print the outline.
5. Move the insertion point to the right of the tab on the "SUBJECT:" line in the heading of the memo. Type "A proposal for" and press [Spacebar].
6. Change the location of macro files to your Student Disk in drive A.
7. Record a named macro (with the name SJ) that inserts the phrase "a new office in San Jose."
8. Move the insertion point to all occurrences of double question marks (??) in the document, delete the double question marks, and use your macro to insert the phrase "a new office in San Jose."

**E**   9. Using the first level-1 heading ("Executive Summary"), create a temporary macro you can use to convert level-1 headings to boldface and all uppercase letters, for example, **"EXECUTIVE SUMMARY."** *Hint:* You record and play a temporary macro in exactly the same way you do a named macro, except you don't include a name in the Record Macro or Play Macro dialog boxes.
10. Use the temporary macro to format the other level-1 headings in the report.
11. Restore the default location of macro files to C:\WPWIN60\MACROS or to the path given by your instructor or technical support person.
12. Insert a footnote reference after the period at the end of the phrase "is well documented." The text for the footnote is the following: See the report, "Networking Hardware Needs in the San Jose Area," attached.
13. Save the draft of the report as S5SANJOS.DFT.
14. Print the draft of the report.

## 2. Outline for a Presentation on Time Management

Valerie Mitchell graduated six years ago with a bachelor's degree in business management and started working as a consultant for T.I.M.E. (Training In Management Excellence), a company that gives management training seminars, especially on time management. Besides giving time-management seminars as part of her job, Valerie also speaks frequently on a voluntary basis at local service organizations, self-help groups, churches, and not-for-profit foundations. Right now, she is creating an outline for a speech she will give to United Way workers in two weeks.

Do the following:

1. Open the draft of the outline of Valerie's time-management speech, P5TIME.OTL, from your WordPerfect Student Disk.
2. Move the insertion point into the outline region of the document, and turn on the Outline Bar.
3. Move the outline family that begins with the paragraph "IV. Time is Money" to paragraph II. (The current paragraph II, "The Ten Key Principles of Time Management," should become paragraph III.)

4. After the outline family that now begins "III. The Ten Key Principles of Time Management," insert the following new paragraph: IV. Applying the Ten Key Principles

5. After the outline family that begins "V. The Ten Secondary Principles," insert the following new paragraph: VI. Applying the Ten Secondary Principles

6. After the phrase "The Ten Secondary Principles," create a footnote reference. The text of the footnote should be the following: Adapted from Lester R. Bittel, *Right on Time! The Complete Guide for Time-Pressured Managers,* McGraw-Hill, New York, 1991.

7. At the phrase "Time is Money," create a footnote reference. The text of the footnote should be: Adapted from Stephanie Culp, *How to Get Organized When You Don't Have the Time,* Writer's Digest Books, Cincinnati, 1986.

**E** 8. Convert the last outline paragraph (which begins "This speech requires . . .") to normal text. *Hint:* Use 🔳, the Body Text button on the Outline Bar.

**E** 9. Insert a blank line between the last outline paragraph and the text paragraph at the end of the document, so that the sentence "This speech requires . . ." is separated from the outline by a blank line. *Hint:* Insert a new line as you would in any normal document. If an outline paragraph number appears in the blank line, use 🔳 to convert the outline paragraph to text.

10. Save the outline as S5TIME1.OTL.

11. Print the outline.

**E** 12. Move the insertion point anywhere within the outline region of the document and click the 1 button to the right of Show on the Outline Bar, and print the outline. Then click the 2 button to the right of Show. As you can see, the numbered buttons to the right of Show allow you to show or hide the various paragraph levels.

## 3. Report on Using a Word Processor

Write a short report (about 700–1,000 words) on the advantages and disadvantages of using a word processor in writing lengthy reports. In writing your report, do the following:

1. Write an outline before you write the report, then revise the outline after you have completed your report. Submit both versions of the outline to your instructor, along with the report itself.

2. Double-space the report.

3. Create a title page that contains the title of your report, your name, the title of your course, the date, and any other information your instructor wants you to include.

4. Include at least two footnotes giving the source of information for your report. Sources of information can be books, articles, or personal communication with family members, teachers, or other students.

5. Include a header and page numbering in the report.

6. Change the location of macro files to your Student Disk in drive A.

7. Record and use at least two keystroke or named macros to help you write the report. *Hint:* The macros may be recordings of phrases commonly used in the report or of format codes for creating headings or titles. Make sure you copy the macro files onto the disk that you submit to your instructor.

**E** 8. Click File, then click Document Info to determine the word count of your report. If necessary, revise your report to make sure it has 700–1000 words.

9. Turn on and use Hyphenation for the entire document.

10. Restore the default location of macro files to C:\WPWIN60\MACROS or to the path given by your instructor or technical support person.

11. Save the report as S5WP.REP.

12. Print the report.

# T U T O R I A L   6

**OBJECTIVES**

In this tutorial you will:
- Create data files and form files for merging
- Merge files to create form letters and labels
- Desktop-publish a document
- Create columns
- Use typographic characters
- Import graphics from another Windows file

# Merging Documents and Desktop Publishing

## Writing a Sales Form Letter and Creating a Newsletter

**CASE**   **Sanders Imports, Inc.**   Immediately after graduating from high school, Whitney Sanders began working as a clerk in an import store owned by International Products, Ltd. (IPL), a large corporation with franchises throughout the United States. During the next six years, Whitney worked her way up to international buyer for IPL. Her job entailed traveling to foreign countries, especially Central and South America, to purchase specialty items, such as rugs, wood carvings, picture frames, ceramics, and cast-iron furniture.

Although she enjoyed her job and was successful at it, Whitney wanted to go back to school and earn a degree in business administration. She felt a degree would improve her professional opportunities. So after seven years with IPL, Whitney resigned and went back to school full time. Four years later, she received a B.S. with a major in business administration and a minor in international relations from Howard University in Washington, D.C.

With degree in hand, Whitney started her own import business, called Sanders Imports, Inc. (SII), headquartered in Gaithersburg, Maryland, just outside Washington, D.C. Now, 18 months later, her business is healthy and growing.

Among Whitney's successes are large contracts with three major discount department stores and more than 20 accounts with specialty shops throughout the United States. Whitney markets to these clients by publishing a quarterly catalog that contains color photographs and descriptions of the items she imports. She also publishes a quarterly newsletter called *SII Update,* which updates catalog information and provides news of the company. Several members of her staff help write and edit the newsletter.

Last week Whitney added two major items, Mexican iced-tea glass tumblers and Ecuadorian hand-carved chess sets, to her catalog. She is not scheduled to publish another catalog for two months, but she wants to inform her customers immediately about these highly marketable new products. She decides to write a letter to her clients (Figure 6-1) and prepare a one-page issue of *SII Update* (Figure 6-2).

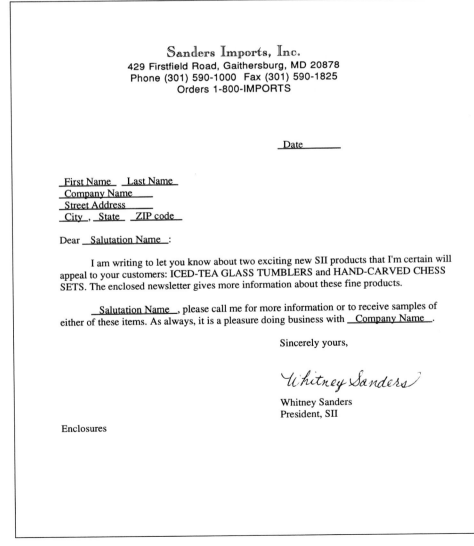

**Figure 6-1**
Whitney's form letter

# SII Update

Vol. 3  No. 2                                                    July 18, 1994

## Sanders Survives Peruvian Jungle

Our CEO and favorite world traveler, Whitney Sanders, risked the humidity, the heat, and the Shining Path (a violent activist group) to venture into the jungles of Peru last December. "It was really not that big a risk," said our courageous chief exec. "Lima and Cuzco are pretty safe, especially since I have a Peruvian friend who helps keep me out of trouble. Besides, the wonderful deals on alpaca rugs and gold jewelry were worth the effort."

Don't let her kid you. It was her side trips to the ancient Inca ruins and the high mountain landscapes that made the trip worth the effort. Besides, December is summer in Peru, so she missed Washington's wintery ice storms. She's no dummy.

Anyway, she did make some marvelous deals on rugs and jewelry. You'll be hearing the details in a future newsletter.

On her way home from Peru, she stopped off in Ecuador and struck a great deal on hand-carved chess sets. She also spent a few days in Mexico City, where she discovered some beautiful glass tumblers. You'll read more about these items elsewhere in this newsletter. We know you'll love them—just as Whitney loved her South American "business trip."

## Guillermo Catlán Joins SII

Sanders Imports, Inc., has increased its number of international buyers from two to three. We welcome Guillermo (Bill) Catlán to our ranks. Bill hails from San Diego. He graduated from La Jolla High School and from San Diego State University with a degree in International Relations. While in college, he attended the Semester Abroad program in Madrid, Spain, where he got first-hand training in buying and selling international products.

While a university student, Bill's main hobby was competing in triathlons, (long-distance swimming, biking, and running). He continues that hobby here in Washington with greater enthusiasm but with slower times. "It's an outlet from the pressures of life," says svelte Bill. "I don't try to be competitive any more—except in the business world!"

Along with running in triathlons, he's running all around Central and South America finding quality items at bargain prices. His hard work and keen business sense help you, our clients, get the best deals available in the import business.

## New Additions to SII Catalog

ICED-TEA GLASS TUMBLERS
- 16 oz.
  - Finely painted patterns
  - Imported from Mexico
  - Suggested retail price $24.75 per set of four
  - Your price $14.80 per set

These drinking glasses have heavy glass bottoms and clear sides and come in six different patterns. They are sold in attractive cardboard carrying boxes. Because they are attractive yet inexpensive, these tumblers will sell well.

HAND-CARVED CHESS SETS
- Staunton pattern
- Weighted and felted bases
- Detailed knights
- Natural-grain wood
- U.S. Chess Federation approved
- Imported from Quito, Ecuador
- Suggested retail price $55.95
- Your price $28.15 per set

These sets are almost identical in appearance to the sets imported from India that sell for twice this amount.

**Figure 6-2**
Whitney's finished newsletter

## Planning the Documents

Whitney wants to write a **form letter,** which is a letter that contains information pertinent to a large number of people (in this case, Whitney's clients) but that also contains information specific to the addressee. The specific information in Whitney's form letter is an inside address and salutation for each client and, in the body of the letter, the client's first name and company name.

Whitney will use WordPerfect's Merge features to generate her form letters. In general, a **merge** is an operation that combines information from two documents to create many slightly different final documents.

The merge operation employs two separate documents: a form file and a data file. A **form file** is a document—such as a letter or a contract—that, in addition to text, contains merge codes to mark where special information—such as a name or an address—will be inserted. In Whitney's case, the form file will be like Figure 6-1, except that the document will contain merge codes to mark the location of the client's name, address, and other data.

A **data file** is a document that contains information, such as names, street addresses, cities, states, and ZIP codes, that will be merged into the form file. In Whitney's case, the data file will be an address list. The data file contains merge codes to help WordPerfect merge the information into the form file.

A final document produced by merging information from a data file into a form file is called a **merged document** (Figure 6-3).

## Merge Operations

During a merge operation, the **merge codes** in the form file instruct WordPerfect to retrieve specific information from the data file. For example, one merge code in the form file might retrieve a name, while another merge code might retrieve a street address. For each set of data (for instance, a name and address) in the data file, WordPerfect usually creates a separate page in the merged document. Thus, if Whitney's data file has, for example, five sets of names and addresses of clients, the merge will produce five different letters, each with a different client name and address and each on a separate page in the merged document.

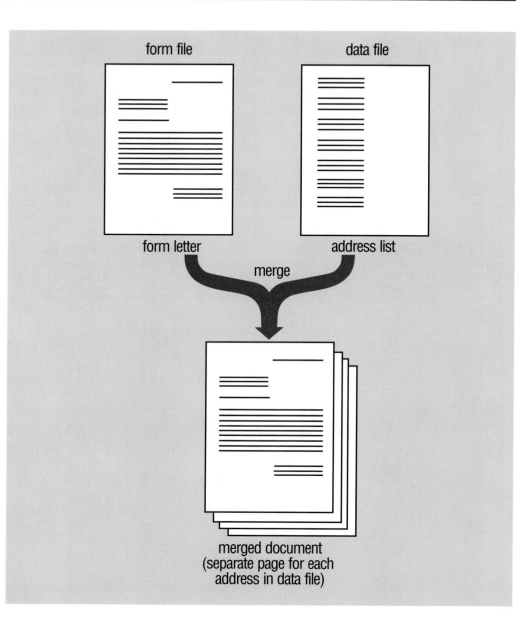

**Figure 6-3**
Merging a form file and
a data file to create the
merged document

### Records and Fields

The set of data about one individual or object in the data file is called a **record.** In Whitney's data file, each record contains information about one client (Figure 6-4). Each item within a record is called a **field.** One field might be the client's name, another field the client's street address, another field the client's city, and so forth. For a merge operation to work properly, every record in the data file must have the same set of fields.

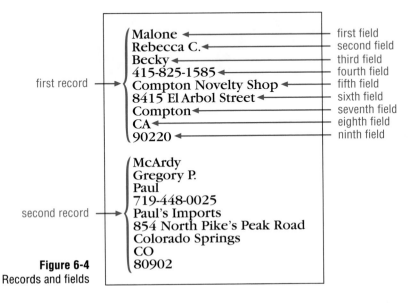

**Figure 6-4**
Records and fields

Data files are not limited to records about clients. You could create a data file with inventory records, records of suppliers, records of equipment, and so forth. Once you understand how to manage and manipulate the records in data files, you'll be able to use them for many different types of applications.

### Merge Codes

Form files usually contain merge codes that instruct WordPerfect which fields of each record to retrieve and where to place those fields in the merged document. Form files may also contain merge codes that insert the current date, accept input from the keyboard, and perform other functions. Data files, on the other hand, contain merge codes that label the fields in each record, as well as mark the end of each record.

Figure 6-5 is a table of some of the most common merge codes. Each merge code consists of the code itself, which appears in the form file or data file as a red, uppercase word, often followed by a set of parentheses. You don't actually type the merge code; instead you use WordPerfect's Merge Codes command to insert the code in your form file or data file.

| Common WordPerfect Merge Codes | |
| --- | --- |
| **Merge Code** | **Action** |
| DATE | Inserts current date |
| FIELD *(FieldName)* | Retrieves data from field named *FieldName* in data file |
| FIELDNAMES *(FieldName1; FieldName2; FieldName3;...)* | Lists names of fields in data file |
| ENDFIELD | Marks end of the field |
| ENDRECORD | Marks end of the record |

**Figure 6-5**

Some merge codes require you to supply a parameter. For example, the FIELD code requires a parameter that names a particular field within a record. You type the parameter between the parentheses following the name of the code. Hence, a form file containing the merge code FIELD(FirstName) would instruct WordPerfect to retrieve the field named "FirstName" from a record in the data file. The merge code FIELDNAMES(Name;Address;Phone) would list the fields named "Name," "Address," and "Phone," in that order, for each record within the data file. The DATE code, which inserts the current date into the document, doesn't require a parameter and therefore appears in a form file without parentheses. In the following section, you'll use merge codes to create the data file.

## Creating a Data File

As Whitney acquires new and potential clients, she types information about them into a WordPerfect data file. She can then merge the data file with a form file to generate her sales letters.

Figure 6-6 shows the first five records of Whitney's data file. As you can see, the file contains merge codes that specify the names of the fields and mark the ends of fields and records. Notice that each field ends with an ENDFIELD code, and each record ends with an ENDRECORD code and hard page break.

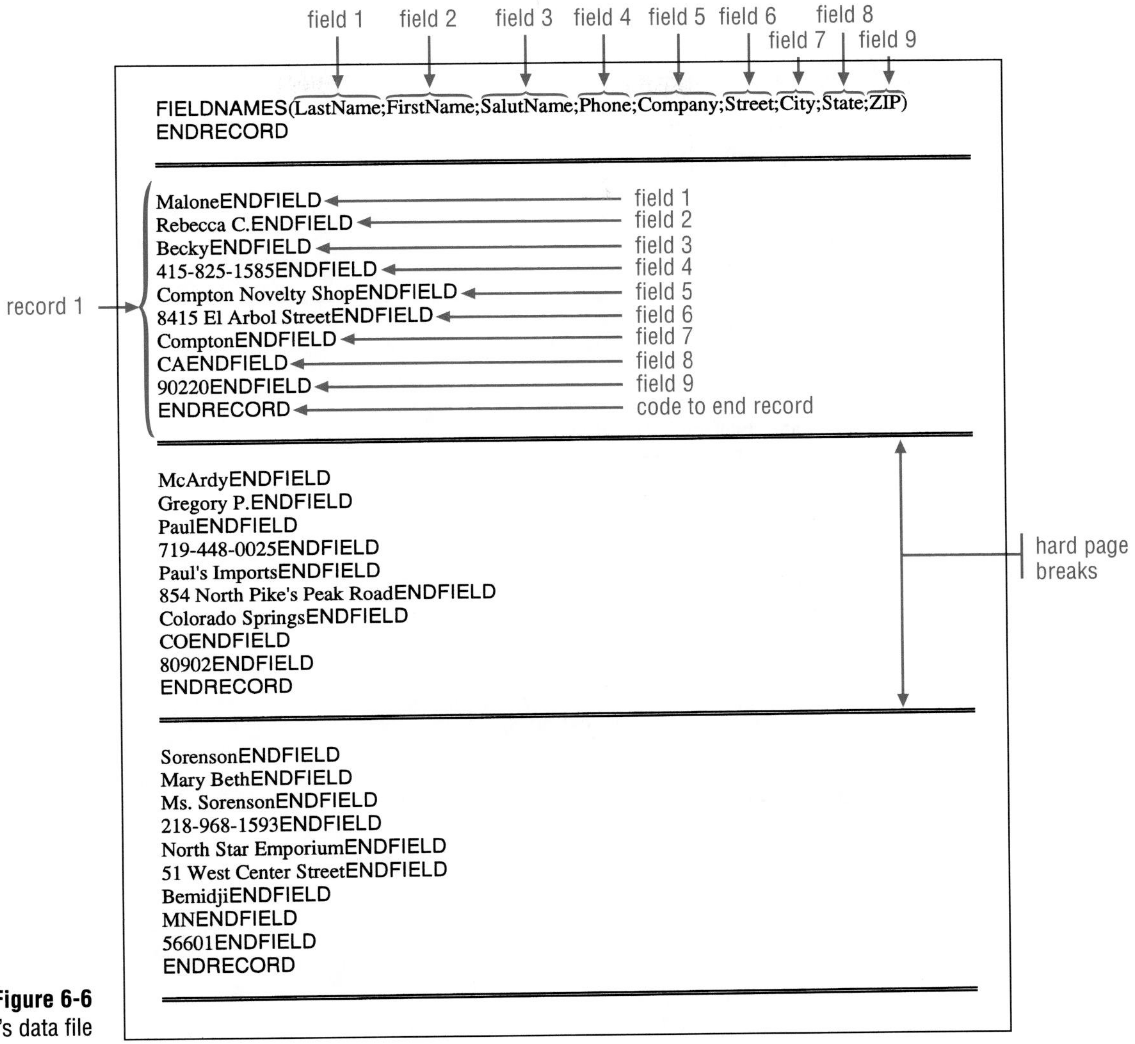

field 1   field 2   field 3   field 4   field 5   field 6   field 8
                                          field 7 | field 9

FIELDNAMES(LastName;FirstName;SalutName;Phone;Company;Street;City;State;ZIP)
ENDRECORD

MaloneENDFIELD ◄————————————————— field 1
Rebecca C.ENDFIELD ◄——————————— field 2
BeckyENDFIELD ◄——————————————— field 3
415-825-1585ENDFIELD ◄—————————— field 4
Compton Novelty ShopENDFIELD ◄————— field 5
8415 El Arbol StreetENDFIELD ◄—————— field 6
ComptonENDFIELD ◄————————————— field 7
CAENDFIELD ◄—————————————————— field 8
90220ENDFIELD ◄————————————————— field 9
ENDRECORD ◄————————————————— code to end record

record 1

McArdyENDFIELD
Gregory P.ENDFIELD
PaulENDFIELD
719-448-0025ENDFIELD
Paul's ImportsENDFIELD
854 North Pike's Peak RoadENDFIELD
Colorado SpringsENDFIELD
COENDFIELD
80902ENDFIELD
ENDRECORD

hard page
breaks

SorensonENDFIELD
Mary BethENDFIELD
Ms. SorensonENDFIELD
218-968-1593ENDFIELD
North Star EmporiumENDFIELD
51 West Center StreetENDFIELD
BemidjiENDFIELD
MNENDFIELD
56601ENDFIELD
ENDRECORD

**Figure 6-6**
Whitney's data file

PilarENDFIELD
F. EmilioENDFIELD
EmilioENDFIELD
602-433-8878ENDFIELD
Grand Canyon ImportsENDFIELD
4851 Caibab Highway Suite 210ENDFIELD
FlagstaffENDFIELD
AZENDFIELD
86001ENDFIELD
ENDRECORD

GutanovENDFIELD
MikhailENDFIELD
MikeENDFIELD
404-921-3722ENDFIELD
Peachtree EmporiumENDFIELD
88 Peachtree PlazaENDFIELD
AtlantaENDFIELD
GAENDFIELD
30304ENDFIELD
ENDRECORD

**Figure 6-6**
Whitney's data file
(continued)

**REFERENCE WINDOW**

### Creating a Data File

- Click the Merge button on the Button Bar to display the Merge dialog box.

- Click the Data button to display the Merge Bar along the top of the document window and the Create Data File dialog box.

- Type the names of the fields that you want in each record of the data file, click the Add button after typing each field name, then click the OK button to accept the field name list and display the Quick Data Entry dialog box.

- Enter data into your data file, click the Close button to close the Quick Data Entry dialog box, then click the Yes button to save the file, enter the desired filename, and click the OK button.

Let's create the data file of information about Whitney's clients. First we'll insert the merge code FIELDNAMES, which names the fields.

To create a data file:

❶ Launch WordPerfect and make sure a blank document window appears on the screen.

❷ Click [icon], the **Merge button** on the Button Bar. WordPerfect displays the Merge dialog box. See Figure 6-7.

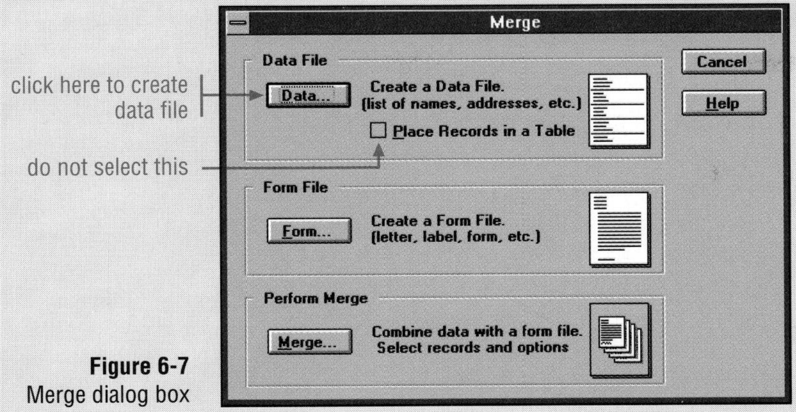

**Figure 6-7**
Merge dialog box

click here to create data file

do not select this

❸ Make sure the checkbox next to Place Records in a Table is *not* selected. You don't want to place the records in a table; you want to type the records as normal text.

❹ Click the **Data button** to create a data file.

The Merge Bar appears along the top of the document window, and the Create Data File dialog box appears on the screen. See Figure 6-8. This dialog box appears automatically so you can insert the FIELDNAMES merge code. The Field Name List is currently blank because you haven't specified any field names yet.

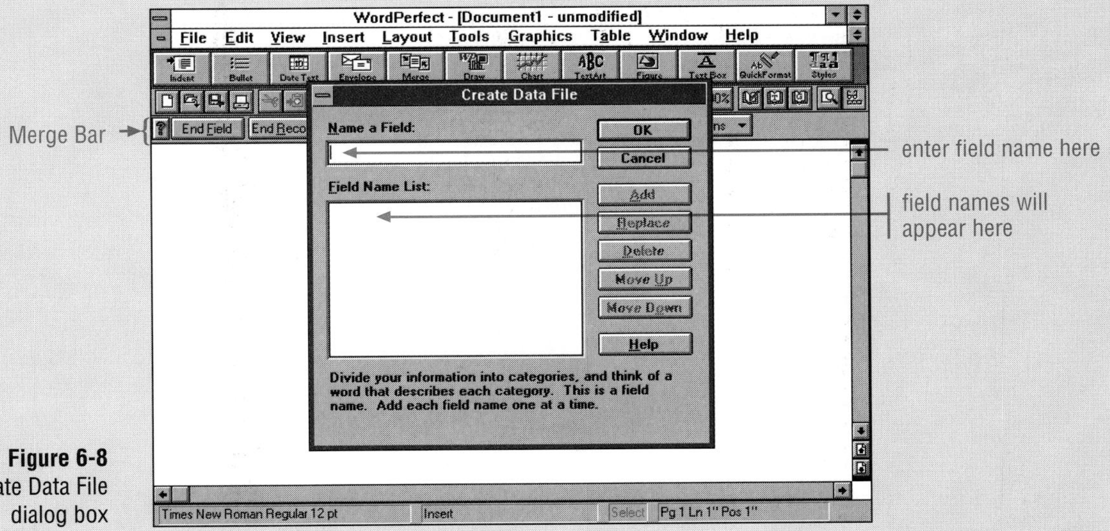

Merge Bar

enter field name here

field names will appear here

**Figure 6-8**
Create Data File
dialog box

❺ Type **LastName** and click the **Add button** or press **[Enter]** to specify that the first field in each record will contain the last name of the client.

The field name "LastName" appears in the Field Name List within the dialog box. The Create Data File dialog box stays on the screen and prompts you to enter another field name.

**TROUBLE?**    If you made a typing mistake, for example, typed "LastName" as two separate words, "Last Name," click the mistyped word in the Field Name List to highlight it, and click the Delete button. With the mistyped word deleted, click I in the Name a Field text box, and type the field name correctly.

**❻** Type **FirstName** and click the **Add button** or press **[Enter]** to add the second field name to the list.

**❼** Type **SalutName** and click the **Add button** or press **[Enter]**. This tells WordPerfect that the third field in each record will contain the name you want to use in the salutation of a letter.

**❽** Type the names of the remaining fields into the dialog box. The field names are "Phone," "Company," "Street," "City," "State," and "ZIP." The Create Data File dialog box should now look like Figure 6-9. Check the list carefully to make sure your field names are identical to the ones in Figure 6-9.

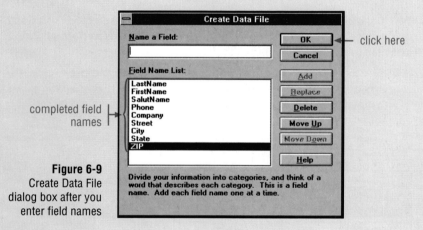

**Figure 6-9**
Create Data File
dialog box after you
enter field names

**TROUBLE?**    If any of the field names is wrong, click the incorrect field name. The name becomes highlighted and appears in the Name a Field text box. Edit or replace the name in the Name a Field text box, then click the Replace button.

**❾** Click the **OK button** in the Create Data File dialog box to accept the field name list.

The FIELDNAMES merge code is inserted into the document window, and WordPerfect displays the Quick Data Entry dialog box. See Figure 6-10. You can't see the FIELDNAMES merge code in the document because it is behind the dialog box.

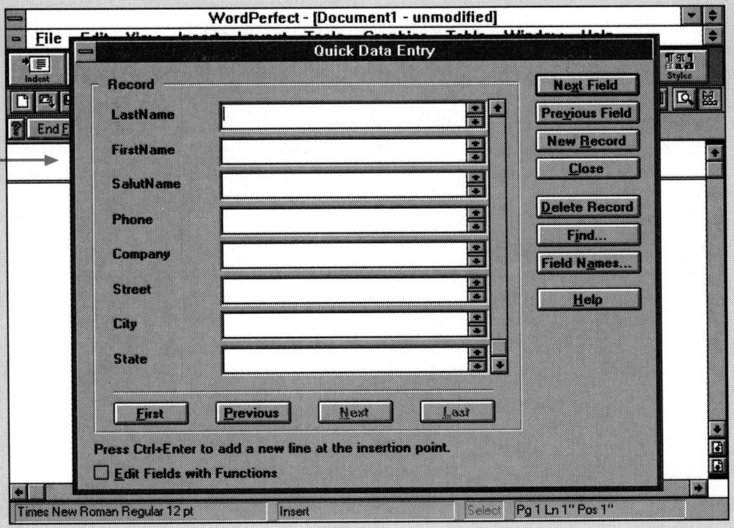

FIELDNAMES merge code in document window hidden behind dialog box

**Figure 6-10**
Quick Data Entry
dialog box

The data file you have just created contains no records yet; you have only named each field. You'll now enter the data for each record.

## Entering Data into a Data File

Whitney is now ready to enter client information into the file, as shown in Figure 6-6. Let's begin by entering data into the first record.

To enter data into a record:

❶ With the insertion point positioned in the LastName text box in the Quick Data Entry dialog box, type **Malone.** This is the last name of the first client.

❷ Click the **Next Field button** or press **[Enter]** to move the insertion point to the FirstName text box.

Notice that pressing [Enter] moves the insertion point to the next field. If you wanted to include more than one line of information within a field, you would press [Ctrl][Enter] rather than just [Enter]. For example, if you wanted to include a department name and the company name on two separate lines in the Company field, you would type the department name, press [Ctrl][Enter], and then type the company name. In this particular file, we will need only one line per field.

❸ Type **Rebecca C.** and press **[Enter]** to insert the client's first name and move the insertion point to the next field. Notice that the FirstName field also contains any middle name or middle initial of the client.

❹ Type **Becky** and press **[Enter]** to insert the client's salutation name and move the insertion point to the next field name. If you know the client well, you would include the first name or a nickname (as you have done here). If you don't know the client well, you would use a more formal salutation name, such as "Ms. Malone."

❺ Type **415-825-1585** and press **[Enter]** to enter the client's phone number and move to the next field name.

❻ Type **Compton Novelty Shop** and press **[Enter]** to enter the client's company name, then type **8415 El Arbol Street** and press **[Enter]** to enter the street address.

❼ Type **Compton** and press **[Enter]**, then type **CA** and press **[Enter]** to insert the city and state into the record.

The list of Records scrolls up so the ZIP field name appears in the dialog box.

❽ Type **90220**. This inserts the ZIP code into the record.

You have now entered all the data for the first record.

❾ Click the **New Record button** or press **[Enter]** to display a blank Quick Data Entry box.

Normally, you would start entering the data for the second record at this point. In this case, however, Whitney realizes she has now worked for about 15 minutes on the document and wishes to save an intermediate version.

To close the Quick Data Entry dialog box and save the data file:

❶ Click the **Close button** in the Quick Data Entry dialog box.

WordPerfect asks you if you want to save the document to disk.

❷ Click the **Yes button.** The Save Data File As dialog box appears on the screen.

❸ If necessary, insert your Student Disk into drive A and choose drive A.

❹ Type **s6addr.dat** into the Filename text box and click the **OK button.** WordPerfect saves the data file to the disk.

The filename extension .DAT reminds you that this is a data file.

Your screen should now look like Figure 6-11. Notice the FIELDNAMES and ENDRECORD merge codes at the top of the document window, with a hard page break underneath them. Below these codes is the first record in your data file. At the end of each field is the ENDFIELD code, and at the end of the record is the ENDRECORD code and a hard page break. The merge codes appear in red. The insertion point is in position for the first field (LastName) of the second record. The status bar gives the name of the field in which the insertion point is located.

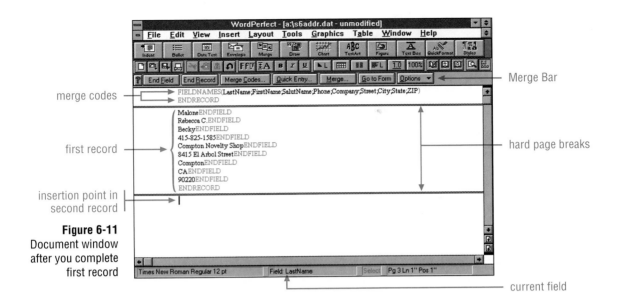

merge codes

first record

insertion point in second record

Merge Bar

hard page breaks

current field

**Figure 6-11**
Document window after you complete first record

*If you want to take a break* and resume the tutorial at a later time, you can exit WordPerfect. When you resume, launch WordPerfect and open S6ADDR.DAT into a document window.

## Creating Additional Records

Having saved an intermediate version of her data file, Whitney is now ready to add more records to it.

To add a new record to a data file:
1. Make sure the data file S6ADDR.DAT is in a document window.
2. Move the insertion point to the end of the document. Your screen should look like Figure 6-11.
3. Click the **Quick Entry button** on the Merge Bar. The Quick Data Entry dialog box again appears on the screen.
4. Type **McArdy** into the LastName text box, and press **[Enter]**.
5. Continue entering information into the dialog box until it looks like Figure 6-12.

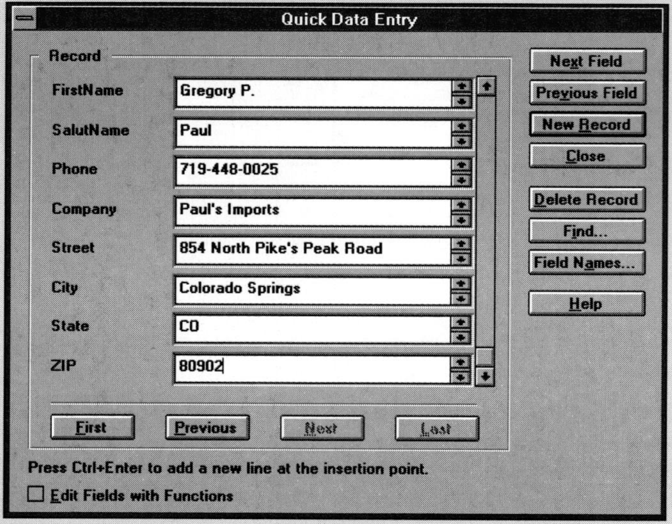

**Figure 6-12**
Quick Data Entry
dialog box after
you enter data for
the next record

❻ Click the **New Record button** or press **[Enter]** after typing the ZIP code.

❼ Type the data for the last three records following this same procedure. Use the information in Figure 6-6.

**TROUBLE?**   If you pressed [Enter] after typing the ZIP code for Mikhail Gutanov, don't worry. A blank record will appear in the Quick Data Entry dialog box. Just ignore this and go on to the next step.

❽ After completing the last record, click the **Close button** to close the Quick Data Entry dialog box and return to the document window.

❾ At the prompt to save the changes to the disk, click the **Yes button,** and save the data file using the default filename S6ADDR.DAT. When WordPerfect prompts you that the file already exists, click the **Yes button** to replace the previous version of the file with the current version.

You should now see the last record of the data file (Mikhail Gutanov) on your screen. Look through all the records of your data file. If you see an error, use the usual insertion-point movement and editing commands to correct the error. Then save the document to the disk again, this time using the Save command.

Although Whitney's data file will eventually contain numerous records (one for each of her many clients), S6ADDR.DAT contains only five records, a sufficient number to demonstrate WordPerfect's Merge features.

## Creating a Form File

A **form file** contains text and merge codes. Creating a form file is similar to creating any other type of WordPerfect document, except that you use the Merge Codes command to insert the merge codes into it.

**Creating a Form File**

- Open a new document window.

- Click the Merge button on the Button Bar to display the Merge dialog box.

- Click the Form button, then click the OK button.

- If you like, type the name of the data file that you want to associate with the form file and click the OK button. Otherwise, click the circle next to the word None, then click the OK button.

- Type the text and insert the desired merge codes into the form file.

Let's begin by inserting the DATE merge code.

To set up a form file and insert the DATE code:

❶ Click 🖹, the **New Document button** on the Power Bar, to create a new, blank document window, then press **[Enter]** until the insertion point is at Ln 2.5" or lower.

This leaves room for the letterhead at the top of the page. If your paper doesn't have a letterhead, the blank space will keep the text of the letter from being too high up on the page.

❷ Press **[Tab]** until the insertion point is at Pos 4.5", where Whitney wants the date to appear.

Now you're ready to instruct WordPerfect to set up a form file.

❸ Click 📑, the **Merge button** on the Button Bar. WordPerfect displays the Merge dialog box. Before inserting merge codes, you have to tell WordPerfect what kind of merge file your document is.

❹ Click the **Form button.** This informs WordPerfect that the current document is a form file. The Create Merge File dialog box appears on the screen.

❺ Make sure the button to the left of Use File in Active Window is selected, then click the **OK button.** The Create Form File dialog box appears. This dialog box allows you to select a data file to be associated with the current form file.

❻ Type **a:\s6addr.dat**, then click the **OK button.**

WordPerfect designates the current document as a form file and displays the Merge Bar along the top of the document window.

Notice that the Merge Bar displayed for a form file has different buttons than the Merge Bar displayed for a data file.

**TROUBLE?**    If WordPerfect informs you that the data file was not found, click the OK button and check the spelling of "s6addr.dat" to make sure you've typed the correct filename. Then click the OK button again in the Create Form File dialog box.

You're now ready to insert the DATE merge code into the form file.

❼ Click the **Date button** on the Merge Bar. WordPerfect inserts the DATE code into the document. See Figure 6-13. The DATE code appears in red to remind you that it is a code, not text. (On a monochrome monitor, the DATE code looks exactly like text.)

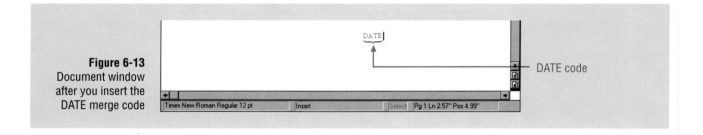

**Figure 6-13**
Document window
after you insert the
DATE merge code

DATE code

When Whitney executes the merge, WordPerfect will insert the current date at the location of the DATE code on each copy of the letter.

Next, you need to insert the FIELD merge code into the form file.

To insert the FIELD merge code into the form file:

❶ Press **[Enter]** three times to leave space between the date and the inside address.

❷ Click the **Insert Field button** on the Merge Bar. The Insert Field Name or Number dialog box appears on the screen. See Figure 6-14.

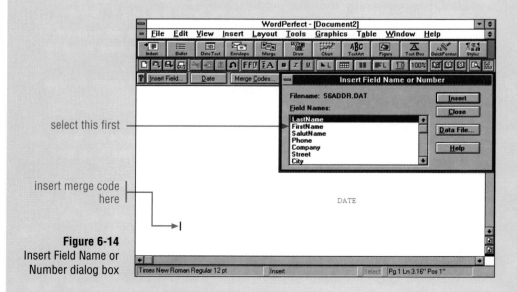

select this first

insert merge code here

**Figure 6-14**
Insert Field Name or
Number dialog box

❸ Click **FirstName** in the Field Names list, then click the **Insert button** at the right of the dialog box. WordPerfect inserts the FIELD(FirstName) merge code into the document at the location of the insertion point. The Insert Field Name or Number dialog box stays on the screen but is inactive.

**TROUBLE?**   The insertion point returns to the document window, but you might not be able to see it if it is behind the Insert Field Name or Number dialog box. If this is the case, simply drag the dialog box out of the way.

When Whitney executes the merge, WordPerfect will retrieve the first name—which includes the first name and a middle name or initial—from the data file and insert it into the document at that location.

Now you're ready to insert the other FIELD merge codes for the inside address and salutation.

To insert the FIELD merge codes for the inside address and salutation:

❶ Press **[Spacebar]** to insert a space between the first name and the last name of the client.

❷ Click **LastName** in the Field Names list, then click the **Insert button** on the Insert Field Name or Number dialog box. The FIELD(LastName) merge code is inserted into the document.

❸ Press **[Enter]** to move the insertion point to the next line.

❹ Double-click **Company** in the Field Names list. The FIELD(Company) merge code appears in the document. Notice that double-clicking the field name is equivalent to clicking the name and then clicking Insert.

**TROUBLE?**     If you insert the wrong name from the Field Names list, use the usual deletion keys to delete the merge code, then repeat the command to insert the FIELD merge code.

❺ Press **[Enter]** and insert the FIELD(Street) code. Insert the other merge codes as shown in Figure 6-15. Don't forget to insert the comma after the City field code. If necessary, scroll the Field Name List in the Insert Field Name or Number dialog box so you can see the desired field name.

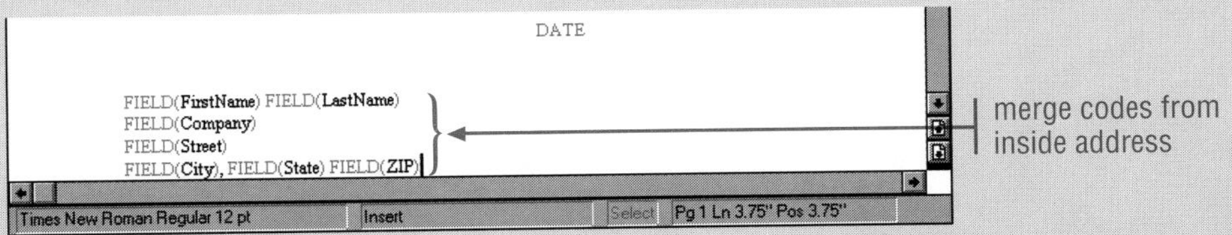

**Figure 6-15**
Document window after you insert the FIELD codes for the inside address

DATE

FIELD(FirstName) FIELD(LastName)
FIELD(Company)
FIELD(Street)
FIELD(City), FIELD(State) FIELD(ZIP)

merge codes from inside address

Times New Roman Regular 12 pt          Insert          Select   Pg 1 Ln 3.75" Pos 3.75"

❻ Press **[Enter]** twice to double-space between the inside address and the salutation.

❼ Type **Dear**, press **[Spacebar]**, insert the FIELD(SalutName) merge code, then type **:** (a colon). This completes the salutation of the form file.

❽ Press **[Enter]** twice to double-space after the salutation.
Carefully check your document to make sure all the field names are correct.

❾ Click the **Close button** on the Insert Field Name or Number dialog box. Your screen should look like Figure 6-16.

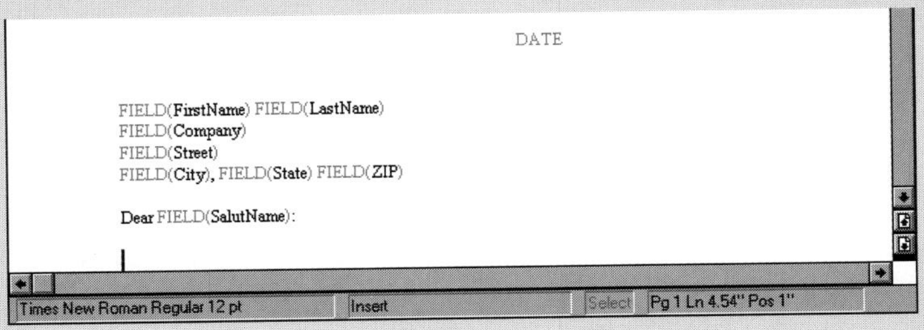

**Figure 6-16**
Document window after you insert the FIELD codes for the inside address and salutation

DATE

FIELD(FirstName) FIELD(LastName)
FIELD(Company)
FIELD(Street)
FIELD(City), FIELD(State) FIELD(ZIP)

Dear FIELD(SalutName):

Times New Roman Regular 12 pt          Insert          Select   Pg 1 Ln 4.54" Pos 1"

**TROUBLE?**     If you see errors, use WordPerfect's editing commands to delete the error, then insert the correct merge code or text.

You'll now retrieve the rest of the form letter (the form file) from the Student Disk and insert the two merge codes needed to personalize the last paragraph of Whitney's letter.

To insert the file:

❶ Make sure the Student Disk is in drive A.

❷ Click **Insert**, then click **File** to display the Insert File dialog box.

❸ If necessary, change the Drives to drive A.

❹ Double-click **c6file1.dft** in the Filename list, then click the **Yes button** to insert the file into the current document.

WordPerfect inserts the file C6FILE1.DFT into the current document window.

You're now ready to insert the last two FIELD merge codes into the form letter.

To insert the last two FIELD merge codes:

❶ Move the insertion point to the comma at the beginning of the second paragraph of the letter.

❷ Click the **Insert Field button** on the Merge Bar.

❸ Double-click **SalutName** in the Field Names list of the Insert Field Name or Number dialog box.

❹ Move the insertion point to the period at the end of the second paragraph.

**TROUBLE?**    If the Insert Field Name or Number dialog box hides the second paragraph, scroll the text so it appears above or below the dialog box or drag the dialog box out of the way.

❺ Insert the merge code FIELD(Company). Then close the Insert Field Name or Number dialog box. See Figure 6-17.

merge codes in body of letter

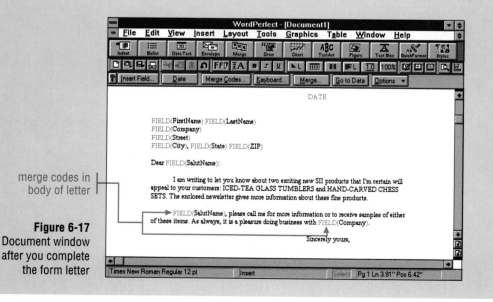

**Figure 6-17**
Document window
after you complete
the form letter

The merge codes in the last paragraph of the document will tell WordPerfect to insert the client's salutation name and company name at these locations in the letter.

❻ Save the file to the Student Disk as S6SLSLET.FRM.

The abbreviation "SLSLET" stands for "sales letter," and the filename extension .FRM stands for "form" to remind you that this is the form file used in a WordPerfect merge operation.

***If you want to take a break*** and resume the tutorial at a later time, you can exit WordPerfect. When you resume, launch WordPerfect and go on to the next section.

# Merging Form and Data Files

Now that she has created her form letter (form file) and her address list (data file), Whitney is ready to merge the two files to create personalized letters to send to her clients.

REFERENCE WINDOW

### Merging a Data File and a Form File

- Click the Merge button on the Button Bar to display the Merge dialog box.
- Click the Merge button in the Merge dialog box.
- In the Form File text box, type the name of the form file and move the insertion point to the Data File text box.
- If necessary, type the name of the data file.
- Click the OK button to perform the merge.

Let's merge S6SLSLET.FRM (the form file) with S6ADDR.DAT (the data file).

To merge a form file and a data file:

❶ Close the two open documents, S6SLSLET.FRM and S6ADDR.DAT.

Because WordPerfect creates the merged file in an empty document window, this step is not essential.

❷ Click     , the **Merge button** on the Button Bar, to display the Merge dialog box.

❸ Click the **Merge button.**

The Perform Merge dialog box appears on the screen.

❹ Type **a:s6slslet.frm** into the Form File text box, and move the insertion point to the Data File text box.

Because you have already told WordPerfect that the form file is associated with the data file S6ADDR.DAT, that name appears in the Data File text box automatically. The Output File text box specifies the location of the merged file, that is, the document that results from the merge of the form and data files. We want the merged file to appear in the current document window rather than in a disk file, so we leave "<Current Document>" in the Output File text box.

❺  Click the **OK button** to perform the merge.

WordPerfect displays the Please Wait dialog box while merging the documents. The merged document contains five letters, one for each record in the data file. The end of the merged document now appears in the document window. See Figure 6-18. As you can see on the status bar, the last letter in the merged document is page 5.

data retrieved from data file

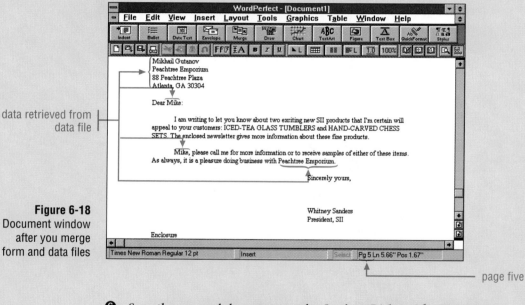

**Figure 6-18**
Document window after you merge form and data files

page five

❻  Save the merged document to the Student Disk as S6MERGED.DOC.
❼  Print all five pages of the merged document.

During the merge operation, WordPerfect retrieved information from the data file— one record at a time—and inserted it into the form file, according to the merge codes, to create five letters. After each letter, WordPerfect inserted a hard page break, so that each letter will print on a separate page. Scroll through the merged document. As you can see, it contains five pages, one page for each of the five records in the form file.

## Printing Address Labels

Whitney wants to mail the form letters and accompanying newsletter (which you'll create later in this tutorial) in 9-by-12-inch manilla envelopes. Rather than typing the address on each envelope, she will use WordPerfect's labels and merge features to create mailing labels.

### Merging the Labels Form File with the Address List

Whitney's first task is to create a form file that specifies the format of the mailing label. The contents of her labels form file is shown in Figure 6-19. As you can see, this form file contains FIELD merge codes similar to those in Whitney's form letter. Let's create the labels form file.

**Figure 6-19**
Document window
with the form file
for labels

To create a form file for labels:

❶ Close the document window containing the merged document.

❷ Click the **Merge button** on the Button Bar, then click the **Form button** on the Merge dialog box. The Create Form File dialog box appears.

❸ In the Associate a Data File text box of the Create Form File dialog box, type **a:s6addr.dat**, then click the **OK button** or press **[Enter]**. The Merge Bar for a form file appears at the top of the document window.

❹ Click the **Insert Field button** on the Merge Bar, then double-click **FirstName** to insert the FIELD(FirstName) merge code.

❺ Press **[Spacebar]** and insert the next FIELD merge code, as shown in Figure 6-19.

❻ Continue inserting the FIELD merge codes and formatting the label exactly as shown in Figure 6-19.

❼ Close the Insert Field Name or Number dialog box.

❽ Save the file using the filename S6LABELS.FRM.

Because the mailing labels contain only the names and addresses of the clients, this form file includes no text except spaces, hard returns, and a comma. Notice that the labels form file uses the same data file as Whitney's form letter. This demonstrates the important point that, whenever you create a data file, you can use it with any number of different form files. Also notice that the labels form file doesn't use all the fields in the data file. WordPerfect provides total flexibility in the creation and use of merge data and form files.

Whitney's next task is to merge the labels form file she has just created with the data file (the client list) she created earlier.

To merge the files:

❶ Close the document window.

❷ Click ⬚, the **Merge button** on the Button Bar, then click the **Merge button** in the Merge dialog box. The Perform Merge dialog box appears on the screen.

❸ In the Form File text box, type **s6labels.frm** and move the insertion point to the Data File text box. The name of the data file automatically appears in the Data File text box, because you already told WordPerfect that the labels form file was associated with the data file S6ADDR.DAT.

❹ Click the **OK button** to perform the merge.

❺ Click **View**, then click **Draft** to view the merged document in draft mode.

WordPerfect merged the form and data files to yield the five labels shown in Figure 6-20, with one page for each record in the data file.

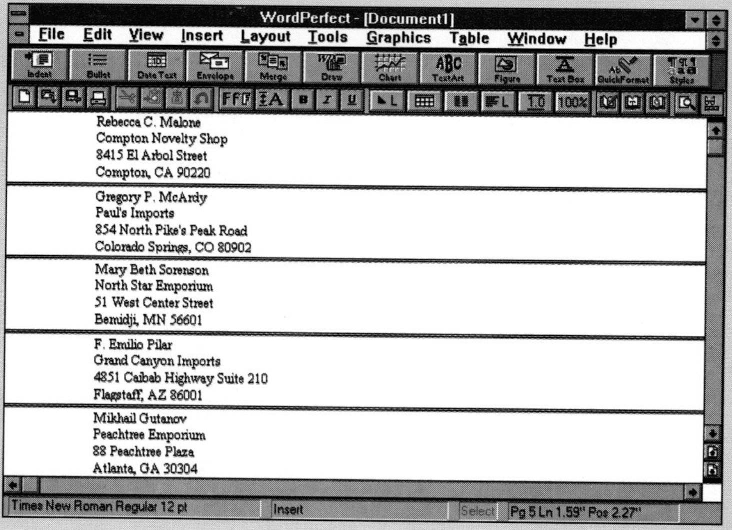

**Figure 6-20**
Document window
after you merge
labels form file
with data file

## Creating the Labels Document

If Whitney were to print the merged labels document as it appears now, she would get one address in the upper-left corner of each printed page. Instead, she wants the addresses to be printed on a standard sheet of gummed labels. Fortunately, WordPerfect provides a method for printing on gummed labels.

To format the merged document for labels, you need to change WordPerfect's default page layout. By telling WordPerfect that you are printing labels and by specifying certain measurements about those labels, you can create a page layout for printing them successfully.

Whitney has purchased Avery Laser Printer Labels number 5162, in sheets, from a local office-supply store. Each label measures 4 inches by 1.33 inches and each sheet has seven rows of labels, with two labels in each row, for a total of fourteen labels per sheet. (See Figure 6-21.) WordPerfect supports most types of commercial label formats. If you use a different type of gummed label from the one illustrated here, you will need to set up your merged document for that type.

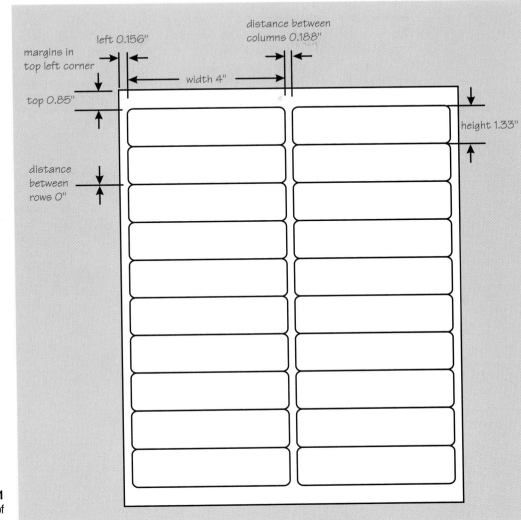

left 0.156"

distance between
columns 0.188"

margins in
top left corner

width 4"

top 0.85"

height 1.33"

distance
between
rows 0"

**Figure 6-21**
Measurement of
typical labels page

### Creating a Labels Document

- Move the insertion point to the beginning of the document.
- Click Layout, then click Labels. The Labels dialog box appears.
- Scroll through the Labels list until you find the name of your labels, and highlight the name of your labels.
- Click the Select button.

You're now ready to tell WordPerfect the type of gummed labels you're using.

To set up the merged document for gummed labels:

❶ Move the insertion point to the very beginning of the merged labels document (Figure 6-20), before any format codes except [Open Style:InitialCodes].

❷ Click **Layout,** then click **Labels.** The Labels dialog box appears.

❸ Scroll through the Labels list until you find the name of your labels, for example, **Avery 5162 Address.**

**TROUBLE?**   If your type of label isn't in the list, choose the label name that closely matches the sheet size (usually 8.5 by 11 inches), the label size, and the number of labels on a page—for example, 2 by 10, which means 10 rows of 2 labels each. Look in the Label Details box for this information as you highlight the various label names. Then click the Edit button from the Labels dialog box and edit the dimensions of your labels. In this example, we will assume that your labels are on the list.

❹ Highlight the name of your labels (for example, Avery 5162 Address) by clicking it. The dialog box displays a diagram of the labels sheet and gives details about it. See Figure 6-22.

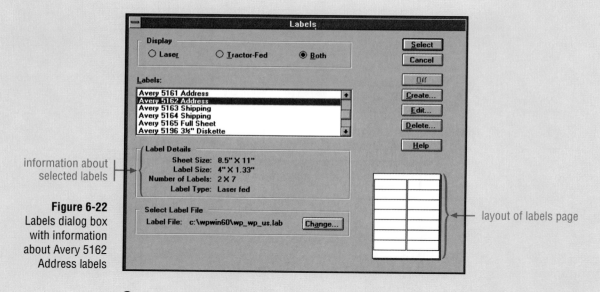

**Figure 6-22**
Labels dialog box with information about Avery 5162 Address labels

information about selected labels

layout of labels page

❺ Click the **Select button** to select the highlighted labels.

❻ Click **View,** then click **Page** to view the labels document in Page view.

Your screen should now look like Figure 6-23.

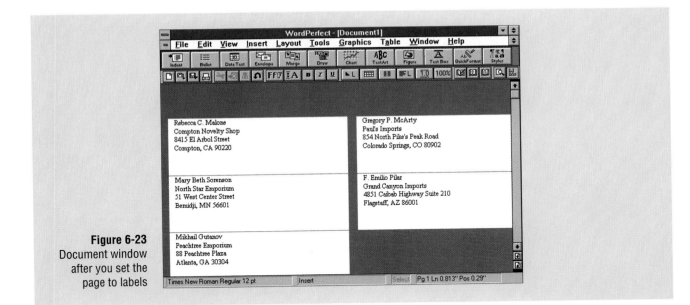

You can now save and print the labels document.

To save and print the labels document:

❶ Save the document as S6LABELS.DOC.

If you don't have a sheet of labels, you can print the labels document on an ordinary sheet of paper. If you're using a sheet of labels, consult your instructor or technical support person about how to feed the sheet into the printer.

❷ Print the labels document.

❸ Close the document S6LABELS.DOC.

With the letters and labels printed, Whitney is now ready to create the newsletter that will accompany her letters.

***If you want to take a break*** and resume the tutorial at a later time, you can exit WordPerfect. When you resume, launch WordPerfect and leave the document window blank.

## Desktop-Publishing a Newsletter

Whitney's next task is to create the issue of the SII newsletter shown in Figure 6-2. To perform this task, you will apply some features of desktop publishing. **Desktop publishing** is the production of commercial-quality printed material using a desktop computer system. The following characteristics are commonly associated with desktop publishing:

- **High-quality printing.** Desktop-published documents are usually printed with a laser printer or high-resolution inkjet printer.
- **Multiple fonts.** Desktop-published documents often include two or three different font styles and sizes.
- **Graphics.** Desktop-published documents often include graphics, such as horizontal lines (called rules in the publishing industry), boxes, computer art, and digitized photographs.
- **Typographic characters.** Desktop published documents use typographic long dashes, called em dashes (—), in place of double hyphens (--) to separate dependent clauses; typographic medium-width dashes, called en dashes (-), in place of hyphens (-) as minus signs and in ranges of numbers; bullets (•) to signal items in a bulleted list; quote marks like "this," not "this"; and so forth.
- **Columns and other formatting features.** Desktop-published documents often contain columns of text and other special formatting features that you don't frequently see in word-processed documents.

You'll see how to incorporate most of these features as you create the SII newsletter.

## Using TextArt to Create the Newsletter Title

Whitney wants the title of her newsletter, *SII Update,* to be eye-catching but easy to read. Using WordPerfect's TextArt feature she can create this title with special effects, including curved and shaded letters. Figure 6-2 illustrates the final version of Whitney's newsletter title.

The WordPerfect TextArt feature allows you almost limitless flexability in designing text that expresses exactly the image or mood you want to convey in your printed document. The TextArt feature creates a **graphics box,** which contains the text you are designing. By selecting from various options within the TextArt dialog box, you can apply color, and shading, as well as alter the shape and size of characters and words.

Let's create the title of the newsletter now. First you'll need to create the horizontal line. The Horizontal Line feature allows you to quickly and easily draw horizontal lines across the document page.

To create the title for the newsletter:
❶  Open a new document window.
❷  Click **Graphics**, then click **Horizontal Line.** WordPerfect draws a horizontal line from the left to the right margin. The insertion point disappears, because WordPerfect automatically collapses the height of the insertion point to the height of the horizontal line.
❸  Press [Enter] to move the insertion point down to the next line. You can now see the blinking insertion point.

Now you're ready to insert the title and apply special effects.

**REFERENCE WINDOW**

## Creating Text with Special Effects Using TextArt

- Click the TextArt button on the Button Bar to display the TextArt dialog box.

- With the insertion point in the Enter Text box, type the text to which you want to apply special effects.

- Using the TextArt dialog box options, change the shape, color, shading, size, justification, and so forth, of the text, in whatever ways you choose.

- After creating the desired text, click File, then click Exit & Return to WordPerfect.

- Click the Yes button to verify that you want to "update the embedded object into WordPerfect"—in other words, to insert the text art into your document window.

Let's use TextArt to create the title of Whitney's newsletter.

To insert the title and apply special effects:

❶ Click 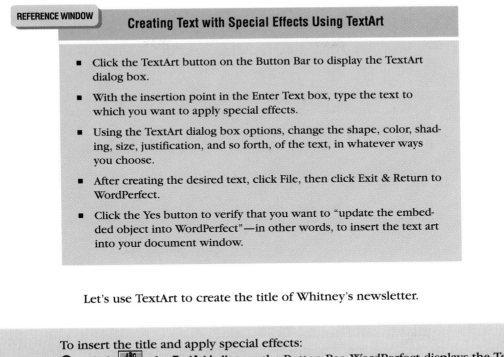, the **TextArt button** on the Button Bar. WordPerfect displays the TextArt dialog box. See Figure 6-24.

change font

change text to "SII Update"

select this shape

shadow grid

click here twice to create shadow

**Figure 6-24**
TextArt dialog box

❷ Move the mouse pointer to the various buttons and icons in the TextArt dialog box. As you do so, note that a description of each option appears in the lower-left corner of the dialog box.

❸ With the insertion point in the Enter Text box and the word TEXT highlighted, type **SII Update.** This is the title of the newsletter.

Now let's change the font.

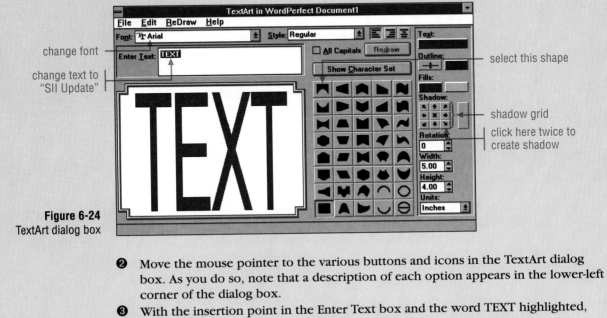

❹  Click the **Down Arrow** to the right of the text box labeled Font. This displays a list of available fonts.

❺  Scroll the list (if necessary) until Arrus BT appears and click **Arrus BT.**

   TROUBLE?   If Arrus BT doesn't appear on your list, choose some other serif font.

In the next step, you'll change the shape of the text so it is straight across the top and rounded along the bottom. The TextArt dialog box provides forty different shapes into which you can "pour" your text.

❻  Click the shape in the upper-left corner of the grid of shapes, as indicated in Figure 6-24.

   TROUBLE?   If the display of the text art seems slow, don't worry. On most computers, changing the attributes of the text art is slow.

Now let's add a shadow to the newsletter title. The Shadow grid is on the right-hand side of the dialog box, as shown in Figure 6-24. Clicking on any of the arrows creates a shadow off-set from the text in the direction of the arrow.

❼  Click the arrow in the lower-right corner of the Shadow grid. After the shadow appears in the dialog box, click the same arrow again to move the shadow farther from the text. The TextArt dialog box now looks like Figure 6-25.

**Figure 6-25**
TextArt dialog box
after you create
the title

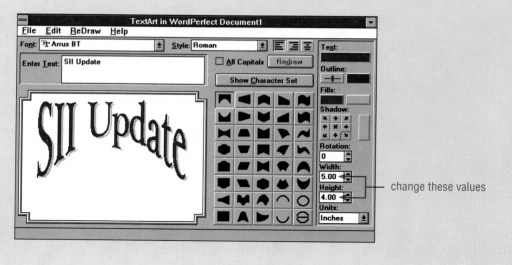

change these values

This completes the design of the text art. Now you're ready to change the size of the title so it spans the entire width of the document. The current width of your text art is probably 5.00 inches, and the height is probably 4.00 inches, as shown in Figure 6-25. You'll change these to 6.50 and 1.50 inches, respectively.

To change the size of the text art:

❶  Double-click the current value in the text box below the word "Width" on the right side of the TextArt dialog box. The value becomes highlighted.

❷  Type **6.5**.

❸  Double-click the current value in the text box below the word "Height," then type **1.5**.

The TextArt dialog box now looks like Figure 6-26.

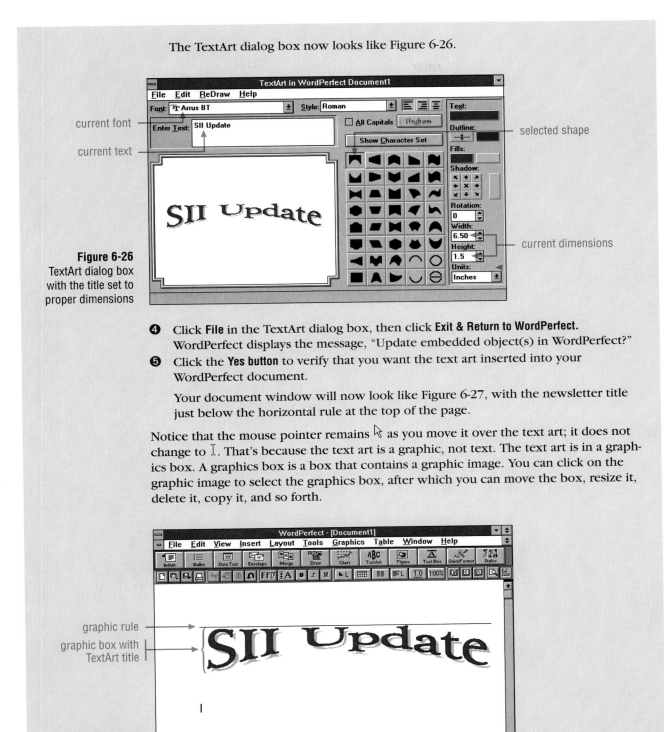

current font
current text

selected shape

current dimensions

**Figure 6-26**
TextArt dialog box
with the title set to
proper dimensions

❹ Click **File** in the TextArt dialog box, then click **Exit & Return to WordPerfect.**
WordPerfect displays the message, "Update embedded object(s) in WordPerfect?"

❺ Click the **Yes button** to verify that you want the text art inserted into your
WordPerfect document.

Your document window will now look like Figure 6-27, with the newsletter title
just below the horizontal rule at the top of the page.

Notice that the mouse pointer remains ⌖ as you move it over the text art; it does not
change to Ⅰ. That's because the text art is a graphic, not text. The text art is in a graphics box. A graphics box is a box that contains a graphic image. You can click on the
graphic image to select the graphics box, after which you can move the box, resize it,
delete it, copy it, and so forth.

graphic rule
graphic box with
TextArt title

**Figure 6-27**
Document window
with title in
graphics box

❻ Click anywhere on the text art. See Figure 6-28.

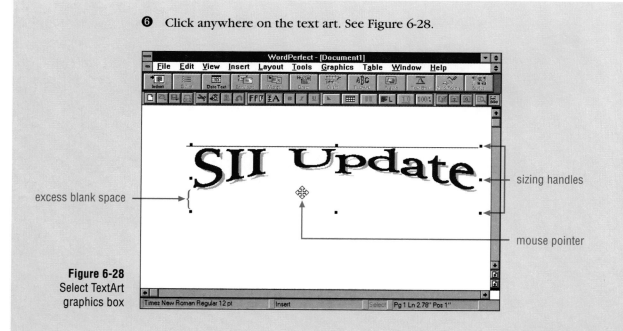

**Figure 6-28**
Select TextArt
graphics box

The graphics box is now selected, with sizing handles on its corners and edges. The mouse pointer becomes ⊕ within the graphics box. If you click and hold the left mouse button, you can drag the graphics box to another location in the document. If you position the mouse pointer directly on top of a sizing handle, it becomes a two-headed arrow. You can then drag a handle to change the size of the graphics box.

Notice that the graphics box includes blank space below the bottom of the title, as shown in Figure 6-28. WordPerfect inserts this space at the bottom of the graphics box to prevent the graphic from being overwritten by text. To avoid this extra space, you can tell WordPerfect that you want to allow text within the graphics box. Let's do that now.

To turn off the Wrap feature for the graphics box:
❶ Move ⊕ anywhere within the graphics box that contains the newsletter title, then click the *right* mouse button. A pop-up menu appears on the screen. See Figure 6-29.

**Figure 6-29**
Pop-up menu after
you click graphics
box with *right*
mouse button

❷   Click **Wrap**. The Wrap Text dialog box appears on the screen.

❸   Click the button to the left of No Wrap (through), which tells WordPerfect to allow text to be typed through the graphics box, then click the **OK button.**

❹   Click I in the blank space below the graphics box to deselect the box.

Now the insertion point appears just below the horizontal line at the top of the page.

❺   Press **[Enter]** about six times until the insertion point is near *Ln 2.2"* as indicated on the status bar.

You're now ready to draw the horizontal line below the title.

❻   Click **Graphics,** then click **Horizontal Line,** and press **[Enter].** Your screen should now look like Figure 6-30.

**Figure 6-30**
Document window
with completed
newsletter title

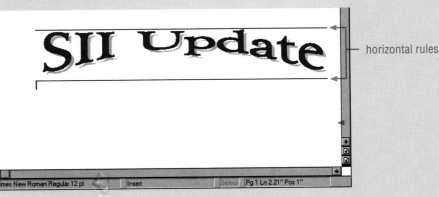

With the newsletter title complete, you're now ready to create the line with the volume, number, and date for this issue and insert the text of the document.

**TROUBLE?**   If you made a mistake creating the newsletter title, you can click Graphics and then click Edit Box. If you have only one graphics box on the screen (which is the case now), the graphics box becomes active, as indicated by the sizing handles on its corners and edges. Double-click the graphics box. WordPerfect activates the TextArt dialog box, where you can make the necessary changes in the text art. (Normally, you can edit the text art by double-clicking the graphics box, but WordPerfect doesn't allow this once you've turned off text wrap.)

## Inserting the Text of the Newsletter

In the business world, the person who creates a newsletter is often not the one who writes the articles included in it. This is the case with *SII Update.* Several workers at Sanders Imports wrote articles for the newsletter and submitted them to Whitney as WordPerfect files.

In the steps that follow, you will insert the text of the articles for the current issue of the newsletter. In this and later sections of this tutorial, you will format the text using techniques of desktop publishing.

To insert the the text into the newsletter:
❶ Make sure the Student Disk is in drive A.
❷ Click **Insert**, click **File**, change the default drive to A (if necessary), click **c6file2.dft** from the Filename list, then click the **Insert button**. At the prompt, click the **Yes button** to verify that you want the file inserted into the current document. WordPerfect retrieves the file from the disk and inserts it into your newsletter document.

The articles that Whitney's staff submitted aren't formatted for the newsletter. But before working on the articles, Whitney decides to format the volume, number, and date of the current issue of *SII Update*.

To format the volume, number, and date:
❶ Make sure the insertion point is immediately to the left of "Vol." and make sure the current font is Times New Roman (or another serif font).
❷ Click [A], the **Font Size button** on the Power Bar, and select **14** to set the font size to 14 points.
❸ Move the insertion point to the "J" in "July," and click **Layout**, click **Line**, then click **Flush Right** to make the date flush against the right margin of the document.
❹ Move the insertion point to the next line below "Vol." and insert a horizontal rule using the procedure you learned in the last section. Then press **[Enter]** to move the insertion point to a new blank line.

Your screen should now look like Figure 6-31. Having created the title and heading for the newsletter, Whitney is ready to format the text.

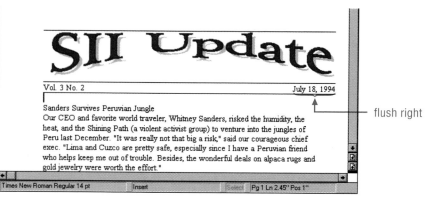

**Figure 6-31**
Document window
after you insert
newsletter text

## Using Columns

Whitney wants *SII Update* to be in a two-column format, as shown in Figure 6-2. Let's set the text of the newsletter to two columns now.

To format the document in two columns:

❶ Move the insertion point to the location where you want the columns to begin. In this case, move the insertion point to the first "S" in "Sanders" in the title of the first news item.

❷ Click ▦, the **Columns Define button** on the Power Bar, and select **2 Columns**.

❸ Scroll the text up by clicking the Down Arrow of the vertical scroll bar. You want to still see the newsletter title, but also more of the body of the text.

You can now clearly see the two-column format of the newsletter text.

## Making Additional Font Changes

Now that the columns are set, Whitney wants to change the fonts to improve the appearance of the newsletter. The font for most of the *SII Update* newsletter is 10-point Times New Roman (or some other serif font). The font for the headings of the three articles of the newsletter is 14-point Arial (or some other sans serif font). Let's make these changes now.

To change the fonts of the various parts of the document and make other formatting changes:

❶ With the insertion point immediately to the left of the "S" in "Sanders" in the title of the first article, click ⅎⅎⅎ, the **Font Face button** on the Power Bar, and set the font to **Arial** or to some other sans serif font. Notice that the status bar indicates that the current font is Arial Regular 14-point.

❷ Move the insertion point to the "O" in "Our," the first word in the line below the title.

Let's set the font for the text of the article to 10-point Times New Roman.

❸ Click ⅢA, the **Font Size button** on the Power Bar, and set the font size to 10-point.

❹ Click ⅎⅎⅎ and set the font to **Times New Roman** or to some other serif font.

Now Whitney can make other formatting changes. While the insertion point is still near the beginning of the newsletter, let's change the justification to full, change the paragraph indent to 0.25 inch, and turn on Widow/Orphan Protection.

To make additional formatting changes:

❶ Click ▤, the **Justification button** on the Power Bar, and set the justification to **Full**. Each column of text becomes aligned along both its right and left margins.

Now you'll set the tab stop so that the first line of each paragraph is indented one-fourth inch rather than one-half inch. (This smaller indent looks better with the narrow columns in the newsletter.)

❷ Click **Layout**, click **Line**, then click **Tab Set**.

❸ Change the value of the Position in the Settings box to **0.25**, then click the **OK button**. The tab at the beginning of each paragraph changes from 0.5 to 0.25 inch. The first paragraph under each heading in the newsletter is not indented, so you'll have to look at the subsequent paragraphs in each article to see the difference in the tab-stop setting.

Now let's set Widow/Orphan Protection. In a multiple-column document, an orphan is the first line of a paragraph appearing alone at the bottom of a column, and a widow is the last line of a paragraph appearing alone at the top of a column. Setting Widow/Orphan Protection is especially important in making desktop-published documents look professional.

❹ Click **Layout**, click **Page**, then click **Keep Text Together.** WordPerfect displays the Keep Text Together dialog box.

❺ Click the checkbox beneath "Widow/Orphan," then click the **OK button.** This prevents the first or last line of any paragraph from being isolated at the top or the bottom of a page.

❻ Select (highlight) each of the other two titles, "Guillermo Catlán Joins SII" and "New Additions to SII Catalog," and change their font to 14-point Arial.

❼ Move the insertion point to the end of the document.

Your document window should now look something like Figure 6-32. Due to slight differences in how printers handle fonts, your document might not be exactly the same as the one shown.

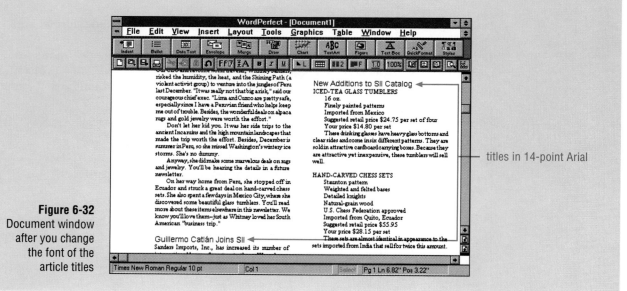

**Figure 6-32**
Document window after you change the font of the article titles

titles in 14-point Arial

## Using Typographic Characters

The employees of SII who wrote the articles for the newsletter used standard word-processing characters, which do not include typographic em dashes, en dashes, quotation marks, or bullets. So Whitney's next task in formatting the newsletter is to insert typographic characters—namely, typographic quotes, em dashes, and bullets (for a bulleted list)—at the appropriate places in the document.

**REFERENCE WINDOW**

## Inserting Typographic Characters

- Move the insertion point to the location where you want a particular typographic character.
- Click Insert, then click Character to display the WordPerfect Characters dialog box.
- Select Typographic Symbols from the Character Set text box.
- Highlight the desired character or symbol, then click the Insert and Close button. WordPerfect inserts the selected character into your document.

Let's first change the regular quotes to typographic quotes.

To insert typographic quotation marks:

❶ Move the insertion point to the beginning of the document.

❷ Click **Edit**, then click **Find**, type a regular quotation mark (") in the Find text box, then click **Find Next.**

WordPerfect finds the first occurrence of a regular quotation mark just to the left of the word "It" in the first paragraph.

❸ Click the **Close button** to close the Find Text dialog box.

❹ With the insertion point to the right of the quotation mark, press **[Backspace]** to delete the mark. Now you're ready to insert the typographic left quote.

❺ Click **Insert**, then click **Character** to display the WordPerfect Characters dialog box.

❻ Change the character set to **Typographic Symbols.**

❼ Scroll the Characters box until you see the quote marks, then click the third quote mark from the left. A blinking dotted-line box appears around the character. Make sure the character Number is 4,32. See Figure 6-33.

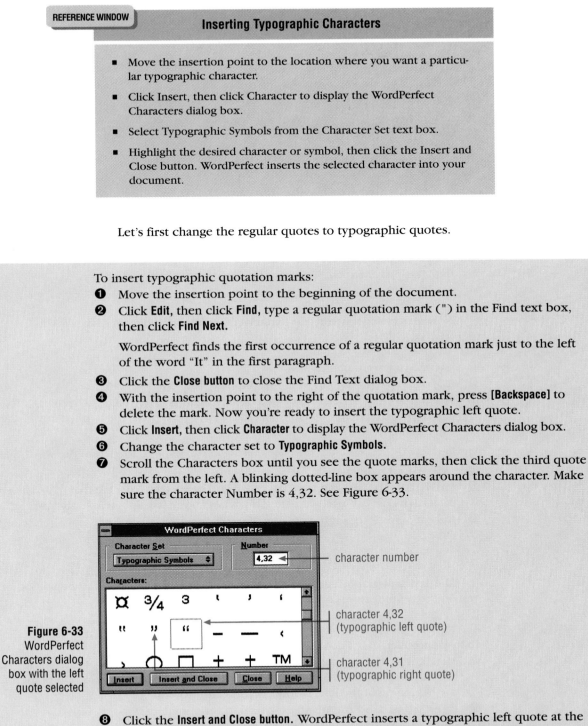

**Figure 6-33**
WordPerfect
Characters dialog
box with the left
quote selected

character number

character 4,32
(typographic left quote)

character 4,31
(typographic right quote)

❽ Click the **Insert and Close button.** WordPerfect inserts a typographic left quote at the location of the insertion point in your document. On the screen, the new mark might not look any different from a regular quotation mark, but it will look very different on the printed page.

You have now changed the first regular quote to a typographic quote. Changing the others in the document will go more quickly if you use shortcut keys. Let's change the rest now.

To insert typographic characters using the shortcut keys:

❶ Press **[Shift][F2]** (Find Next) to find the next occurrence of a quotation mark.

You could also click Edit, click Find, then click the Find Next button, but in this case, using the shortcut keys is obviously much faster.

❷ With the quotation mark highlighted, press **[Ctrl][W]** (WordPerfect Characters) to open the WordPerfect Characters dialog box.

Again you could use the menu commands Insert and Character, but using the shortcut keys saves you time.

❸ Type **4,31** to select the typographic right quote, and click the **Insert and Close button.** WordPerfect replaces the regular quote with the typographic right quote.

❹ Repeat Steps 1 through 3 until all the quote marks have been changed. For a left quote, use character 4,32. For a right quote, use character 4,31.

Now let's change the regular hyphens (--) to typographic em dashes (—).

To change hyphens to em dashes:

❶ Move the insertion point to the beginning of the document.

❷ Search for the first occurrence of a double hyphen ([- Hyphen][- Hyphen]). (To insert the [- Hyphen] code in the Find text box, just press the hyphen key to the right of the 0 (zero) key on your keyboard.)

WordPerfect finds the first occurence of a double hyphen to the left of the word "just."

❸ Delete both hyphens.

❹ Press **[Ctrl][W]** (WordPerfect Characters) and insert character number 4,34, the em dash. WordPerfect inserts an em dash between the words "them" and "just."

❺ Repeat Steps 2 through 4 once more to change the other double hyphen to an em dash.

The last typographic character you'll insert is a bullet (•) at the beginning of each item in the list of features of SII's two new products.

To insert a bullet:

❶ Move the insertion point to the beginning of the line to the left of the phrase "16 oz.," just below "ICED-TEA GLASS TUMBLERS." Make sure the insertion point is at the beginning of the line, before the Hd Left Ind code.

❷ Insert a bullet (•), the WordPerfect character number 4,0.

❸ Using the same procedure, insert a bullet before each of the other four items under "ICED-TEA GLASS TUMBLERS" and each of the eight items under "HAND-CARVED CHESS SETS."

Your document window should now look like Figure 6-34.

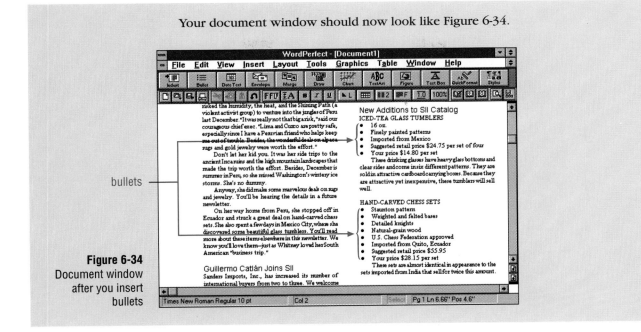

**Figure 6-34**
Document window
after you insert
bullets

## Changing the Paragraph Spacing

One formatting feature that helps improve the appearance and readability of documents is paragraph spacing. This feature allows you to insert white space between paragraphs within the document. Whitney wants her newsletter to be easy to read and attractive, so her clients will read it rather than just throw it away. Let's change the paragraph spacing in the newsletter.

To change the paragraph spacing:

❶ Move the insertion point to the location in the document where you want the paragraph spacing change to begin. In this example, move the insertion point to the "S" in "Sanders" in the title of the first article in the newsletter.

❷ Click **Layout**, click **Paragraph**, then click **Format**. WordPerfect displays the Paragraph Format dialog box.

   Notice that the current spacing between paragraphs is 1.

❸ Double-click the text box labeled Spacing Between Paragraphs.

❹ Set the spacing between paragraphs to **1.2**. This adds a small amount (2/10ths of a line) of white space between the paragraphs.

❺ Click the **OK button.**

WordPerfect inserts extra white space between each paragraph in the newsletter. Whitney has now worked on the newsletter for more than 15 minutes and wants to save her changes.

❻ Save the newsletter as S6NEWS.LET.

*If you want to take a break* and resume the tutorial at a later time, you can exit WordPerfect. When you resume, launch WordPerfect and open S6NEWS.LET into a document window.

■          ■          ■

## Importing Graphics

Whitney's final task in creating the newsletter is to import a graphic image, a map of Peru. She purchased a graphics file of the map from a commercial clip-art supplier. The clip art in this case was supplied in a Windows Meta File format, which is a format for transferring information or graphics from one Windows application to another.

REFERENCE WINDOW

### Importing Graphics

- Move the insertion point near the location where you want the graphics image to appear in your document.
- Click the Figure button on the Button Bar to display the Insert Image dialog box.
- Using the normal procedure for opening a document, select the desired graphics image, then click the OK button.

Let's import the map of Peru now.

To import graphics:

❶ Make sure the Student Disk is still in drive A.

❷ Make sure the insertion point is still at the beginning of the body of the newsletter, just below the title. The exact location of the insertion point is not important, because you can position a graphic image almost any place on a page, regardless of the exact location of the code for the graphic box.

❸ Click [Figure], the **Figure button** on the Button Bar. The Insert Image dialog box appears on the screen.

❹ Change the Drives option to drive A.

❺ Change the text in the Filename text box to **\*.wmf** and press **[Enter]**. This tells WordPerfect to display a list of all the files with the filename extension .WMF (Windows Meta File).

❻ Click **perumap.wmf** in the Filename list box, then click the **OK button.** WordPerfect inserts the file into a graphics box within the newsletter document and displays the Graphics Bar along the top of the document window. See Figure 6-35.

Graphics Bar →

sizing handles

**Figure 6-35**
Document window
after you insert
graphic image

Although the graphic image is now in Whitney's document, it is not the proper size, nor is it in the right position. Whitney feels the map would be more attractive if it were located between the two columns, with the text wrapping around the contour of the map. Let's make these changes to the graphics box now.

To edit the graphics box:

❶ Click the **Size button** on the Graphics Bar. WordPerfect displays the Box Size dialog box.

❷ In the text box to the right of Set in the dialog box, change the value from 3.25 inches (or whatever it happens to be on your screen) to **2.25** inches.

❸ Make sure the button next to Size to Content in the Height box is on. (This causes the height of the graphics box to automatically change in proportion to the change in the width.) Then click the **OK button**. The dimensions of the graphics box in the document window decreases.

❹ Click the **Position button** on the Graphics Bar. The Box Position dialog box appears on the screen.

❺ Click the button to the left of Put Box on Current Page, just beneath Box Placement. This tells WordPerfect that you want to specify a position on the page for the graphics box.

❻ Click the button to the left of Across Columns. This tells WordPerfect that you want the graphics box to span the two columns in your newsletter.

❼ Click in the text box to the right of Place and set the value to **−0.5**, and then to the right of that value, change the "from" under Across Columns setting to **Center of Column**. The number 0.5 causes WordPerfect to position the graphics box one-half inch to the left of the center of the two columns. Whitney chose this value because she felt the map looked better when it was slightly off-center.

❽  Change the Place value under Vertical to **0** (zero), and then change the "from" setting in the Vertical box to **Center of Margins**. This tells WordPerfect to center the graphics box between the top and bottom margins of the page. The zero keeps the graphics box exactly in the center, whereas a positive value would position the box below the vertical center, and a negative value would position the box above the vertical center of the page. The dialog box should now look like Figure 6-36.

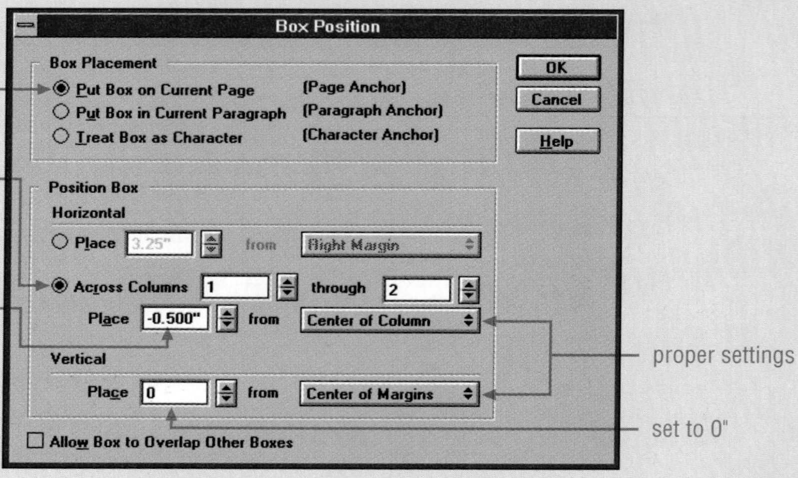

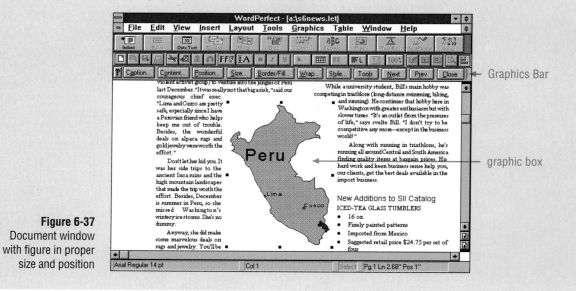

**Figure 6-36**
Box Position dialog box with the proper box position settings

selected ——
set to -0.5" ——
selected ——
proper settings
set to 0"

❾  Click the **OK button** to accept these settings for the position of the graphics box. Your screen now looks similar to Figure 6-37.

**Figure 6-37**
Document window with figure in proper size and position

Whitney decides she wants the text to wrap around the contour of the map itself, rather than around the graphics box that holds it. To accomplish this, let's change the method by which WordPerfect wraps text around the figure.

To change the method of wrapping text around the graphics box:

❶ Click the **Wrap button** on the Graphics Bar. WordPerfect displays the Wrap Text dialog box.

❷ Click the button to the left of Contour. The Contour method of wrapping causes the text to follow the contour of the graphic image.

❸ Click the **OK button** to close the Wrap Text dialog box, then click the **Close button** on the Graphics Bar to close the bar and deselect the graphics box.

❹ Click ⬚, the **Page Zoom Full button** on the Power Bar, to get a full-page view of the newsletter. Your screen should now look like Figure 6-38.

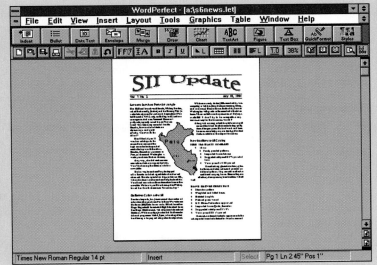

**Figure 6-38**
Document window
in full-page view
showing completed
newsletter

Whitney is satisfied with this edition of *SII Update*. She saves and prints the newsletter.

❺ Save the newsletter using the default filename S6NEWS.LET and print it.

Whitney and her staff enclose personalized copies of the form letter along with the newsletter into envelopes and mail them to their clients.

# Questions

1. Define or describe each of the following:
   a. form file
   b. data file
   c. merge code
   d. record
   e. field
   f. merged document
2. Explain how you would set up a data file and insert the FIELDNAMES merge code into the file.
3. What is the purpose of the FIELDNAMES merge code in a data file?
4. Suppose during a merge you wanted to insert information for a field named "Company" into the form file. Explain how you would do this.
5. When entering data into a data file without using Quick Entry, how do you mark the end of a field? the end of a record?
6. With a data file in the document window and the Quick Data Entry dialog box on the screen, how would you quickly find a record that contains the word "Emporium" in the Company name?
7. How do you initiate a merge between a form file and a data file?
8. Explain in general (without listing keystrokes) how you would use a data file to create mailing labels.
9. List the major features that differentiate a desktop-published document from a regular document.
10. When would you use each of the following symbols? How would you insert each symbol into a document?
    a. em dash
    b. typographic quotes
    c. bullet
11. What is WordPerfect's TextArt feature? When would you use it?
12. How would you format a document so the text appears in two columns?
13. How would you do the following:
    a. insert a graphic image into a document
    b. change the size of a graphics box
    c. change the position of a graphics box
    d. change how text wraps around a graphics box

# Tutorial Assignments

*If you have completed all the tutorials and end-of-chapter exercises, you might run out of disk space. If you get a message telling you that the disk is full when you try to save a file, get a new, blank, formatted disk and save the file to it.*

With a blank document window on the screen, do the following:
1. Set up a merge data file and create the following field names: "Last," "First," and "HomePhone."
2. Create a record for each of the following Sanders Imports employees:
   Zapata, Guillermo E., 286-1121
   Lim, Ching, 286-8442
   Mustoe, Geoffrey, 285-9142

Apgood, Arnold, 285-3435
Trifiletti, Katherine, 287-4501
Qiad, Ke, 285-3318

3. Save the file as S6EMPLOY.DAT.
4. Close the document window.

Open the file T6FILE1.DFT and do the following:

5. Set up a merge form file using the document in the active document window, and associate it with S6EMPLOY.DAT.
6. To the right of "MEMO TO:," press [Tab] and then insert the FIELD merge code for the field "First" (for the first name), press [Spacebar], and insert the FIELD code for the field "Last" (for the last name).
7. To the right of "DATE:" in the memo, press [Tab] and insert the DATE merge code.
8. At the beginning of the body of the memo, before the word "here," insert the FIELD code for the field "First," followed by a comma and a space.
9. Save the file as S6MEMO.FRM.

Clear the document window and do the following:

10. Merge the files S6MEMO.FRM and S6EMPL2.DAT.
11. Save the merged document as S6MEMO.MRG.
12. Print the file S6MEMO.MRG.

Make sure the document window is blank, and then do the following:

13. Create a merge data file with the following FIELDNAMES: "ProductName," "RetailPrice," "WholesalePrice," "Country," and "QuantInStock."
14. Create a record for each of the following products. In the list below, each line is a record. Fields in each record are separated by semicolons. (Don't include the semicolons in your data file record.)
    Teapot, Irish; 48.98; 28.80; Ireland; 258
    Rug, Alpaca; 185.95; 105.40; Peru; 188
    Mug, Designer Ceramic; 6.49; 3.20; Taiwan; 467
    Sweater, Turtleneck; 38.95, 20.60; Germany; 1,285
    Bowl, Wooden; 25.95, 15.80; Ecuador, 858
15. Save the file as S6PRODS.DAT.

**E** 16. Click Quick Entry on the Merge Bar, then click the Find button to find the record that contains "Turtleneck" in the product name. Change the quantity in stock for this item from 1,285 to 1,197. Then close the Quick Data Entry dialog box.

Clear the document window and do the following:

17. Open the document T6FILE2.DFT.
18. Make the document a merge form file, using the document in the active window as the merge file.
19. Associate the data file S6PRODS.DAT with the form file.
20. On the second line of the document, below the title, insert the DATE merge code, centered between the left and right margins.
21. Move the insertion point to the right of "Product Name:," press [Tab] to move the insertion point to position 4", and insert the FIELD merge code using the field name "ProductName."
22. Move the insertion point to the right of "Suggested Retail Price:," press [Tab] to move the insertion point to position 4", and insert the FIELD merge code using the field name "RetailPrice."
23. Continue inserting a tab and a FIELD merge code after each of the items in the document, using the field names "WholesalePrice," "Country," and "QuantInStock."
24. Save the file as S6PRODS.FRM.
25. Clear the screen and do the following:
26. Merge the files S6PRODS.FRM and S6PRODS2.DAT.
27. Save the merged document as S6PRODS.MRG.
28. Print the file S6PRODS.MRG.

Clear the document window, and do the following:

29. Create a TextArt title for the newsletter *Sander's Spotlight,* written by and for employees of Sanders Imports. Use any font and shape you like. Adjust the width of the title to 6.5 inches and the height to 2.0 inches.
30. Insert the file T6FILE3.DFT into the newsletter.
31. Insert horizontal rules above and below the line with the issue, volume, number, and date.
32. Make the date flush right.
33. Set the font for the body of the newsletter to 10-point Times Roman or to some other serif font.
34. Change the font of the title of the two articles to 14-point Arial or to some other sans serif font.
35. Set the layout of the body of the newsletter to three columns.
36. Change all the regular quotation marks (") to typographic quote marks (" . . . ").
37. Change the double hyphens to an em dash.
38. Change the hyphens to the left of each item in the list of "points to success" to bullets (•).
39. Import the graphics file KNIGHT.WMF from the Student Disk into the newsletter.

**E**

40. You can change the size and position of a graphics box using the mouse. Click the figure to select it. A selected graphics box displays corner and edge "handles," which you can drag with the mouse pointer to size the box. With the graphics box selected, you can drag the entire box to a new location on the page.
    a. Use the mouse and the graphics box handles to make the graphics box of the chess knight smaller—approximately 1.5 inches in width and 2 inches in height.
    b. Use the mouse to position the graphics box to the right of the article on the sale of chess sets, between the two columns.
41. Set the method of wrapping type to Contour, so that the text follows the contour of the knight in the graphics box.
42. Save the newsletter as S6NEWS2.LET and print the newsletter.

# Case Problems

## 1. Form Letter to Small-Business Review Panel

Robyn Palkki is managing director of the National Entrepreneurial Foundation (NEF), headquartered in Denver, Colorado. She receives grant proposals from entrepreneurs who have innovative ideas for developing and marketing new products. The NEF funds several of these ideas each year. The proposals are reviewed by a panel of small-business experts. Ms. Palkki is preparing a data file of the current members of the review panel and a form letter to accompany a set of proposals.

Do the following:

1. Create a data file with the following field names: "Name," "NickName," "Title," "Company," "Street," "City," "State," and "ZIP."
2. Enter the following records into the data file. Each paragraph below is one record. The fields in each record are separated by semicolons. (Don't include the semicolons in the records.)

   Michael Richardson; Mike; President; R&U Toy Company; 1630 Chicago Avenue; Evanston; IL; 60201

   Lisa C. Holmes; Lisa; Employment Manager; The David J. Wang Company; 300 Pike Street; Cincinnati; OH; 45202

   Susan Whitman; Sue; Chief Financial Officer; The Glidden Company; 925 Euclid Avenue; Cleveland; OH; 44115

   Elizabeth Kreischer; Liz; Director, Research and Development; Kwasha Lipton, Inc.; 2100 North Central Road; Fort Lee; NJ; 07024

3. Save the data file as S6PANEL.DAT.
4. Open the document P6PANEL.DFT, which is the body of the letter to the review panel.
5. Make the letter a merge form file and associate it with the S6PANEL.DAT data file.
6. Insert blank spaces at the beginning of the document to allow room for the letterhead. The insertion point should be below Ln 2".
7. Insert the DATE merge code and press [Enter] three times to leave blank lines between the date and the inside address.
8. Insert FIELD merge codes for the complete inside address. Include fields for each panel member's name, title, company, street, city, state, and ZIP code.
9. Insert a blank line below the fields for the inside address and create the salutation of the letter. Use the field name "NickName" in the salutation. Insert another blank line between the salutation and the body of the letter.
10. Before the comma at the beginning of the second paragraph, insert the NickName field again.
11. Save the document as S6PANEL.FRM.
12. Merge the form file and the data file to create a set of letters to the review panel.
13. Save the letters file as S6PANEL.MRG.
14. Print the first two letters.
15. Create a file of mailing labels for the panel members. Format your labels document for Avery 5162 Address labels.
16. Save the labels file as S6PANEL.LBL.
17. Print the labels file onto a plain sheet of paper.

## 2. Form Letter and Flyer to Announce a Class Reunion

You have agreed to serve on the organizing committee of your high-school-class reunion. Do the following:
1. Create a data file containing the names and addresses of at least five classmates. You can use fictitious names and addresses.
2. Save the data file as S6REUN.DAT.
3. Write a one-page form letter describing a high-school-class reunion that you are helping to organize. Include the following in the letter:
    a. Merge code for the current date.
    b. FIELD merge codes for the inside address and salutation of the letter.
    c. At least one FIELD merge within the body of the letter.
    d. Information to classmates about the cost, time, date, and location of the reunion.
4. Save the form file as S6REUN.FRM.
5. Merge the form file and the data file.
6. Save the merged document as S6REUN.MRG.
7. Print the first two pages (letters) of the merged document.
8. Create a labels form file. You can use any printer label type you like, as long as each name and address fits on one label and all the labels fit on one page.
9. Save the labels file as S6REUN.LBL.
10. Print the labels file onto a plain sheet of paper.
Now create the desktop-published flyer (a single-page advertisement) announcing your high-school reunion. The flyer should contain information about the cost, time, date, and location of the reunion.
11. Use TextArt to create a title for the flyer.
**E** 12. Using the TextArt dialog box, rotate the title of the flyer 90 degrees.
**E** 13. Move the mouse pointer over the text art, click the *right* mouse button, and choose Feature Bar to display the Graphics Bar. Use the Position button on the Graphics Bar to position the title along the left margin of your flyer page. Use the Size button on the Graphics Bar to set the title to the desired size.

14. Use a large, sans serif font and bullets to create a bulleted list of the key information about the reunion.
   a. Import one of the WordPerfect graphics files included in the default graphics directory, usually C:\WPWIN60\GRAPHICS. You might want to use FATHRTME.WPG (an image of Father Time in a party costume), OCTBFEST.WPG (an image of a woman serving beer), ROSE.WPG (an image of three roses), or some other .WPG image.
   b. Adjust the size, position, and wrapping style of the graphic to fit in the design of your flyer.
   c. Save the flyer as S6FLYER.DOC and print it.

## 3. Managing Computer Supplies

Bruce Warrenton is the administrative assistant to the office manager of Valtech International. One of his duties is to keep track of computer supplies at corporate headquarters. Bruce decides to do this using WordPerfect's Merge feature. He decides to generate a merged document that lists the current inventory and the cost of each item.

Do the following:

1. Create a data file with the field names "Type," "Name," "Copies," and "Cost."
2. In your data file, include at least ten records of office supply items. Names, quantities, and costs can be fictitious.
3. Save the data file as S6SUPPL.DAT.
4. Create a form file (associated with S6SUPPL.DAT) with the following features:
   a. The title "COMPUTER SUPPLIES" centered at the top of the page.
   b. The DATE merge code centered below the title.
   c. A line with the text "Type of item:" for the type of office supply. Item types should include such items as disks, laser paper, toner cartridges, software, and so forth.
   d. A line with the text "Product Name:" for the name of the product. For example, if the type of item is software, the product name might be "WordPerfect," "Microsoft DOS 6.0," or "Lotus 1-2-3."
   e. A line with the text "Number in stock:" for the quantity of that particular item on hand.
   f. A line with the text "Cost per item:" for the cost of each item.
   g. To the right of each of the above lines of text, insert a tab and a FIELD merge code with the field names "Type," "Name," "Stock," and "Cost."
5. Save the form file as S6SUPPL.FRM.
6. Merge the form and data files.
7. Save the merged document as S6SUPPL.MRG.
8. Print the first two pages of the merged document.

## 4. Desktop-Publishing a Catalog

Maria Camberlango is an assistant production manager for Ocean Breeze Publishing, Inc., a small textbook-publishing company. One of her duties is to desktop-publish the catalog pages that advertise the publisher's books. She is currently working on the catalog page that describes "C++ Programming: A Primer," which is an introductory textbook on the C++ computer programming language.

Do the following:

1. Use horizontal rules and the TextArt feature to create a title for the catalog page. The text of the title is the name of the textbook, "C++ Programming: A Primer."
2. Below the title, insert the first draft of the text that describes the book. The text is in the file P6CBOOK.DFT on your Student Disk.
3. Change the initial quote by Parley Smith to 13-point bold italics text. Keep the body of the text, which begins after the quote, in a sans serif font.

4. Change the hyphen next to the name Parley Smith to an em dash.

5. Change the quote marks to typographic quote marks.

6. At the beginning of the body of the catalog description, change the paragraph spacing to 1.2.

7. Change the first tab stop from 0.5 inch to 0.3 inch.

8. Set the justification to Full.

**E**

9. Set the body of the text to two balanced newspaper columns. *Hint:* To define balanced newspaper columns, click Layout, click Columns, then click Define. Then set the Type to Balanced Newspaper.

10. Change the occurrence of double hyphens to an em dash.

11. Change the three uppercase headings to a 14-point bold sans serif font.

12. Insert a bullet and an indent at the beginning of each item in the three lists.

13. Import the graphic file CBOOK.WMF. Position the graphic between the two columns. Adjust the size of the graphic to a width of 2 inches, with height automatically changing size proportionately.

14. Save the document as S6CBOOK.DOC and print it.

# Index

# TASK REFERENCE
### WordPerfect 6.0 for Windows
*Italicized page numbers indicate the first discussion of each task.*
*When you see * in the Button, CUA Template, or DOS Template column, continue with * in the Menu column.*

| TASK | BUTTON | MENU | CUA TEMPLATE | DOS TEMPLATE |
|---|---|---|---|---|
| Bold, toggle on or off *WP 68* | Click [B] | Click Layout, click Font, click the Bold checkbox, click the OK button | [Ctrl][B] | [Ctrl][B] or [F6] |
| Bookmark, create *WP 169* | | Click Insert, click Bookmark, *click Create, type name of bookmark, click the OK button | | [Shift][F12]* |
| Bookmark, move to *WP 170* | | Click Edit, click Go To, *click Down Arrow by Bookmark, click desired bookmark, click the OK button | [Ctrl][G]* | [Shift][F12]* |
| Button Bar, hide or display *WP 21* | Click [icon] | Click View, click Button Bar | | |
| Button Bar, move *WP 17* | Drag Button Bar using [icon] | Click File, click Preferences, double- click Button Bar, click Options, click one of the locations, click the OK button | | |
| Button Bar, select *WP 164* | Move mouse pointer to Button Bar, click the *right* mouse button, select desired Button Bar | Click File, click Preferences, double-click Button Bar icon, select desired Button Bar, click the Select button, click the Close button | | |
| Center a line of text *WP 109* | | Click Layout, click Line, click Center | [Shift][F7] | [Shift][F6] |
| Center page top to bottom *WP 140* | | Click Layout, click Page, click Center, click Current Page or Current and Subsequent Pages, then click the OK button | | |
| Character (typographic), insert *WP 258* | | Click Insert, click Character, *select character, click the Insert and Close button | [Ctrl][W]* | [Shift][F11]* |
| Close a document without saving changes *WP 23* | Double-click the Control menu box* | Click File, click Close, *click the No button | [Ctrl][F4]* | [F7]* |
| Coach, use *WP 46* | | Click Help, *click Coach, click a feature, then click the OK button | [F1]* | [F1]* |
| Columns, create *WP 256* | Click [icon] * | Click Layout, click Columns, click Define, *set number of columns, click the OK button | | |
| Conditional end of page set *WP 157* | | Click Layout, click Page, click Keep Text Together, click Conditional End of Page checkbox, type the number of lines, click the OK button | | |
| Copy text *WP 127* | Select text, click [icon], move insertion point, click [icon] | Select text, click Edit, click Copy, move insertion point, click Edit, click Paste | Select text, press [Ctrl][C], move insertion point, press [Ctrl][V] | Select text, press [Ctrl][C], move insertion point, press [Ctrl][V] |

# TASK REFERENCE
## WordPerfect 6.0 for Windows
*Italicized page numbers indicate the first discussion of each task.*
*When you see * in the Button, CUA Template, or DOS Tenplate column, continue with * in the Menu column.*

| TASK | BUTTON | MENU | CUA TEMPLATE | DOS TEMPLATE |
|---|---|---|---|---|
| Cut and paste text *WP 123* | Select text, click 🗒, move insertion point, click 📋 | Select text, click Edit, click Cut, move insertion point, click Edit, click Paste | Select text, press [Ctrl][X], move insertion point, press [Ctrl][V] | Select text, press [Ctrl][X], move insertion point, press [Ctrl][V] |
| Data file, create *WP 230* | Click ▣ Merge * | Click Tools, click Merge, *click the Data button, add names of fields, click the OK button | [Shift][F9]* | [Shift][F9]* |
| Date, insert today's *WP 16* | Click ▣ Date Text | Click Insert, click Date, click Date Text | [Ctrl][D] | [Shift][F5] |
| Draft mode, select *WP 156* | | Click View, click Draft | [Ctrl][F5] | |
| Drag and drop (to move text) *WP 129* | Select text, drag highlighted text with ▯ | | | |
| Exit WordPerfect *WP 38* | Double-click the WordPerfect Control menu box | Click File, click Exit | [Alt][F4] | |
| Field merge code, insert *WP 240* | Click the Insert Field button on Merge Bar, click desired field name, click the Insert button | | | |
| Find text *WP 110* | | Click Edit, click Find, *type the find string, click the Find button | [F2]* | [F2]* |
| Flush right, set text *WP 109* | | Click Layout, click Line, click Flush Right | [Alt][F7] | [Alt][F6] |
| Font, change appearance *WP 60* | Click FFF, select the font | Click Layout, click Font, *click the font, click the OK button | [F9]* | [Ctrl][F8]* |
| Font, change the size *WP 60* | Click ⫴A, select point value | Click Layout, *click Font, click font size, click the OK button | [F9]* | [Ctrl][F8]* |
| Footnote, create *WP 208* | | Click Insert, click Footnote, click Create, type text of footnote, click the Close button | | |
| Footnote, edit *WP 211* | Click I in footnote, edit the footnote, click I in main text | Click Insert, click Footnote, click Edit, type number of desired footnote, click the OK button, edit the footnote, click the Close button | | |
| Form file, create *WP 238* | Click ▣ Merge | Click Tools, click Merge, *click the Form button, type associated data file name, click the OK button | | |
| Grammatik *WP 96* | Click 🔳 | Click Tools, click Grammatik | [Alt][Shift][F1] | [Alt][Shift][F1] |
| Graphics, import *WP 262* | Click ▣ Figure * | Click Graphics, *click Figure, select graphic file, click the OK button | [F11] | |
| Hard page break *WP 140* | | Click Insert, click Page Break | [Ctrl][Enter] | [Ctrl][Enter] |

# TASK REFERENCE
## WordPerfect 6.0 for Windows
*Italicized page numbers indicate the first discussion of each task.*
*When you see * in the Button, CUA Template, or DOS Tenplate column, continue with * in the Menu column.*

| TASK | BUTTON | MENU | CUA TEMPLATE | DOS TEMPLATE |
|------|--------|------|--------------|--------------|
| Header or footer, create *WP 146* | | Click Layout, click Header/Footer, desired header or footer, click the Create button, type the text of the header or footer, click the Close button | | |
| Help, get *WP 43* | | Click Help, click Contents, click the desired Help category | [F1] | [F1] |
| Horizontal line, insert *WP 250* | | Click Graphics, click Horizontal Line | [Ctrl][F1] | |
| Hyphenate *WP 213* | | Click Layout, click Line, click Hyphenation, select Hyphenation On, click the OK button | | |
| Indent a paragraph *WP 77* | Click [Indent] | Click Layout, click Paragraph, click Indent | [F7] | [F4] |
| Insert file into document window *WP 198* | | Click Insert, click File, type pathname of file, click the Insert button, click the Yes button | | |
| Italic font, toggle on or off *WP 71* | Click [*I*] | Click Layout, click Font, click the Italic checkbox, click the OK button | [Ctrl][I] | [Ctrl][I] |
| Justification, change *WP 65* | Click [L], click Justification type | Click Layout, click Justification, click Justification type | [Ctrl][L] or [Ctrl][R] or [Ctrl][E] or [Ctrl][J] for left, right, center, or full justification | [Ctrl][L] for left justification |
| Labels document, create *WP 246* | | Click Layout, click Labels, select the desired printer labels, click the Select button | | |
| Line spacing, change *WP 140* | Click [1.0], click desired spacing | Click Layout, click Line, click Spacing, set desired spacing, click the OK button | | |
| Macro, play keystroke macro *WP 204* | | | [Ctrl][*letter* or *digit*] or [Ctrl][Shift] [*letter* or *digit*] | |
| Macro, play named macro *WP 207* | | Click Tools, click Macro, click Play, type name of macro, click the Play button | [Alt][F10] | [Alt][F10] |
| Macro, record *WP 202* | | Click Tools, click Macro, click Record, type name of macro, click the Record button, record desired commands and keystrokes, click Tools, click Macro, click Record | [Ctrl][F10] | [Ctrl][F10] |

# TASK REFERENCE
## WordPerfect 6.0 for Windows
*Italicized page numbers indicate the first discussion of each task.*
*When you see * in the Button, CUA Template, or DOS Template column, continue with * in the Menu column.*

| TASK | BUTTON | MENU | CUA TEMPLATE | DOS TEMPLATE |
|---|---|---|---|---|
| Macros, change default location *WP 200* | | Click File, click Preferences, double-click 🗁, select macros, click 🗐, select desired path, click the OK button, click the OK button, click the Close button | | |
| Margins, change *WP 62* | With Ruler Bar on screen, drag left or right margin markers | Click Layout, click Margins, *set the new values, click the OK button | [Ctrl][F8]* | |
| Merge data file and form file *WP 243* | Click [Merge]* | Click Tools, click Merge, *click the Merge button, type the name of the form file, press Tab, type the name of the data file, click the OK button | | |
| New document window, open *WP 195* | Click 🗋 | Click File, click New | [Ctrl][N] | |
| Number pages *WP 145* | | Click Layout, click Page, click Numbering, click Position, select desired page numbering position, click the OK button | | |
| Open a document *WP 40* | Click 🗐 * | Click File, click Open, *type the filename, click the OK button | [F4]* | [F5]* |
| Outline, create *WP 185* | | Click Tools, click Outline, change Paragraph to Outline on Outline Bar | | |
| Outline family, move *WP 191* | Drag ⬍ to new location | | | |
| Page mode, select *WP 171* | | Click View, click Page | [Alt][F5] | |
| Page number, set new *WP 148* | | Click Layout, click Page, click Numbering, click the Value button, change the New Page Number, click the OK button, click the Close button | | |
| Paragraph spacing, change *WP 261* | | Click Layout, click Paragraph, click Format, set Spacing Between Paragraphs, click the OK button | | |
| Print a document *WP 37* | Click 🖥 | Click File, click Print, *click the Print button | [F5]* | [Shift][F7]* |
| Print multiple copies *WP 101* | Click 🖥 * | Click File, click Print, *change Number of Copies, click the OK button | [F5]* | [Shift][F7]* |
| Records, adding new records to data file *WP 237* | With the insertion point at the end of the document, click the Quick Entry button, enter information, click the New Record or Close button | | | |

# TASK REFERENCE
## WordPerfect 6.0 for Windows

*Italicized page numbers indicate the first discussion of each task.*
*When you see * in the Button, CUA Template, or DOS Template column, continue with * in the Menu column.*

| TASK | BUTTON | MENU | CUA TEMPLATE | DOS TEMPLATE |
|---|---|---|---|---|
| Replace text *WP 112* | | Click Edit, click Replace, *type the find string, press [Tab], type the replace string, click the Find, Replace, or Replace All button | [Ctrl][F2]* | [Alt][F2]* |
| Reveal codes, hide or display *WP 73* | | Click View, click Reveal Codes | [Alt][F3] | [Alt][F3] |
| Save a document for the first time *WP 25* | Click 🖫 | Click File, click Save, *type the filename, click the OK button | [F3]* | [F10]* |
| Save a document that already has a filename *WP 35* | Click 🖫 | Click File, click Save | [Shift][F3] | [Ctrl][F12] |
| Save a document with a new filename *WP 42* | | Click File, click Save As, *type the new filename, click the OK button | [F3]* | [F10]* |
| Select block of text *WP 118* | Drag I over block of text | | Move insertion point to beginning of block, press [F8], move insertion point to end of block | Move insertion point to beginning of block, press [Alt][F4], move insertion point to end of block |
| Select page | | Click Edit, click Select, click Page | | |
| Select paragraph *WP 128* | Quadruple-click I in paragraph or double-click ⬀ in left margin | Click Edit, click Select, click Paragraph | | |
| Select sentence *WP 126* | Triple-click I in sentence or click ⬀ in left margin | Click Edit, click Select, click Sentence | | [Ctrl][F4] |
| Speller *WP 87* | Click 📖 | Click Tools, click Speller | [Ctrl][F1] | [Ctrl][F2] |
| Style, apply *WP 155* | Click [Styles]* | Click Layout, click Styles, *click name of desired style, click the Apply button | [Alt][F8]* | [Alt][F8]* |
| Style, create *WP 151* | Click [Styles] | Click Layout, click Styles, *click Create, type the style name and description, assign a style type, insert the desired format codes into the Contents box, click the OK button | [Alt][F8]* | [Alt][F8]* |
| Suppress page numbering, headers and footers *WP 147* | | Click Layout, click Page, click Suppress, click desired boxes, click the OK button | | |

# TASK REFERENCE
## WordPerfect 6.0 for Windows
*Italicized page numbers indicate the first discussion of each task.*
*When you see * in the Button, CUA Template, or DOS Tenplate column, continue with * in the Menu column.*

| TASK | BUTTON | MENU | CUA TEMPLATE | DOS TEMPLATE |
|---|---|---|---|---|
| Tab stops, change *WP143* | | Click View, click Ruler Bar, drag tab stop markers to desired location; or click Layout, click Line, click Tab Set, *set the tab stops, click the OK button | | [Ctrl][F11]* |
| Table, create *WP 161* | Click ▦ , drag to select table size | Click Table, click Create, *set desired Table size, click the OK button | [F12]* | [Alt][F7] |
| Table, format *WP 163* | Click *right* mouse button on Button Bar, click Tables, click ✛ | Click Table, click Format, click the Table button, *choose desired format, click the OK button | [Ctrl][F12], click the Table button* | |
| TextArt, create *WP 50* | Click **ABC** TextArt | Click Graphics, click TextArt | | |
| Thesaurus *WP 94* | Click 🔲 | Click Tools, click Thesaurus | [Alt][F1] | [Alt][F1] |
| Tiles, display document windows *WP 197* | | Click Window, click Tile | | |
| Undelete text *WP 82* | | Click Edit, click Undelete | [Ctrl][Shift][Z] | [Ctrl][Shift][Z] |
| Underline, toggle on or off *WP 70* | Click ⊻ | Click Layout, click Font, click the Underline checkbox, click the OK button | [Ctrl][U] | [Ctrl][U] or [F8] |
| View the document at Full Page Zoom *WP 36* | Click 🔍 | Click View, click Zoom, click Full Page, click the OK button | [Shift][F5] | |
| Widow/Orphan protection, set *WP 160* | | Click Layout, click Page, click Keep Text Together, click Widow/Orphan checkbox, click the OK button | | |